# DODGE CITY A
## OF THE WI

# DODGE CITY AND THE BIRTH OF THE WILD WEST

ROBERT R. DYKSTRA

AND

JO ANN MANFRA

UNIVERSITY PRESS OF KANSAS

Published by the University Press of Kansas (Lawrence, Kansas 66045), which was organized by the Kansas Board of Regents and is operated and funded by Emporia State University, Fort Hays State University, Kansas State University, Pittsburg State University, the University of Kansas, and Wichita State University.

Library of Congress Cataloging-in-Publication Data

Names: Dykstra, Robert R., 1930– author. | Manfra, Jo Ann, author.
Title: Dodge City and the birth of the wild west / Robert R. Dykstra and Jo Ann Manfra.
Description: Lawrence, Kansas : University Press of Kansas, 2017. | Includes bibliographical references and index.
Identifiers: LCCN 2017020136
ISBN 9780700624751 (cloth : alk. paper)
ISBN 9780700624768 (pbk. : alk. paper)
ISBN 9780700624775 (ebook)
Subjects: LCSH: Dodge City (Kan.)—History—19th century. | Frontier and pioneer life—Kansas—Dodge City. | Violence—Kansas—Dodge City—History—19th century.
Classification: LCC F689.D64 D95 2017 | DDC 978.1/76—dc23
LC record available at https://lccn.loc.gov/2017020136.

British Library Cataloguing-in-Publication Data is available.

Printed in the United States of America

10 9 8 7 6 5 4 3 2 1

The paper used in this publication is recycled and contains 30 percent postconsumer waste. It is acid free and meets the minimum requirements of the American National Standard for Permanence of Paper for Printed Library Materials Z39.48-1992.

*In memory of*
*Anna Marrocco Manfra and Joseph Manfra*

# CONTENTS

Introduction: Gettin' Outta Dodge   *1*

1. Pioneers   *6*

2. Year of Living Dangerously   *22*

3. Deadly Prose   *45*

4. Case Histories   *66*

5. Circle Dot Cowboys   *84*

6. Dodge City's Sensations   *104*

7. End Games   *143*

8. Contesting Boot Hill   *162*

Epilogue: Homicide, Moral Discourse,
Cultural Identity   *179*

Appendix: Homicide Victims, 1872–1886   *183*

Acknowledgments   *185*

Notes   *187*

Index   *223*

*A photo section appears following page 126.*

# DODGE CITY AND THE BIRTH
# OF THE WILD WEST

# INTRODUCTION:
## GETTIN' OUTTA DODGE

Dodge City's very first gunfight, so far as anyone knows, occurred in the wee hours of September 3, 1872. A fragmentary news report out of nearby Hutchison verifies the encounter.

> SHOOTING AFFAIR AT DODGE.—We learn from persons who came down the road yesterday, that there was a lively shooting affray at Dodge on Tuesday, in which four or five persons were wounded, one or two perhaps fatally. We did not learn the names of any of the parties concerned.[1]

Decades later a pioneer named George Brown, once the co-owner of one of the low-end saloons that hugged the riverbank in early Dodge, found himself recalling all the names and details. It started, he said, with the harassment of gambler Charley Morehouse by John Langford and two of Langford's pals. "They pulled Morehouse out of bed one night, where he was enjoyin' himself with a dance-hall girl, and made him drink with them," Brown remembered. Intent on payback, later that night as drinkers crowded the makeshift bar,

> Morehouse and his bunch came into my saloon and inquired for Johnnie Langford. I told them he had just left about two minutes ago. They stepped to the front door and [spotted Langford and friends] going down the street. The Morehouse party opened fire on them. Langford returned the fire and bullets were flyin' around pretty thick.

Brown wryly itemized the fallout.

> One man was shot in the heel as he was goin' out the back door. A man was on a cot near the door on the outside. Next morning they found five bullet holes through his coat, and the man wasn't touched. In all this shootin' there wasn't a man killed.

Morehouse suffered only an inconsequential wound in the arm and remained a regular in Dodge City saloon life until almost the end of the year. Not so his antagonist.

> Langford was shot five times, but he crawled off and hid himself in some brush down near the river. He was rescued next morning and was taken to the hospital at Fort Dodge.[2]

Offloaded at the fort after a five-mile wagon ride from Dodge City, the dirt- and blood-encrusted Langford might just have got lucky. Dr. William Tremaine, the post's Canadian-born physician, happened to be a pioneering American student of the "Lister system," the surgical reforms urged by the prominent Scots physician Joseph Lister. Calling for operating-room cleanliness and strict antiseptic surgical procedures, Lister's innovations failed to take hold in the United States until the 1890s. In 1882 the American Surgical Association declared them unproven at best, nonsense at worst. Hence most surgeons ignored filthy hospital conditions, failed to sterilize their instruments, and even neglected to scrub their hands before operating. Not so Dr. Tremaine, who had trained himself in the dangers of unclean equipment, dirty hospital bedding, and soil in open wounds.[3]

Due for leave in September 1872, Tremaine may still have been on post when Langford was brought in on the third of that month. If so, he would have directed an assistant to continuously spray the patient's wounds with an antiseptic carbolic acid solution, while he himself removed pistol slugs, dead tissue, and microbe-laden soil. Afterward Langford lay in the post infirmary "for quite a while," remembered George Brown, "and finally recovered."[4]

John Langford's name then disappears from the record. When he painfully dragged his bleeding carcass into the undergrowth he desperately feared being hunted down by Morehouse and finished off. At the military hospital, once it became clear he would recover, one can imagine a friend of Langford's stopping by to warn him that Morehouse was still around town and to give him some good advice:

"Johnnie, you better get outta Dodge."

———————

That colorful figure of speech, however conjectural in Langford's case, is still with us. Just as "Rome wasn't built in a day," it's foolish to "carry

2 : *Introduction*

coals to Newcastle," so-and-so has been "sent to Coventry" or "gone Hollywood," and something "won't play in Peoria," so "get out of Dodge" is one of the rare place-name aphorisms in use among English speakers worldwide.

The Dodge City metaphor, with its echo of the Old West, dates from the Vietnam War. For young service personnel nurtured on television series featuring Dodge City—*Gunsmoke, Bat Masterson, The Life and Legend of Wyatt Earp*—the phrase advised or described a hasty escape from some fearsomely defended enemy area or, as it came to be used, from any disagreeable situation. It remained popular among military professionals through the post-Vietnam decades.[5]

By then it had infiltrated American popular speech, movies, magazines, newspapers, and books. For instance, in tracking the appearance of words or phrases year by year in millions of publications, Google's Ngram Viewer shows "get out of Dodge" on a steady climb from 1985 to 2008. And between 1979 and 2008 one metropolitan newspaper, the *Boston Globe*, cited metaphorical Dodge City, in one context or another, sixty-nine times. As recently as 2013 members of the New York City "Preppers Network," readying themselves for the city's next natural disaster, employed as one of their mantras "GOOD" (Get Out of Dodge).[6]

Back in the 1970s and 1980s, as the drug wars heated up, frontier Dodge City carried the figurative burden for urban violence. Those who spoke for metropolitan areas with the highest homicide rates felt called on to deny the trope's applicability. The president of the Dade County Crime Watch insisted that "Miami is not Dodge City, U.S.A." The beleaguered mayor of the nation's capital strongly asserted that "Washington is not Dodge City." And New York's chief executive growled that "things are not out of control [here], and this is not Dodge City."[7]

Overseas journalists soon weighed in. A Welsh commentator described a "showdown with guns that would not have been out of place in Dodge City." An Australian newsman probing Melbourne's drinking culture concluded that his town was "like Dodge City on a bad night." A Glasgow writer disputed the belief that he and his neighbors lived in a civilized place. "This is Dodge City, Scotland," he glumly remarked. A British editor summarized crime data from Nottingham with a headline that said it all: "Not Dodge City."[8]

Neither was the metaphor limited to the Anglo-American world when it came to shorthand assessments of nasty or violent settings. "Life in Jaffna," wrote a reporter from Sri Lanka, "is like Dodge City without the sheriff." In one war-ravaged Serbian town in 1997 a foreign correspondent noted that its most flourishing business was prostitution. "Dodge City," muttered a citizen. A senior American commander in Iraq, downplaying concern about Baghdad's 2003 crime rate, said that it was no worse than that of any major city in America. "Maybe *Dodge* City," sniffed an Iraqi businessman. And at the height of the occupation a journalist at the Cannes Film Festival overheard two French couples joke about "Cowboy George" Bush and term the United States "*un grand* Dodge City."[9]

Interestingly, the history behind the trope seems little known. In 1999 the Random House website advised a baffled reader that the word "dodge" in the phrase "get the hell out of Dodge" should be capitalized, because it "is a reference to Dodge City, Kansas." Other sites posted similar information in 2005 and 2006. And the following year a discussion of "get out of Dodge" erupted on forum.wordreference.com with postings from Canada, Argentina, Ireland, and Switzerland, as well as from Pennsylvania, California, and Maine. An Oregonian finally cut through the puzzlement by noting that "Dodge City is very real and has a very real history apart from the glamorization in films."[10]

Books have explored that history with varying degrees of success. *Dodge City: The Cowboy Capital* (1913) is a pioneer memoir to which all subsequent works are indebted. General treatments by academics appeared in 1952 and 1977, followed by four books on special aspects of the town's frontier experience written by a Kansas scholar. Dodge City's own resident historian offered lively and informative works in 1972 and 2009. The latter year also saw publication of an encyclopedic book by a retired businessman residing in Arizona.[11]

Any number of fictional treatments of Dodge in its legendary era have emerged over the years, but historical novelist Mary Doria Russell's *Doc*, released by Random House in 2011, turned out to be a surprise addition to this ten- or twenty-foot shelf. The best-selling novel informs readers that frontier Dodge City's cast of complex and varied characters proved far larger than its few celebrity gunfighters, who still bestride the Old West of the imagination.[12]

————⟨∞⟩————

Dodge City was not the Old West's only notorious "border town" by any stretch of the imagination. But its frontier era lasted for almost fifteen years, a longer span than enjoyed (or suffered) by many such settlements. And from the first Dodge seemed to attract more than its share of media attention, probably because of journalists' and tourists' easy access to it by rail—in contrast to its two main competitors in the popular notoriety sweepstakes, Deadwood and Tombstone, both of them remote mining villages. Of these three most famous western towns only Dodge City came to possess a distinct metaphorical existence.

In the final ten years of its adolescence Dodge flourished as a nationally prominent cattle-trading center. Three other Kansas settlements similarly, but only briefly, existed as major cattle towns. The onslaught of rural settlement wiped out the cattle trade at Abilene (in 1871), Ellsworth (in 1874), and Wichita (in 1875) by overrunning grazing lands and cutting off the trails. Consequently, between 1876 and 1879 Dodge held a virtual monopoly on the Texas cattle business, broken only by a latecomer, Caldwell, in 1880; both settlements flourished as cattle towns through the last five shipping seasons.[13]

The economic structure and social experience of the Kansas cattle centers differed little, yet Dodge City's four years as a major point for shipping buffalo hides, followed by its unique longevity as a cattle town, made it far more vulnerable than the others to media exploitation. Garnished by fourteen years of publicized violence and disorder, real and imagined, the Dodge City of old gave birth to, and remains, a cultural metaphor grounded in a reality all its own. It deploys images of violence and civic anarchy in a legendary West that still engages deeply held imaginings of belligerent individualism and freedom from social restraint.

This book examines the discursive space between historical Dodge City and these metaphors, exploring how the settlement became a setting for symbol, for public memory, and for instructed fantasy—for good or ill an important item in the nation's presentation of itself.

*Gettin' Outta Dodge* : 5

# PIONEERS

When Dodge City came to life in the summer of 1872 an expatriate Pennsylvanian named Henry Sitler, as his biography put it, "owned the ground where it now stands." Within the decade Sitler would see his modest corner of the world ascend to international celebrity or, perhaps better, international notoriety.[1]

Until his mid-twenties Henry still lived at home, helping out on the family's prospering Pennsylvania stock farm that produced feed grain, butter, and beef, and, like his father before him, working as a carpenter. Unlike his father, who labored some twenty years at his craft to earn enough to buy the Sitler place, the son enjoyed better local prospects. The very week Henry turned twenty-two the nation's first drilled oil well at Titusville, thirty miles east of the farm, began bringing up quality black crude. The oil extraction and refining business touched off a local building boom that led to unprecedented wages for construction work.[2]

But the outbreak of the Civil War disrupted whatever immediate future Henry may have anticipated. Late in 1861, six months after the firing on Fort Sumter, Sitler and his brother enlisted in the 2d Pennsylvania Cavalry. An enrolling officer jotted down Henry's particulars: age twenty-four, height almost five feet seven inches, complexion light, hair dark, eyes brown. Henry was made a regimental bugler, a position of some responsibility that carried with it promotion to noncommissioned officer.[3]

Sergeant Sitler survived almost three years' soldiering before falling into enemy hands during a fighting retreat at the battle of Samaria

Church southeast of Richmond, Virginia. Not long afterward he stepped down from a railroad boxcar and faced the Civil War's ultimate horror: the Confederate prison camp at Andersonville, Georgia. The stockaded enclosure hit its peak population of around 33,000 POWs when Sitler arrived in late June 1864. That August alone nearly 10 percent of them died from confinement in this open-air sewer crowded with makeshift tents and lean-tos shrouded in woodsmoke, where sight-seers gawked from stockade platforms as Yankees in their multitudes died of illness, malnutrition, exposure, and what record keepers recorded as "nostalgia," a sad euphemism for lethal despair.[4]

Released in a prisoner exchange after five hazardous months in captivity, Sitler spent Christmas 1864 at home on leave, then waited out the lengthy processing of his discharge at a transition camp near Philadelphia. Here, not yet fully recuperated from his imprisonment, he spent two weeks in the hospital, being treated for acute constipation and ecthyma, an ulcerating skin disease. In March 1865 the army finally turned him loose with $100 unused clothing allowance in his pocket.[5]

Although prepared to resume his trade as a carpenter, Sitler ultimately chose not to stay in northwest Pennsylvania. A two-week delay in a project he had signed on for at Meadville prompted him to indulge in a quick trip (about two days by rail) to see a brother in Illinois. "On that visit," it was later said of Sitler, "he became inflicted with the western fever." Instead of returning home he lit out for the trans-Mississippi frontier.[6]

---

Henry Sitler ended up at the edge of the High Plains, a region long in contention among native peoples of diverse cultures and languages. In the 1400s, at the close of a centuries-long drought and consequent depopulation, successive waves of tribal migrants began drifting into the area from ancient homelands. The Apache peoples established permanent villages at the headwaters of the Arkansas River in what is now Colorado. The Comanches, having followed the Rocky Mountain foothills southward, arrived in the 1820s on the upper Arkansas and systematically destroyed the Apache settlements. Although by 1780 mounted Comanche hunters, raiders, and traders dominated the Plains from Kansas to southern Texas, on their northern flank the Kiowas, then the

Plains Apaches (distant cousins of the early inhabitants), then the linguistically related Arapahos and Cheyennes drifted in from the Dakotas.

By the 1830s intertribal war raged along the Arkansas River, finally exhausting all combatants. In 1840 Arapaho and Apache intermediaries brokered a cease-fire among the five tribes that informally ceded the Plains above the Arkansas River to the Arapahos and Cheyennes, with the Comanches, Kiowas, and Plains Apaches sharing control over everything to the south.[7]

Already by 1821 heavily armed Saint Louis trading caravans had laid out the storied Santa Fe Trail, which cut across southern Kansas on its way to New Mexico. After thirty years of small-scale raids and retaliations, all affected Indian groups, in return for a shared federal payment of $18,000 a year for ten years, formally promised to stop impeding commerce on the trail. But in 1856 war between the Cheyennes and the US Army broke out in Wyoming. Then the Pike's Peak gold rush in Colorado engulfed the Arapahos. In 1864 the Kiowas and Plains Apaches joined the Cheyennes and Arapahos in closing off the Santa Fe Trail, and the violence spread eastward to the Kansas settlements.[8]

So it was that when Sitler staked a claim in the lower Solomon River valley of central Kansas the region had been hastily evacuated by the fear of raids. Undaunted, Henry broke sod and raised a crop. But, as he later said of his own pioneering innocence, "The country was a complete wild prairie, and not a railroad was then in operation in the State of Kansas; farming was therefore a slow way of making a fortune." He retreated to Topeka, where the new state capitol was under construction and work plentiful.

In 1867, as the Indian war subsided and the Kansas Pacific Railway snaked up the Smoky Hill River valley heading for a newly relocated army post at Ellsworth, Sitler responded to the call of the quartermaster for some 300 "mechanics and laborers" to finish building Fort Harker. As soon as that military project was up and running in January 1867, Sitler and others progressed further along the rail line to Hays City, where another relocated army post offered skilled employment.

Just as Fort Hays reopened for business in the summer of 1867 the Indian war flared up again, requiring a different kind of well-paid work for men willing to face the danger. Sitler, crediting "a chance job at driving a team of 'shave tails' [second lieutenants] to Fort Dodge," joined a rag-tag procession of teamsters freighting military supplies down to that solitary post in 1868. Here one of Henry's old corps commanders, General Philip Sheridan, was organizing an area defense of the southwestern Kansas frontier.[9]

Fort Dodge had been laid out well beyond the line of population advance in the closing days of the Civil War. The compound stood on the site of an old Santa Fe Trail campground, fronting the meandering, low-banked Arkansas River (pronounced by Kansans, then as now, the Ar-*kan*-sas River). Embroidered with quicksands and potholes, the quarter-mile-wide flow proved especially treacherous each spring as Rocky Mountain snowmelt briefly sent the river boiling eastward. Civilian employees constructed log-roofed dugouts along its bank for their quarters, keeping a wary eye out for flooding.[10]

When in 1869 the army's defeat of the Cheyenne Dog Soldier faction brought another cease-fire that would last until 1874, Sitler spent the next several years hauling goods, at ninety cents per hundredweight, from the railroad at Hays City down to Fort Dodge and from there to army detachments policing the Texas Panhandle and Indian Territory. As he later recalled, he also secured military contracts, bidding successfully on various short-term and lucrative quarrying, lumbering, hay-cutting, and construction jobs. On one contract alone, probably in 1869, he earned $1,020 (around $16,728 in 2015 currency) supplying the fort with sixty cords of wood at $17 a cord. After hostilities resumed the work proved hazardous. When supervising the harvest of a hay crop Sitler took an Indian bullet in the leg, resulting in a bad wound that required hospitalization at Fort Dodge and postponement of marriage to Emma Harper of Pennyslvania. The two finally married in 1875 in Kansas City.[11]

While working his government contracts Sitler nurtured plans for making it big in cattle raising, figuring that once the buffalo had been swept from the region by over-hunting and the Plains tribes had been sequestered on Indian Territory reservations, it would be prime grazing country.

Wanting to keep his day jobs, Henry decided to stake a land claim as close as possible to the fort's compound. An irregular 43,000-acre military reservation surrounded Fort Dodge, established to preserve its timber, stone, and hay for government use. The tip of the reservation's western panhandle ended at the Arkansas River five miles from the fort complex. At this intersection Henry for a second time became a squatter, preempting, as allowed by federal law, 160 acres of land. In 1871 he built a three-room sod house and released a few head of cattle, signaling his intent to apply to the US land office at Wichita for formal possession of his quarter-section of riverside pasture.[12]

In his capsule biography Sitler implied that his remembered "five months and twenty days" in unspeakably crowded rebel confinement still rankled. The immense sky and vast, empty surfaces of southwestern Kansas must have suited him. He stayed the rest of his life.[13]

Before long Sitler's claim profited from two transforming developments.

In the spring of 1872 commercial buffalo hunting on the Great Plains expanded from a seasonal to a year-round enterprise. Although prime bison pelts had been an item of commerce for half a century, the market was limited to consumer goods (rugs, lap-robes, coats) made from skins harvested and processed by Plains Indians in winter when the animals' fur was at its thickest. But eastern demand abruptly accelerated when in 1871 tanners developed new chemical processes for converting buffalo hides into tough, low-cost belting for transmitting energy from one factory machine to another.

Word promptly spread from eastern tanners to traveling hide buyers to western hunters that commercially valuable bison skins could be collected year round. One to two thousand well-armed groups of self-styled "buffalo runners" flocked west. Many ignored treaty restrictions on access to tribal lands and invaded Indian hunting grounds along the Arkansas River. That first season alone, based on the Sante Fe Railroad's transportation of 165,721 bison hides in 1872 and Richard Dodge's estimate that over a third of the buffalo killed that year proved unsalable due to improper skinning, roughly 250,000 bison died in Kansas and Colorado on both sides of the river from large-caliber gunshot wounds. The military at Fort Dodge and other posts looked the other way.[14]

Also in 1872 the Atchison, Topeka & Santa Fe Railroad began building southwestward through Kansas, roadbed graders ahead, track-layers spiking down iron rails over white oak ties ten days behind, advancing a mile per day. In mid-June the graders reached Hutchinson. From there the company's right-of-way headed toward Fort Dodge. Then it cut diagonally across the military reservation, sidling up to the north bank of the Arkansas River precisely at Henry Sitler's claim before swinging north again. This made Henry's homestead the southernmost point on the Santa Fe line.

Suddenly Sitler's ordinary preemption appeared to be pure gold— not as a ranch but as prospective urban real estate, a feasible entrepôt for the roughly 90,000 square miles of buffalo range to the south and for the government agencies in Indian Territory. Weeks before the rails actually reached Sitler's backyard, hunters had begun piling stretch-dried bison skins along the line of the surveyors' stakes. And on the morning of June 17, 1872, the first pioneer businessmen began to gather. Within forty yards of Sitler's house George Hoover pitched a tent enclosing a barrel of whiskey and a makeshift bar, over which he and a partner retailed shots to the railroad builders for twenty-five cents each. That afternoon two more entrepreneurs arrived on site.[15]

Sitler the would-be cattle baron wisely relinquished his individual claim in favor of a corporate body that could add to and transform his 160 acres into a townsite speculation. With that end in sight, eleven men joined Sitler at Fort Dodge on July 8, 1872, to form the Dodge City Town Company, offering 600 shares of stock at $10 each.[16]

··◦∞◦··

Although Sitler's signature led the list of shareholders, the second signatory, Robert Wright, was by all accounts the venture's prime organizer and promoter. Wright served as the post trader at Fort Dodge, holding a government license to operate a profitable commercial enterprise there.[17]

All but one of the additional ten shareholders also possessed military connections. Three were resident army officers, including post commandant Richard Dodge, a native North Carolinian and West Point graduate, of no relation to the Civil War general for whom the fort had been named. Like Sitler and Wright, four others worked as civilians at Fort Dodge. Two of the three absentee investors also had links to the military, one an army major and paymaster at Fort Leavenworth, the other a former clerk in the post trader stores at Forts Dodge and Larned.[18]

With newcomers daily setting up shop on Sitler's claim the share-holders moved fast to forestall any rival preemption. Following federal and state rules for town site acquisition, they asked that Judge H. J. Mc-Gaffigan of nearby Ellis County, to which the politically unorganized Ford County was attached for judicial purposes, act as their agent. The judge "for and in behalf of the occupants and Town Company of the town of Dodge City" submitted to the Wichita land office a "declaratory state-ment" dated July 16, 1872, for what the land office registrar certified as the site location. Wichita then forwarded the claim to the General Land Office in Washington, DC.[19]

The company, however, as one of its shareholders later testified, had been "compelled to file upon the wrong land . . . knowing it to be wrong, but owing to an error in the maps in the [Wichita] Land Office." Indeed, those maps omitted the most desirable portion of Sitler's preemption: 81.33 acres hard against the military reservation border. According to Wichita's survey, that prime acreage—destined to become the town's Front Street business district and the fabled "south side" entertainment quarter—lay *within* the reservation. Relying on an 1868 army survey, the Dodge City Town Company disagreed.[20]

While awaiting a new survey the company's directors not only went ahead and applied to the Kansas secretary of state for a corporate char-ter on August 15, 1872, but they also confidently included the disputed acreage in their description of the proposed town.

By November a definitive resurvey had proved that the original survey had erroneously extended the military reservation's southeastern pan-handle 400 yards past its true boundary, meaning the coveted 81.33 acres did indeed lie just beyond the reservation, and the lengthy process of altering the original land claim could begin. Anticipating a positive out-come the town company, by now an official corporation, opened for busi-ness, selling space to those already in occupation as well as to newcomers. "Lots on the principal streets and near the center of business command $200 each," reported a Leavenworth correspondent. "The prices of lots 25 feet front by 125 feet deep range from $50 to $200, and the demand is very active and promises to increase rather than diminish."[21]

It took a good three months for the company's attorney to arrange a hearing before the Wichita land registrar for himself and two of the corporation's more credentialed shareholders, both of them commissioned officers from Fort Dodge. In a February 1873 affidavit all three swore that the old declaratory statement "was made in error," and asked that the description of the tract—home to supposedly 300 inhabitants, 200 more than legally required—be changed to include the prized downtown acreage. That location, the statement declared, had already been laid out into blocks, lots, streets, and alleys on which stood some forty commercial establishments: "drug stores, general supply stores, grocery stores, saloons, barber shops, hotels &c." The registrar agreeably mailed this rather embellished declaration to the commissioner of the General Land Office, recommending that "the change be allowed."[22]

Anxious to take title, the company sought to speed up the process. One shareholder, Fort Leavenworth's Major David Taylor, persuaded his friend US senator Alexander Caldwell to put in a good word with the General Land Office commissioner. Another investor, Captain Tullius Tupper, an Ohioan stationed at Fort Dodge, had similar luck with Ohio congressman John Beatty. Ultimately Judge McGaffigan was pressed back into service, sending a revised declaratory statement to the Wichita registrar for transmittal east. The registrar complied, again adding that "we respectfully recommend that the change be allowed."[23]

On May 24, 1873, almost a year after submission of the original paperwork, the General Land Office finally approved the revised claim. A month later the company paid just $378.47 for 302.78 acres abutting the military reservation that included downtown Dodge.[24]

Following the dictates of federal and state law, McGaffigan on August 21, 1873, deeded the tract to its nineteen adult male "occupants," those inhabitants or their assigns who had made improvements on platted town lots. Six of the nineteen happened to be original shareholders still on site. Two others, both Fort Dodge officers, had bought in a few months after the company's July 1872 founding. The rest most likely purchased shares between then and August 1873, some of them after the corporation had increased its capital stock from $6,000 to $8,000.

On August 30, 1873, all nineteen men deeded their individual allotments to the Dodge City Town Company for collective exploitation.[25]

Henry Sitler, who numbered among the nineteen, spent a few years working his Fort Dodge contracts while overseeing a brickyard in town, then realized his dream by launching himself into the cattle business. He divided his time between a ranch southwest of Dodge and a stock farm in the Flint Hills of central Kansas. Although often a welcome visitor, Sitler would not return permanently to Dodge until liquidating his cattle interests in 1882 and becoming a major shareholder in the town's first commercial bank. Three years later he got back into brick making, and bricks imprinted with his monogram—H. L. S.—can still be seen on buildings in Dodge today.[26]

---

"It is the first fellows who settle in a Kansas town who make or break it," declared a newspaper editor at a new village just up the tracks from Dodge.[27]

Of Dodge City's first fellows, eleven of the nineteen occupants anchored the town's business community. Converging on Kansas from several points of the compass, all had arrived on site by the close of 1872 and still lived in Dodge a decade later. Relatively young, with an average age of thirty-one at the founding, none possessed more than a grade-school education. Four, perhaps five, had fought in the Civil War; five had worked as business clerks, reflecting, as historians have noted, the "spread of advanced literacy"; and eight had married before receiving a town allotment.[28]

George Hoover, Dodge City's original businessman, hailed from a hardscrabble Ontario farm just west of Niagara Falls. His was a troubled household. When he was twelve, his mother, suffering from postpartum psychosis, slashed her throat with a kitchen knife. At age twenty-one, disgusted with his father's economic fecklessness, Hoover left home, carrying only "an axe over his shoulder," as family tradition has it. In 1869 he passed through Detroit, then followed the Wabash River into central Indiana. There the 1870 census-taker identified him as a "com[mon] laborer."[29]

During the next two years Hoover continued his trek southwestward across Indiana and Illinois to Saint Louis, where he and a former Pony Express rider—familiar with the territory to the west—decided to open a saloon in frontier Kansas. Their first stop was Coffeyville, a railhead on the Indian Territory line. Probably finding it overcrowded with taverns, they traveled farther west, following the railroad survey out to Fort Dodge, then on to Sitler's land. Railroaders, hunters, and soldiers from the fort proved so immediately lucrative a clientele that they soon could afford to put up a saloon and liquor store on Front Street, advertising "foreign and domestic wines and liquors," with "pure Kentucky bourbons a specialty."[30]

Three more founding entrepreneurs, all original shareholders, had like Henry Sitler arrived before 1872 to work at Fort Dodge.[31] Robert Wright, as mentioned, operated its post exchange, where Herman Fringer and Alfred Peacock clerked.

Born to a village merchant in a suburb of Washington, DC, Wright in 1856 "took a notion to come west," as he laconically put it. He spent the next three years on his Uncle Henry Wright's farm near Saint Louis, just up the road from ex-captain Ulysses S. Grant's brief and unsuccessful venture into husbandry. Here Robert met and in 1859 married his cousin Alice Armstrong, the daughter of an Irish immigrant father and Ohio-born mother, who had left her parents' home in Louisiana to live in Uncle Henry's household.

That same year, employed as a teamster, Wright made his first trip overland to Denver. During the Civil War he worked in Colorado and western Kansas as a wagon master, stagecoach driver, and way-station manager on the Santa Fe Trail, later selling wood, hay, and lime to various army posts. Alice and the couple's two children lived sometimes at Uncle Henry's place, sometimes with Robert. It proved a dangerous life. On one occasion Alice had to help defend a stage station from a Cheyenne assault. On another, Robert, urged to abandon a wagonload of his goods on the approach of a war party, coldly refused. "A man might as well be dead," he remarked, "as to lose his property."

In 1868 the Wrights settled at Fort Dodge, where Robert had been appointed post trader, giving him a virtual monopoly on sales of civilian merchandise, including liquor, and laying the foundation for his future as early Dodge City's wealthiest merchant.

Once the town's business district had been platted, Wright laid claim to its premier location, the northwest corner of Front Street and Second Avenue. At that strategic site he erected a two-storey general store in July 1872. Later rebuilt in brick, it became the centerpiece of Wright's regional commercial empire.[32]

Herman Fringer, a native of Pennsylvania Dutch country, was the youngest of three children raised by a widowed mother. Moving the family in the 1850s to a village near Canton, Ohio, she worked as a domestic and the teenaged Herman as a clerk. During the war Fringer signed on with a "hundred-day" unit, the 162d Regiment of the Ohio National Guard, that never saw combat. Eighteen-sixty-seven found him at Fort Dodge serving as a civilian quartermaster's clerk before being taken on at Wright's concern.[33]

In 1856, Alfred Peacock, age eighteen, a "pipe maker" born on the outskirts of London, landed in New York with almost 800 other converts to the Church of the Latter Day Saints, all headed for the Mormon settlement at Salt Lake. After reaching Iowa City by train, the immigrants found themselves assigned (by the church authorities' cost-cutting effort) to the famously ill-fated handcart expedition—1,300 miles to be covered on foot, possessions pushed and pulled in handcarts. In central Wyoming, after exhausted and famished members of Peacock's company began dying or dropping out, he and another English teenager joined the deserters and trudged back to Fort Laramie.[34]

Never publicly revealing his desperate apostasy, Peacock claimed to be a native New Yorker who had made his way to Kansas from Massachusetts and married an Ohioan named Emma Payne. By 1870 his parents had emigrated to a Mormon settlement north of Salt Lake and Peacock worked as a clerk in Hays City. He soon migrated down to Dodge, taking a job in the same capacity at Wright's place. Emma joined him there.[35]

In early July 1872 Peacock and Herman Fringer hired carpenters from the fort's worker pool to raise a frame structure on Front Street. It soon contained a drugstore where Fringer offered "drugs, medicines, notions, perfumery, stationery, paints, oils, dye-stuffs, &c., &c., &c." And Dodge Citians picked up their mail there once Fringer had been appointed postmaster.

In short order Alfred Peacock erected a second building in which he opened a billiard saloon, a combination pool hall and tavern where players were promised "round balls! and straight cues!"—the first of Peacock's long sequence of drinking establishments that, as a local historian puts it, "catered to a class slightly below the 'genteel' customers of his competitors."[36]

Another three businessmen—James Kelley, Alonzo Webster, and Richard Evans—arrived from Hays City in August.

Born in Manchester, England, the world's first great industrial city,

James Kelley emigrated with his Irish-born parents to the United States in 1853 at age twelve. The family supposedly settled in Connecticut.

Although an old friend later claimed that Kelley "was a confederate soldier," an obituary said he "enlisted in the U.S. regulars in 1864 or '65 and was sent with his regiment to the west." Military records in the National Archives confirm neither assertion, but Kelley most likely was a so-called Galvanized Yankee, a Confederate soldier who, as the price of release from a Union prison camp, agreed to enroll in the regular army's "U.S. Volunteer Infantry." In 1864–1865 the authorities organized six units of these turncoats—universally despised in the postwar North as well as the South—to help fight Indians on the Plains. Two of the six units served in Kansas as wagon train guards along the Santa Fe Trail, with one of them helping to establish Fort Dodge in 1865.[37]

By the late 1860s Kelley was in Leavenworth, most likely having been demobilized at the nearby fort, where he bought a frame structure destined to be shipped by rail from one army garrison to another. First came Junction City, where the cavalry stationed at Fort Riley promised good saloon and restaurant patronage, then Ellsworth and its army post, next Hays and its fort, where reports claim Kelley served as a civilian scout. (Unfortunately, the fort's monthly returns for the late 1860s fail to identify the numerous "guides and scouts" employed there.) Finally Kelley and his remarkably durable structure made it to Dodge City, where he and a partner resumed the restaurant and saloon business, with Kelley managing the bar. In 1879 they added a second-floor auditorium.[38]

Alonzo Webster, the son of New Englanders, spent his childhood in western New York's famously reformist "Burned-Over District" before his widowed mother turned him over to a legal guardian in Michigan. There the teenager worked as a farmhand.

At age nineteen Webster enlisted in General George Custer's 7th Michigan Cavalry, probably not in time to help Custer's Wolverine Brigade turn the tide at Gettysburg by fighting off encircling Confederate cavalry. Four months later severe illness (variously diagnosed as typhoid fever, rheumatism, and other maladies) caused him to be in and out of army hospitals through most of 1864, including a stay at the state-of-the-art Carver General Hospital in Washington, DC, where Walt Whitman comforted the dying. After Appomattox, orders transferred Webster's regiment to the Far West. In 1866 he was demobilized at Salt Lake City, paying the government $12.50 to retain his service revolver and its holster.[39]

Webster settled in Kansas, first employed as a dispatch rider at Fort Hays, then clerking at the Hays City post office. He earned a reputation as a fierce proponent of law and order. In 1869 when two armed ruffians entered the post office to warn him off, Webster pulled a gun from under the counter, killed one and chased away the other. Not long afterward he eloped with Amanda Treat, born in the Amish country of northeast Ohio, from where her grocer father had resettled the family at Hays.

The couple arrived in Dodge City, and in a new frame building Webster began retailing "dry-goods, clothing, notions, hats, caps, boots & shoes, ladies' and gents' furnishing goods, etc., etc., etc."[40]

Richard Evans, a Presbyterian clergyman's son, emigrated with his parents in 1853 from the rugged and remote Gwynedd County of northwest Wales to a farm in upstate Illinois. He spent his teens working as a clerk and messenger boy before landing a job with the Union Pacific Railroad, then building west toward Wyoming. Somewhere along the line Richard gave up pushing a wheel barrow and veered off to the newly discovered Pike's Peak goldfields. While panning in a creek above Denver he learned of the firing on Fort Sumter.

In July 1862 he helped organize the 2d Colorado Infantry, which marched overland into Kansas. There the regiment and detachments from two other units linked up with the 1st Kansas Colored Infantry and a Native American brigade made up of Cherokees, Creeks, and Seminoles. Commanded by General James Blunt, this uniquely multiracial column advanced into Indian Territory to forestall a rebel invasion of Kansas. At Honey Springs, where Evans was slightly wounded, the Union troops decisively pushed the Confederates back to Arkansas.

In 1863, converted to cavalry, the 2d Colorado hunted down marauding guerrillas in Missouri, in 1864 it harassed invading Confederates from Arkansas, and in 1865 it chased Cheyenne and Arapaho war parties in Kansas.[41]

Following his Fort Riley discharge, Evans found employment there as a post trader's clerk. He next ran a Kansas City restaurant, then worked in a lumberyard, and finally went into general merchandising, specializing in outfitting buffalo runners at Hays City. He and Sarah Old, whose Cornish parents farmed next door to the Evanses back in Illinois, married in 1870. Within two years Sarah assisted Richard as he shifted operations to Dodge, largely because so many hunters, many of whom owed him money for supplies advanced, had done so. His Front Street emporium offered an eclectic array of "staple & fancy groceries, produce, grain, canned goods, tobacco, hides and meat," as well as "Seidenberg & Co's celebrated Key-West cigars."[42]

By October 1872 another three entrepreneurs—Frederick Zimmerman and the Collar brothers, Morris and Jacob—had relocated to Dodge from Kit Carson, a failing boomtown just across the Colorado line.

A Saxon sheep farmer's son born in the Black Forest of southwest Germany, Zimmerman arrived in the United States in 1863 as a seasoned gunsmith, having followed that trade from a teenage apprenticeship in Prussia to overseer jobs in Paris and London. In wartime America he found ready employment at armories in New York City, Trenton, Springfield, and New Britain. While in Connecticut he met and in 1865 married Matilda Messinger, a native Würtemberger, who had come to the United States to live with a brother. Three years later Frederick headed west, seeking the patronage of hunters and sportsmen in Wyoming, northwest Kansas, and, finally, Kit Carson, Colorado, where Matilda and their first child joined him.

The Zimmermans then arrived in Dodge with $3,000 worth of arms and ammunition. With a load of lumber hauled down from Russell, Frederick had a shop built near Hoover's saloon. A larger-than-life model of a buffalo gun topped a pole in front of the building, whose signage advertised "Guns, Pistols, Ammunition, Hardware and Tinware." Representing further diversification, he offered "clocks, jewelry, lumber, flour, grain, and agricultural implements."[43]

Of the Collar brothers little is known. Morris, the elder, born in Austria, and Jacob, birthplace Hungary, had settled in Kit Carson at the end of the sixties. There Morris ran a dry goods business. Jacob, married to the Prussian-born Jennie, identified himself as a tailor. Like many itinerant merchants of Middle European background, the brothers were nonobservant Jews. When fire destroyed Morris's establishment he, Jacob, and Jennie followed the Zimmermans to Dodge.[44]

Morris opened the O.K. Clothing Store next to Peacock's saloon, offering "millinery, staple and fancy dry goods," as well as "a full assortment of furniture, crockery, and window glass." Jacob established his own retail outlet, the Blue Front Store, which featured "general merchandise, furniture, coffins, and undertaker's goods."[45]

In 1873 Morris and Mary Arenson, born in Paris of Russian-Polish parents, married in Saint Louis where the Arensons lived. Mary reunited with Morris in Kansas after the birth of their son Jake, his uncle's namesake.[46]

George Cox, the last of the eleven founding businessmen to arrive at Dodge, moved into town from nearby Larned in November 1872.

Born in the Georgia countryside southeast of Atlanta, Cox claimed to have volunteered for the prestigious 4th Georgia Infantry, a regiment that fought with Lee's Army of Northern Virginia from the Seven Days battles to the surrender at Appomattox. No documentary evidence supports this. Cox also said that after the war he had "drifted about in various places" until he came to Kansas from Alabama, where his parents now lived.

Actually, Cox ended up on the frontier because the War Department sent him there. In 1867, while working as a clerk in Cincinnati, he had enlisted in the 3d US Infantry, unnecessarily subtracting four years from his age. The regiment soon deployed to Fort Leavenworth, then to Fort Larned. A year after his 1870 discharge with the rank of sergeant, Cox married Amy Bennett, a New Jerseyan from the outskirts of Trenton, whose family had hit on hard times, the 1870 census listing her father as a day laborer. Together with a business partner Cox opened a hotel in the nearby town of Larned and played a leading role in Pawnee County's organization as a formal political entity in November 1872, being elected to its charter board of commissioners.[47]

Within weeks of the election George and Amy had relocated to Dodge, having seized the opportunity to purchase the town's principal hostelry, the Essington House, whose owner had been fatally shot. Cox renovated the establishment at a cost, he said, of $11,452 in time for a January 1873 reopening as the Dodge House. With thirty-eight rooms capable of accommodating ninety guests and enclosing a restaurant, billiard parlor, and saloon, the Dodge House commanded the east end of Front Street as the settlement's quality hotel.[48]

---

What of the women? As C. Robert Haywood has noted, "the Victorian true woman rarely has been placed in the western-cattle-town setting."

He might have added that she rarely appeared in the cattle town newspapers unless involved in good works, if middle class, or in male violence, if a member of the demimonde. What little we know otherwise confirms Haywood's observation that the woman of the West, including at the Kansas cattle towns, was "not so much the product of that peculiar environment as of her past associations and the values and manners of current times."

In the "separate spheres" cultural ideology of the late nineteenth century, homemaking and child care, safely confined within the domestic boundaries of the household, were deemed a woman's proper concern. The one sure exception: moral uplift, considered an appropriate activity for women, who, in Haywood's words, "could assume traditionally non-feminine roles with the added authority of a mother figure."[49] So it was that in Dodge some middle-class women and girls finally emerge from historical obscurity in the 1880s by publicly certifying their association with the anti-liquor movements of that decade. But there they seemed to stay. As late as the 1920s, newspaper reports of entirely secular contention in Dodge obviously included women activists but, unlike their male counterparts, none of them are identified by name.

---

And so, in 1872, Dodge City made its debut. On the north side of the railroad tracks, fronting the train station and its high-rise water tank, the big Stars-and-Stripes atop Robert Wright's general store fluttered over what was already the heart of downtown, a nucleus of a dozen or so one- and two-storey wood buildings. Across the tracks toward the Arkansas River a less cohesive straggle of smaller structures and tents inaugurated the town's dives and dance halls district. Landscaping was nonexistent. For decades shade trees were mere fantasies conjured up by leafy street names on the surveyor's plat—Pine, Maple, Locust, Chestnut, Walnut, Spruce, Vine, Cedar, Elm.[50]

While it was still early days, by autumn 1872, as a newspaper reporter paraphrased George Hoover's recollections, "the town had quite a number of buildings and was in a flourishing condition."[51]

The same could not be said of Dodge City's civic situation, which was bad and getting worse.

# YEAR OF LIVING DANGEROUSLY

In the interim between the Dodge City Town Company's organization in August 1872 and the desired land at last coming into its formal possession a year later, the frontier settlement's main challenge was to create from scratch a civil society regulated by law.

An often unruly population congregated at early Dodge. Buffalo hunters, railroad workers, government contractors, and soldiers came to town now and again to spend the dollars jingling in their pockets. Another semitransient thirty to forty men, according to Colonel Dodge's later estimate, eked out a living at gambling and petty criminality or were marginal businessmen, minor artisans, and casual laborers. The so-called hard characters among them, young men of dangerous reputation and fractious nature, proved special troublemakers. Unrestricted access to both liquor and handguns without the close supervision of peace officers became a prescription for bad behavior.[1]

Years later two of Dodge City's pioneers, George Hoover and Robert Wright, assessed the extent of gun violence during the settlement's first twelve months of existence. Hoover said shooting deaths in 1872–1873 totaled "no less than 15." Wright offered an estimate of "twenty-five, and perhaps more than double that number wounded."[2]

Although there is no official body count from early Dodge City, no extant file of coroner's inquests, for example, to verify or discount those estimates, scattered sources do exist. A number of individuals in diaries and letters, in accounts to eager newspaper stringers, and in interviews and memoirs, recorded what they saw and what they heard about violent incidents that ended in bloodshed—gunshot deaths and nonfatal wounds.

Their words, reported here in the earliest surviving versions, provide a contemporary narrative unencumbered by later perceptions about interpersonal violence in the Old West. These verbatim accounts also reveal the grim civic predicament of the town's business community as it desperately sought to rein in the violence by establishing a political and legal structure.[3]

⸺ ⟨∞⟩ ⸺

The callous murder of an African American some time in August 1872, according to both Hoover and Wright, was Dodge City's first shooting fatality. In Wright's words:

> The first man killed in Dodge City was a big, tall, black negro by the name of Tex. . . . He was killed by a gambler named Denver. Mr. Kell[e]y had a raised platform in front of his [business] house, and [Tex] was standing in front and below, in the street, during some excitement. There was a crowd gathered, and some shots were fired over the heads of the crowd, when this gambler fired at Texas [from above] and he fell dead.
>
> No one knew who fired the shot . . . until Denver bragged about it, a long time afterwards, and a long way from Dodge City, and said he shot him in the top of the head just to see him kick.

George Hoover added that Tex, who he remembered as "Black Jack," was the first person interred on Boot Hill, the pioneer burial ground on the western outskirts of town.[4]

In September the editor at nearby Hutchinson published an account of what was later billed as the "first shooting affair" at Dodge: the September 3, 1872, street brawl recounted in the Introduction that ended in the wounding of three men (Charley Morehouse, John Langford, and an unnamed bystander).[5]

Two days later the second documented fatality occurred. The *Topeka Commonwealth,* published at the state capital, broke the story.

> For some time, a notoriously mean and contemptible desperado, named Jack Reynolds has been "beating" his way on the western di-

vision of the A., T. & S. Fe road by murderous threats, backed by a six shooter. On one occasion, he tried his "little game" on Conductor Jansen . . . who tackled the brute, took the six-shooter away from him and pitched him off the train.

Jack, with all his other meannesses was very quarrelsome. On Thursday last [September 5], he got into a quarrel at Dodge City with one of the tracklayers, who, without any "ifs or ands," put six balls, in rapid succession, into Jack's body. The desperado fell and expired instantly; and thus the law-abiding people of the southwest were rid of a terror.

Only a few days before, Jack had shot a man at Raymond [near Great Bend] for some supposed injury.[6]

---

These shootings prompted the members of Dodge City's growing business community, or at least the more reflective among them, to realize that they faced a law-and-order emergency. Gun violence ignited their fears—not for their lives, but for their pocketbooks. Their investments in buildings and goods, to say nothing of the settlement's entire future as a collective real-estate venture, stood at risk.

The State of Kansas nominally sheltered Dodge City by placing it under the political and legal jurisdiction of Ellis County. But Ellis lay a hundred miles away. Civic order, and thus population growth and prosperity, required stewards close at hand: a sheriff, a county prosecutor, judges. Before that could happen the Kansas governor and legislature would have to certify that the virtually empty geographic entity surrounding Dodge—that is, Ford County—legally qualified for self-government.

In October 1872 forty self-identified Dodge Citians initiated the formal process for civic organization. They signed and sent to Governor James Harvey a petition dubiously certifying that Ford contained the legally mandated 600 inhabitants. Harvey obligingly took the next step by appointing Isaac Young, proprietor of a Front Street saddle and harness shop, to take a census. Young spent the next three months—October 21 through January 11—collecting the necessary number of names.[7]

Meanwhile, gun violence continued to plague the village. The *Leav-*

*enworth Commercial* in two sensational sentences reported that "Dodge City is winning the laurels from Newton. Three men were shot at a dance house there the other night and thrown into the streets, while the dance went merrily on." The next day the *Wichita Beacon*, confusing Dodge City with Fort Dodge, published details of this saloon fight that ended in two more homicides and another wounding.

A shooting affair of a desperate character occurred at Fort Dodge on Thursday last [November 14], which grew out of an attempt, our information says, of a party of herders to capture and run the dance house of Kelley & Hunt. Three or four Texas men took [over] the out-fit, one of them made whiskey and sugar free to everybody while the others kept up the dance, music and condiments until daylight.

The dance-room was also occupied by a gambling outfit run by one [Matt] Sullivan and a partner called Billy [Brooks]. One of the Texas men after a game charged Sullivan with cheating and grabbed up the entire wealth of the concern to appropriate it, when Sullivan drew a six shooter and struck him above the left temple, fracturing the skull and penetrating the temporal lobe of the brain with the hammer of the revolver, inflicting a mortal wound.

The other [cowboys] went to the rescue of their companion, one of them came out from the dance, drawing his revolver in the rear of Sullivan, when . . . Billy, who had a six shooter cocked in his hand, raised [it] and shot him dead, the ball entering the cheek bone and coming out at the base of the brain; in the meantime Sullivan shot the other one approaching from the front, through the neck, the ball just grazing the jug[ula]r vein.

The last one shot, is dangerously though not fatally wounded; he passed up on the train to Topeka Friday evening for medical atten-dance there.[8]

A follow-up in the Leavenworth paper denied that the dead and wounded "were thrown out into the street."

As soon as a surgeon could be called their wounds were dressed. The one first shot was taken to the Essington House and the other two, both of whom were considered dangerously wounded, were taken up to [Fort Dodge] and placed in charge of the Post Surgeon for treatment.

Missouri's *Kansas City Times* noted that "one of these men was brought to this city last night to be forwarded to his friends in New Orleans."[9]

A week later came another violent death reported by the *Newton Kansan.*

> A shooting affray took place at the Essington House in Dodge City last Friday night [November 22–23], in which a carpenter, builder and partial owner of the building, was while drunk and in a fuss shot and killed instantly by the cook. He was shot in the head.

The estate of the victim, H. Essington, sold the place to George Cox, who remodeled and reopened it as the Dodge House.[10]

Within a fortnight a bloody bar fight resulted in two more slayings. The *Commonwealth*, also confusing Dodge City with Fort Dodge, described the incident.

> On Tuesday evening last [December 3] a very extensive row occurred in a saloon at Fort Dodge between a squad of soldiers and a number of the citizens of that place. All were in a saloon near the railroad depot, and were engaged in drinking and carousing, as is customary in the early days of all border towns.
>
> A soldier named Hennessy, belonging to company G, of the Third infantry, and who is considered the bully and fighting man of the company, was spoiling for a muss. He got it. We did not learn the particular cause of the row, but a general melee ensued; about forty or fifty shots were fired promiscuously in the room, and the affray terminated with the killing of Hennessy and the fatal wounding of a man named [Charley] Morehouse.
>
> Hennessy was buried on Thursday by his comrades, and Morehouse is momentarily expected to die from the effect of a ball which penetrated his left lung. No one knows who shot either of the men, as the firing was done by all. We are assured that the respectable, law-abiding portion of the community regret the circumstances very much, and are determined to prevent a repetition of such outlawry.

Having recovered from a minor wound in the gunfight at Dodge on September 3, Morehouse this time took a fatal round. Six days later, on December 9, his father wrote from Hannibal, Missouri, asking a Dodge City contact what his son had been doing in Dodge, whether he had a family there, and what "worldly effects" might have survived him. As for Hennessy's death, Robert Wright claimed everyone considered it "good riddance."[11]

A few weeks later Billy Brooks, now anointed "Bully" Brooks, again made the news for his involvement in a contest ending in the wounding of himself and two other men. That the *Oxford Press* featured the story provides an example of how Dodge City's growing notoriety, transmitted orally over some distance, might reach print.

> T. E. Clark, delegate from Oxford to the Western Kansas convention [at Solomon City], arrived home last Thursday evening. . . .
>
> We are indebted to [him] for the particulars of a shooting affray that occurred at Dodge City on Monday night of last week [December 23–24], between "Bully" Brooks, ex-marshal of Newton, and Mr. Brown, yardmaster at the former place, which resulted in the death of Brown. Three shots were fired by each party. Brown's first shot wounded Brooks, whose third shot killed Brown and wounded one of his assistants. Brooks is a desperate character, and has before, in desperate encounters, killed his man.

But Brown did not die. According to Wright:

> A man by the name of Brooks, acting assistant-marshal, shot Browney, the yard-master. . . . The ball entered the back of his head, and one could plainly see the brains and bloody matter oozing out of the wound. . . . The ball entered one side of his head and came out the other, just breaking one of the brain or cell pans at the back. . . . As soon as the old blood and matter was washed off, they saw what was the matter, and he soon got well and was back at his old job in a few months.[12]

Both Billy Brooks, whom Wright here referred to as acting assistant marshal, and Jack Bridges, remembered as the acting marshal, had earlier held law enforcement positions. Brooks served as city marshal at the tough cattle town of Newton until shot in the chest and arm while running two Texas troublemakers out of town. Bridges had been a deputy US marshal, working out of Hays City, before being dangerously wounded while making an arrest at Wichita. He returned to family in Maine to recuperate, but was back in western Kansas by October 1872, apparently on temporary assignment chasing horse thieves and whiskey traders preying on the tribes in Indian Territory. Isaac Young listed him and a wife and child as Ford County residents, presumably occupying quarters at Fort Dodge.[13]

Yet neither Brooks nor Bridges was an official law-enforcement officer at Dodge. Since the town was not yet legally organized, nobody had the power to hire bona fide officers, nor were there public funds to pay them. In short, as summarized many years later, Bridges and Brooks "held no commissions of authority from the community," so it was strictly a private arrangement. Both men, the same source explained, "were hired by saloon keepers and gamblers to preserve some semblance of order among their boisterous patrons."[14]

These unofficial appointments proved ineffective and short-lived. Bridges held a demanding federal job, requiring him to be away much of the time. Brooks remained in Dodge several months longer, but continued to indulge his private quarrels, which local businessmen evidently tired of subsidizing.[15]

At the end of December, as the *Commonwealth* revealed, Brooks may have murdered Matt Sullivan, with whom he had been running a gambling outfit a month earlier.

> Passengers who came in from "the front" yesterday, on the A. T. & S. F. railroad, brought intelligence of another shooting affray at Dodge City. On Saturday evening last [December 28], as Matt. Sullivan, a saloon keeper, was standing in his place of business, a gun was pointed through the window and discharged, the ball striking Sullivan and killing him almost instantly.
>
> It is supposed that the unknown assassin was a character in those parts called Bully Brooks, but nothing definite is known concerning the affair, or what led to it.

A young German-American buffalo hunter from Texas may well have witnessed the Sullivan killing. He claimed that

> one night as I walked up to the front door of the dance hall I saw a man standing with a gun in hand. Inside two men had just stepped up to the bar to take a drink, but he shot one of them through the head, got on his horse and rode off. The music stopped until the floor could

be scrubbed and everything was going again as if nothing had happened.[16]

The *Kansas City Times* offered another possibility for the killing of Sullivan, generally known as a "cowardly rough."

> A short time ago an express messenger [for the railroad] was walking past Sullivan's saloon, when Sullivan's mistress stepped out and spoke to the messenger. While they were conversing Sullivan came up behind the messenger and dealt him a blow over the head with a pistol, cutting a deep gash and slightly fracturing the skull. It is thought that this affair had something to do with his assassination.

A week later, however, the paper printed a more definitive account, with Brooks again as the likely culprit.

> It appears that Bully Brooks . . . walked into a saloon where his victim was in the act of taking a drink, placed a carbine to his ear and shot a bullet clear through his head from ear to ear, killing him instantly. The man had said he intended to kill Brooks, so Brooks took this summary way of preventing it.[17]

---

The new year intensified the race between the mounting body count and citizens' acquisition of a suitable law-enforcement infrastructure.

On January 11, 1873, Herman Fringer, the town's postmaster and notary public, swore to the accuracy of Isaac Young's completed Ford County census, enumerating 609 "bonifide inhabitants." Besides Fringer, the census included seven other founding businessmen: Jacob Collar, Alfred Peacock, James Kelley, Frederick Zimmerman, George Cox, Richard Evans, and Robert Wright. Happily for the town's entrepreneurial elite, a new Kansas governor, Thomas Osborn, passed the document on to the legislature.[18]

Within the week Dodge witnessed yet another bloody brawl in which one man died and two were seriously injured. Back in August, Edward Hurley had been jailed at Great Bend after attempting to rob a railroad subcontractor of $700, and upon release had drifted down the line to Dodge. Testified the *Commonwealth*:

Another terrible shooting affray occurred at Dodge City last Friday night [January 17–18]. As usual, the affair took place at one of the Woodhulleries [dance halls] that infest so many of the temporary outposts of a new railroad. There were some five or six men engaged in the melee, and all had been drinking more or less.

How the trouble commenced our reporter could not learn, but its results are sufficiently deplorable. Two men named Barney Cullen and Edward Hurley were killed on the spot, and another named Southers was wounded so dangerously that it is believed he will not recover. Cullen was an employee of the railroad.

But Cullen did not die. As later reported by a Leavenworth journalist, he was one of "the healthiest looking men we ever saw."[19]

Some residents now began to talk up the need for the town's business and professional men to take matters into their own hands. As the *Newton Kansan* reported:

The orderly citizens of Dodge City have in contemplation the organization of a vigilance committee, and the roughs and rogues generally who have a horror for such proceedings, are beginning to scatter. Several came here on Monday morning's train [January 20], but Marshal Johnson told them there was no room here for such, and they left that night.[20]

Shortly thereafter Hurley's killer fell dead. As its Great Bend correspondent wrote to the *Commonwealth* on January 30:

Another shooting affair has occurred at Dodge, which has proved the death of one McDermott. We cannot give you full particulars, but will give you an inkling of the tragedy, which is purely an item of far frontier life. Sometime since, a man by the name of H[u]rley was shot by McDermott. The "code" is very peculiar in our frontier towns, as you are aware. Consequently a friend of Hurley . . . "plugged" said McDermott.

An observer claimed that Hurley's friend was "a desperado named 'Scotty,'" who killed McDermott in Alfred Peacock's saloon a week after McDermott killed Hurley.[21]

---

The business community had had enough. The result: two extralegal executions. A special dispatch from Dodge promptly made its way to the *Commonwealth*.

A vigilance committee was organized here a few days since. This evening [February 9] they proceeded to the dance house and killed two men named Charles Hill, *alias* Texas, and one Ed. Williams [alias Antelope], and gave five others permission to leave before daybreak or take the consequences, which advice I think they have taken, as they are not to be seen.

These two men were the ringleaders of a gang that have kept the town in an uproar ever since it has been started, but we think they have got them pretty well cleaned out now.[22]

The *Kansas City Journal of Commerce*, the *Kansas City Times*, and the *Leavenworth Commercial* then elaborated.

The trouble, all three agreed, began at Sargeant, a railroad camp a hundred miles to the west of Dodge where "a gang of desperadoes" from Dodge had gathered. They began destroying property and roughing up citizens until, on the morning of February 7, a saloon keeper and former army scout named Christopher Gilson took them on, killing three with a shotgun and blasting the arm off a fourth. According to the *Journal of Commerce* correspondent, "The roughs then left and went to Dodge City where they again undertook to run the town. Their first exploit was to shoot into the house of a Mr. Brooks"—the pugnacious Billy. Perhaps Brooks wired Gilson for help. In any event the former army scout arrived, said the *Commercial* reporter, "where he was met by many friends. Taking his trusty shot-gun, he went around and stirred up the citizens of Dodge."

The *Kansas City Times* printed the best summary of what happened next.

On Sunday last [February 9] they notified the outlaws to leave, but the roughs, deeming themselves the strongest party, refused to go. On Sunday night a Vigilance Committee, twenty in number, went to a dance hall and shot a rough named Williams and wounded another, a Texan [named Hill], who ran over to a dance hall kept by one Tom Sherman. He was pursued by the Vigilantes and shot dead.

"Over two hundred shots were fired inside of ten minutes," claimed the Leavenworth writer, noting that "twenty balls were found in each of their bodies." The *Kansas City Times* reporter added that the very next day "a suspicious character, named Pony Spencer, and his companion were found in Dodge. They received ten minutes' notice to leave town or be shot. They left."

Two days later the *Denver Times* ran a short paragraph on the incident: "Two men of a party of roughs disturbing the peace at Sarge[a]nt, Kansas, were shot by a saloon-keeper. The party then went to Dodge City, where a vigilance committee killed two more."[23]

As Colonel Dodge later reported, the vigilantes had "banded together and taken certain obligations as to secrecy[,] mutual protection &c." In other words, they had organized according to the model seen from time to time in the West since being popularized by the San Francisco business community in 1851, although copycat associations usually insisted on membership secrecy. By the accepted rules any one of the group could initiate an action, and a majority vote then bound all members, by formal oath, to join in support. That both Dodge City victims, Texas Hill and Antelope Williams, suffered exactly twenty bullet wounds confirms that the vigilance committee numbered twenty, each member having fired one round into each body to establish shared culpability, an insurance against betrayal to the authorities.[24]

Except for Gilson, the identities of the original vigilantes remain uncertain, but many years later Robert Wright hinted at his own participation.

> To protect ourselves and property, we were compelled to organize a Vigilance Committee. Our very best citizens promptly enrolled themselves, and, for a while, it fulfilled its mission to the letter and acted like a charm, and we were congratulating ourselves on our success. The committee only had to resort to extreme measures a few times, and [before doing so] gave the hard characters warning to leave town.[25]

A month later the vigilantes eliminated another troublemaker. Henry Raymond, a hide hunter, recorded the confrontation.

Last night [March 11–12] the vigilance committee shot McGill, a buffalo hunter for firing pistol in dance hall. I went down town [and] saw him.

Years later Raymond amended this diary entry.

It later proved that Magill did not fire in the dance hall, but was handling his gun in a menacing manner when his youthful pardner got him outside where he attempted to shoot in at the window. The boy pulled his arm down and [the] shot did no harm.[26]

The *Atchison Patriot* reported the incident in more detail.

An unmitigated scoundrel and desperado, named McGill, was shot and killed at Dodge City. . . . On Tuesday night last, he visited Dodge City, and amused himself by shooting into almost every house he passed. The citizens became alarmed, and concluded to arm themselves, and thus put a stop to his villainous career.

Jim Hanrahan, Tom Kelley, Mr. Scott, Chris Gillson, and a few others started in pursuit of the desperado, and brought him to bay near the city. He opened fire on the party with his needle gun. They responded; and the result was, he was brought into town riddled with bullets.[27]

Three of the four vigilantes named by the *Patriot* are clearly identifiable. Saloon keeper James Hanrahan would soon be appointed one of Ford's interim county commissioners, after which he won election as its first legislative representative. John "Scotty" Scott had been taken on as a business partner in Alfred Peacock's popular Billiard Saloon. And Gilson had led the vigilante raid of February 9. The fourth, Tom Kelley, was more than likely saloon proprietor James Kelley.[28]

It was Scott and his ilk that Robert Wright later accused of having corrupted the vigilance committee. As he put it:

Hard, bad men kept creeping in and joining [the organization] until they outnumbered the men who had joined it for the public good— until they greatly outnumbered the good members, and when they felt themselves in power, they proceeded to use that power to avenge their grievances and for their own selfish purposes, until it was a farce as well as an outrage on common decency.[29]

The night after McGill's killing the death toll rose again: Tom Sherman was the killer and a young man named Burns, the late McGill's partner, the victim. As Henry Raymond explained:

At a late hour in the night [of March 12–13] we heard shooting in town. Shots were fired at irregular intervals.

I hastily rose and ran down town. . . . I could see some fellows gathering and, as I drew closer, could discern a man down and moving his legs & arms. Possibly he may have had consciousness enough to feel that he was fleeing from his pursuer with whom I almost collided. This was Tom Sherman, a big lubbery fellow, who ran with a limp. He had a large calibre revolver in his hand which he was emptying into the boy that was down at every glimpse he could get of him. . . .

Tom, panting for breath, said to those gathering, "I'd better shoot him again, hadn't I boys?" He stepped at once to where he lay struggling; stood over him holding the big revolver in both hands, aimed at his forehead and fired. The bullet went a little high and scattered his brains in his hair. . . . All I could learn was that Sherman had killed [McGill] a friend of Burns and thought it would be safer to have him out of the way.

. . . The body of Burns was allowed to lie behind a hog shed all night. . . . The boys counted where nine bullets had hit him. . . . In the afternoon of the next day some plain boards were brought and nailed together. Into this rough box the body, boots and all, was placed and he was carried up to Boot Hill, with blood oozing from cracks in the box.[30]

Although differing about details on the removal of the corpse to Boot Hill, a young Swedish immigrant may have described the aftermath of the Burns killing:

One night after I had fallen asleep, I was awakened by several pistol shots and I heard the next morning that there had been a fight that night in a dance hall and a man had been killed. That morning as I was going to work, and had to go past that dance hall, I saw a form lying outside. When I got nearer I saw that it was a dead man. . . . When I went home at noon the dead man still lay there, but when I had stopped work for the day and was going home, they had fastened the body to a big pole. As two men carried it with the head and the feet hanging down, I followed them. Each man had a shovel and when they got to the cemetery they dug a grave, not over three feet deep, threw the body into it, and filled it up. When I asked if they knew who the dead man was, I was told that it was no concern of mine.

On March 21 a garbled account of the slayings of McGill and Burns appeared in the *Commonwealth's* gossipy "Various Items" column.

A man by the name of Burns was killed at Dodge City last week; he was shot from his horse by a government guide [Gilson?] whose blood he was searching for at the time. Burns fell from his horse shot through the brain; the guide went up to him and stuck the muzzle of his carbine to his bosom and slid another half pound ball through his form to kill him good. The man was left lying an entire day where he struck the ground.[31]

------◦◦◦------

April brought much-needed good news. Governor Osborn finally declared Ford County organized, appointing four interim officers, among them Herman Fringer as acting county clerk. At the end of the month the new officials scheduled an election for early June.[32]

Then came a setback. On May 12 the Kansas attorney general contested Ford's organization, alleging that both the October petition to the governor and Isaac Young's census were "false and fraudulent." In other words, he questioned that Ford County actually contained the required 600 inhabitants, so he filed a *quo warranto* action against the newly appointed commissioners, challenging their right to exercise the functions of office. This maneuver invited the Kansas supreme court to "inquire into [the alleged] falsehood and fraud." If the court found the charges true, it would declare the organization of Ford County "illegal and void."[33]

According to Colonel Dodge it was widely believed that the Santa Fe Railroad provoked this legal gambit. Its corporate officers correctly feared that as owners of the only local real estate of substantial value outside of the tax-exempt Fort Dodge Military Reservation, the company would bear the main tax burden of a new Ford County government.

Although the supreme court agreed to hear the action, it could not do so until after the election of permanent officers on June 5.[34]

———⋄———

Dodge, like many other Kansas towns, mirrored the Victorian era's racism. But its small number of black residents, only forty-two in 1880 and sixty-eight five years later, appear to have tempered racial tensions.

Racial separation did become more pronounced by the end of the cattle-trading era, when Dodge's African Americans organized their own residential district south of the Arkansas River. A black-owned dance hall opened to accommodate black cowboys. And reputable African Americans held their own dances and parties. As the record reveals and historian C. Robert Haywood confirms, if the white community believed a black individual had demonstrated sufficient respectability, that person was generally accorded at least formal recognition. Especially was this true with respect to the town's few black entrepreneurs.

William Taylor, age thirty-seven, an African American from Leavenworth, numbered among Dodge City's established businessmen. He owned a restaurant and operated a heavily patronized shuttle service between Dodge City and Fort Dodge. On June 3–4, hours before the scheduled election of Ford County's charter public officials, the vigilance committee's hooligan element instigated William Taylor's brutal murder, resulting in the first homicide indictment in Dodge City.[35]

A local correspondent for the *Topeka Commonwealth* was the first to report the affair. With weighty sarcasm he masqueraded as one of the killers, exposing their extravagantly sadistic racism. While the reporter termed the killers "b'hoys," by way of identifying them as Irish, their treatment of the dying black man mimicked the racial savagery of a Deep South lynching. The mob

> dragged [Taylor] out and emptied a half dozen revolvers into him. And then such a good time as we had. We knocked all his teeth out and pounded him with pistols and boot heels until he was near cold. . . . After we all got tired beating him, we just by way of a lark went through him. He had a good business and several horses and mules, and might have money, so we took his watch, pocket book, etc.

This morning the "cuss" was found in front of Fringer's store, where we left him. . . . Gentlemen must have their little sprees.[36]

Another Dodge Citian later reconstructed the cruel affair for the *Kansas City Times.*

The night of the murder [June 3–4] "Scotty" and some of his friends had engaged [Taylor's] wagon to take them down to the Fort. They had been drinking hard all day, and were in a beastly state of intoxication, and in this condition they started, at a late hour of the night, to visit the Fort. [Soon] they commenced maltreating the driver, finally knocking him out of the wagon with the butt end of a revolver, and taking entire charge of the team. The driver run up to Taylor's place, and informed him of what had occurred. When Taylor came to protest someone shot one of his mules.

Just then another shot was heard, and the night watch at the depot called out that the "damned negro had shot him;" when they instantly fired upon Taylor, the shot taking effect, and in its course passing through his kidneys. Taylor, as soon as shot, turned and fled, and attempted to get into the house of a colored woman.

Denied refuge by the terrified woman, he limped to Herman Fringer's drug store, which also housed the offices of Dr. Thomas McCarty, the town's physician.

He was followed and found by [Bill] Hicks, the brother of the night watch at the depot, who was going to shoot him on sight, but was restrained from doing so by Dr. McCarty and Mr. Finnigan [Fringer], who were busily engaged in dressing the poor man's wounds. Hicks left, but soon returned with "Scotty" and several others. "Scotty" exclaimed upon seeing the poor man, "Here you are, you black son of a bitch," raised his heavy rifle and fired . . . the shot knocking Taylor out of the chair, when several more shots were fired. . . . Taylor was dragged out and left lying in front of the store, . . . no one daring to go near him, to remove the body until next morning.

McCarty and Fringer took to their heels, the latter recalling that

when he ran out of his store he could see the mob coming from all directions, armed and breathing vengeance against the poor negro, and that a man would not have lived a moment that dared to have the temerity of interfering in behalf of the man. It was afterward ascertained that Hicks, the night watch at the dep[o]t, accidentally shot himself.[37]

Early on the morning of the killing, Colonel Dodge, utilizing a wire that since March had linked the fort and the town's telegraph office, fired off a furious message to Governor Osborn.

A most *foul* & cold blooded murder committed last night by *ruffians* in Dodge City[;] County organized but no election yet had[;] no body with power to act[;] please authorize the arrest of murderers[.]

Osborn immediately replied in the affirmative:

Until Ford County is fully organized you are authorized to arrest and hold, subject to the orders of the civil authorities of the proper Judicial District, all persons notoriously guilty of a violation of the criminal laws of this State.[38]

Dodge promptly endowed Deputy US Marshal Jack Bridges with a military posse and ordered him to make arrests. Diarist Henry Raymond briefly recorded the outcome.

[June 4] This morning the town surrounded by soldiers trying to arrest the murderer of Taylor who was killed last night.
[June 5] Soldiers again surrounded the town [and] put five men in jail, viz. Sherman, Gilson, Cook and the two Hicks's.[39]

The *Newton Kansan* reported the immediate aftermath.

Judge Brown, C. E. Millard, of this county, the sheriff of Chase county, and others went up Friday morning last [June 6] to arrest and give the murderers a [preliminary] examination. They returned Tuesday, having found evidence to convict but one, Hicks, excepting Scotty, who escaped. Parties from Dodge report the law abiding citizens in the majority, but they are of the milk and water order, and that the druggist [Herman Fringer] might have had more arrested but was afraid to disclose them.[40]

A month later the *Kansas City Times* published a rumor about how Scott had avoided capture.

It is thought by Col. Dodge and the citizens of the town, [that Scott escaped] through the connivance of Bridges, the Marshal—as he was seen on the back streets when the arrests were being made.

Local legend reveals details about both Scott's disappearance and Hicks's guilt. It was said that when the troops moved in Scott hid in a large ice-box in Peacock's Billiard Saloon and fled town that night. He was never captured despite a $500 reward posted by the state. The story on Hicks: He walked up to Taylor's body, threw aside its buffalo-hide shroud, pointed to one of the bullet holes, and said, "I shot him there."[41]

By then Colonel Dodge had sent Governor Osborn a full report, beginning with some background.

Everyone who has had experience of life in Rail Road and mining Towns, in unorganized counties or Territories beyond the reach of civil Law is perfectly aware of the necessity of "vigilance committees" so called—organizations which take upon themselves the right and onus of punishing crime, where otherwise it would [go] unpunished & unpunishable. . . .

So long as these organizations confine themselves to the legitimate object of punishing crime, they are not only laudable but absolutely necessary—[yet] there is a difficulty.

It is not often that the property owning and valuable class of citizens are strong enough to do this work alone. They are obliged to receive into their organization some of the roughs. These in turn take in others worse than themselves until as I have often seen it, a vigilance committee organized by good men in good faith, has become after a while simply an organized band of robbers and cutthroats[.] Another difficulty—Having banded together and taken certain obligations as to secrecy[,] mutual protection &c. the good men sometimes find themselves obliged to aid and abet what in their own hearts they know to be cold blooded crimes perpetrated by their associates.

Then the colonel offered specifics, although with no mention of racial enmity.

The Town of Dodge City is under the control of such a band of vigilantes—some good men, some bad. The murder of Taylor was committed by these vigilantes who were called together on the first alarm, then dispersed to search for Taylor, and while Scott & Hicks (vigilantes both) dragged him from the Drug Store, and shot him to death, at least a dozen other vigilantes stood by ready—and obliged—to take a hand in the shooting if necessary. Among these were good men, who would be shocked at the thought of committing individual crime, and yet who aided, abetted and became "particips criminis" in the most cowardly and cold blooded murder I have ever known in an experience of frontier life dating back to 1848.

Of course these vigilantes are only a small portion of the population of Dodge City. It is probable they do not number over thirty or forty men, but being organized and unscrupulous they are able to exercise a complete tyranny of terror over the much larger number of really good citizens who lack organization [and are] utterly powerless to do anything.[42]

In the only murder trial coming out of Dodge's year of living dangerously, Bill Hicks pleaded not guilty. Dr. McCarty, Robert Wright's business partner Charles Rath, and three founding entrepreneurs—Herman Fringer, Alfred Peacock, and James Kelley—testified at the preliminary hearing. Tom Sherman, one of the four men released for lack of evidence of murdering Taylor, also appeared as a witness for the prosecution. The jury brought in a verdict of second-degree (malicious but unpremeditated) murder.

Hicks was then granted a new trial on unspecified legal grounds and a change of venue to Great Bend. Unable to make bail, he spent a year in jail and then pleaded guilty to third-degree manslaughter: He'd helped kill Taylor, but only "in the heat of passion, without a design to effect death." The penalty for that was up to three years' hard labor in the state penitentiary. The judge credited Hicks with time served and gave him another two years. He was discharged from prison in April 1876.[43]

--------·◦◦◦·--------

For six weeks after their June 5 election Ford County's new officials, intimidated by the Kansas attorney general's impending case, proved reluctant to take on their obligations. As the county attorney complained in mid-July, "Several of the officers elect were very dilatory about entering upon the duties of their respective offices owing to the writ of *Quo Warranto* served upon the Commissioners."[44]

Meanwhile, Colonel Dodge implored Governor Osborn to pressure those elected to assume their jobs, since racial violence continued. "There have been two more attempts at murder in Dodge City, a Negro being the sufferer in each case," he wrote. "The man shot last night [July 4–5] will probably die, being wounded in head and lungs." (These injuries no doubt proved fatal.) Dismissing racial animosities, the editor of the *Newton Kansan* offered details on the second victim, who identified his assailants as a remnant of the bad vigilantes.

> Wallace Dade, a colored man, came in from Dodge City last Saturday evening [July 5], having been shot there by some person through the hand, and also with a cut upon his head from a pistol, as he says. He says the roughs did it from no cause whatever, but we can hardly credit the story.[45]

Governor Osborn heeded Colonel Dodge's advice and urged Ford's new officers to undertake their duties and begin "working harmoniously together in the preservation of order and enforcement of law." Implicit in this instruction was that the Kansas attorney general's *quo warranto* action should be ignored. If the state supreme court eventually voided Ford County's organization (as it would in January 1874), the legislature could pass a statue legalizing its organization and all acts its elected officials had performed in good faith (as it would in March 1874).[46]

⸻ ⬥ ⸻

Ford's elected authorities were finally on the job and legal procedures in place when in late July 1873 two more men died violently. The lethal confrontation between Bill Ellis and Dave Burrell occurred on the night of July 20–21 outside George Cox's hotel. Ellis died the next day, and Justice of the Peace P. T. Bowen convened a coroner's jury. It concluded that the badly wounded Burrell had acted "in self defense," adding that "we the jurors do agree that [Ellis's death] was brought on through carrying firearms—which we emphatically condemn." Signatories to this plea for gun control included businessmen George Hoover and Alfred Peacock, as well as two unlikely advocates of good order: the renegade vigilante Tom Sher-

*Year of Living Dangerously* : 41

TABLE 1

*Gun Violence in Dodge City, June 1872–July 1873*

| Incident | | Dead | | Wounded | |
|---|---|---|---|---|---|
| N | Type | N | Name | N | Name |
| 1 | Racial | 1 | Texas | 0 | — |
| 2 | Street Brawl | 0 | — | 3 | Langford Morehouse Unnamed |
| 3 | Quarrel | 1 | Reynolds | 0 | — |
| 4 | Barroom Brawl | 2 | Unnamed Texans | 1 | Unnamed Texan |
| 5 | Quarrel | 1 | Essington | 0 | — |
| 6 | Barroom Brawl | 2 | Hennessy Morehouse | 0 | — |
| 7 | Quarrel | 0 | — | 3 | Brooks Brown Unnamed |
| 8 | Quarrel | 1 | Sullivan | 0 | — |
| 9 | Barroom Brawl | 1 | Hurley | 2 | Cullen Southers |
| 10 | Quarrel | 1 | McDermott | 0 | — |
| 11 | Vigilantism | 2 | Hill Williams | 0 | — |
| 12 | Vigilantism | 1 | McGill | 0 | — |
| 13 | Quarrel | 1 | Burns | 0 | — |
| 14 | Racial Vigilantism | 1 | Taylor | 1 | Hicks |
| 15 | Racial Vigilantism | 1 | Unnamed African American | 0 | — |
| 16 | Racial Vigilantism | 0 | — | 1 | Dade |
| 17 | Quarrel | 2 | Burrell Ellis | 0 | — |
| | | 18 | | 11 | |

man and the belligerent Billy Brooks. (A year later Brooks was hanged by a Sumner County mob for belonging to a gang of mule thieves.)[47]

A correspondent for the *Commonwealth* reproduced the evidence considered at the inquest.

Ellis, the man killed, was a herder. . . . He came into town on the morning of Sunday, and had been drinking more or less all day. At night he was pretty full, and, in company with "Charley [Hungerford], the butcher," and two prostitutes, went to the barroom of the

[Dodge House] and asked for the drinks for the party. He was refused by Da[ve] Burrell, the barkeeper. Some words followed and the party then left and went to French Peter's saloon where they stowed away some beer.

In returning they had to pass by the hotel on the porch of which the bartender was sitting. It seems that from the harsh words spoken as the party was leaving the hotel, the bartender must have apprehended some trouble, as he armed himself with a Manhattan pistol and had it on his person when the party returned.

The confrontation then became personal.

Ellis boasted of his prowess and said he could whip any damned s— of a b— around the hotel. The remark coming from a drunken man, or any other, for that matter, should have remained unnoticed, but Burrell, who is rather inclined to be quick-tempered, immediately took it up, and replying, told Ellis he had better not talk so loud, and that he was a G—d—d liar. Starting down the steps he pulled off his coat, evidently intending to use his fists in any contest that might ensue, but on [Burrell's] reaching the ground Ellis drew his revolver, and of course Burrell followed suit. . . .

Ellis fired first. Burrell immediately returned the fire and fell upon the ground, exclaiming—"My God, I am shot!" . . . There are those who think that Burrell missed Ellis and he was afterwards shot by "Curley," *alias* Johnny Murr[a]y [who] immediately after the firing jumped off of the porch and grappled with Ellis, taking his pistol away from him. . . .

Three shots were fired. [Possibly] Ellis came to his death by a ball from his own pistol while in the hands of Murr[a]y. . . .

P.S.—Later—July 22d.—David Burrell died this afternoon at four o'clock from the effects of a wound received in the affray on Sunday night.[48]

---

With Burrell's demise the yearlong carnage ended. Was there gun violence resulting in bloodshed at Dodge not recorded in these randomly preserved accounts? No doubt. Undocumented incidents leading to gunshot deaths or injuries most likely occurred. Yet the violent encounters enumerated here are probably not far off the mark, since the number of fatalities fits neatly within the homicide estimates offered by George Hoover (fifteen) and Robert Wright (twenty-five).

Eighteen men lost their lives in the seventeen documented incidents and another eleven suffered nonfatal gunshot wounds. Shootings resulting from barroom brawls claimed five lives. Seven killings stemmed from long-term or impromptu quarrels. Vigilantes gunned down three white men and instigated three of the four racially motivated assaults, of which all but one ended in the murder of a black man (see Table 1).

In Dodge, as elsewhere, evening hours saw the most drinking and thus the most violence. Unlike many other western venues, however, Dodge's weekend was not a specifically dangerous moment. At mining camps in Colorado and Arizona, wage workers tended to overindulge and quarrel most lethally on Saturday nights and Sundays.[49] Not so in Dodge City, where a lack of steady jobs among the saloon-and-dance-hall regulars permitted them to overindulge, quarrel, and sleep late the next morning. They killed and were killed every day of the week. Only one fatal shooting, that of Matt Sullivan, occurred on a Saturday night.

The absence of a law enforcement infrastructure had brought Dodge City a very dangerous year indeed; its establishment sharply reversed that situation.[50] From August 1873 through 1875 apparently no violent deaths occurred. During the final eleven years of Dodge's frontier era, the cattle trading period of early 1876 through early 1886, the known body count totaled eighteen, or 1.6 violent deaths per year, substantial but not shocking.[51]

Yet the public memory of that exceptionally lethal first season would color perceptions throughout Dodge City's frontier years.

# DEADLY PROSE

The narrative context for the West of myth and metaphor, in which Dodge City would surface as a prominent feature, emerged as early as the mid-nineteenth century.

In the 1850s eastern journalists touring the West reported exaggerated accounts of violence that sometimes reflected a receptive ear for local "tall stories" and at other times revealed their own disapproval of indiscriminate handgun display. "Street affrays are numerous," wrote travel writer Frederick Law Olmsted from San Antonio, "[and] murders, from avarice or revenge, are common here." Journalist Albert D. Richardson, also writing from Texas, was told by his stagecoach driver, "If you want to obtain distinction in this country, kill somebody!" *New York Tribune* editor Horace Greeley commented from Denver that "there have been, during my two weeks' sojourn, more pistol shots with criminal intent than in any community of no greater numbers on earth."[1]

Western editors themselves underscored the perception of bullet-riddled corpses piled up like cordwood in the trans-Missouri West by occasionally publishing highly inflated body counts. In 1854 a San Francisco editor confidently stated that there had been no less than 300 murders there over the past five years. (We now know the number was 78.) In 1866 a Montana editor maintained that precisely 102 persons had died feloniously in the territory since the discovery of gold there. (The actual body count was 8.)[2]

Beginning in the 1860s dime novels with a western theme and blank-cartridge showmanship on the stage commodified the Wild West for a mass market by appealing to boys, working-class men, and Civil War soldiers. In the postwar years some of the prolific authors of westerns began taking actual persons as characters, Jesse James, "Buffalo Bill" Cody, and J. B. "Wild Bill" Hickok being favorites. In 1872 Cody, three years before he also began penning westerns, went before the footlights, playing himself in an Indian-fighting melodrama that enthralled eastern audiences, an endeavor he briefly enticed a reluctant Hickok to join.[3]

Around the same time, two literary lions of the 1870s introduced the nation's middle and upper classes to the casual gun violence supposedly common in the West.

Bret Harte's very first collection of short stories opened with the lethal antics of French Pete and Kanaka Joe, whose fatalities—they shot each other—served as light comic introduction to sentimental tales of assorted California characters. A book reviewer for the *Atlantic Monthly*, as an example of East Coast elite opinion, found Harte's stories absolutely enchanting: "The revolver-echoing cañon, the embattled diggings, the lawless flat, and the immoral bar might well have been believed secure from notice. [But] here we have them in literature not overpainted, but given with all their natural colors and textures."

More to the point was humorist Mark Twain, whose account of his western travels hit the nation's bookstores in the same year Buffalo Bill went on stage. In Virginia City, Nevada, Twain asserted, a fellow was not respected until he had "killed his man." Local celebrities such as Sugarfoot Mike, Pock-Marked Jake, and Six-Fingered Pete each "kept [a] private graveyard," were always "on the shoot" (ready for a fight), and cheerfully expected to die "with their boots on." Clearly, Twain had invented the legendary gunfighter, although the culturally essential term for him would not appear in print for another twenty-two years.[4]

---

Dodge City's reputation as a major theater of western violence—a "'red hot' town," as one editor put it—began to take shape when in 1872–1873 the newspapers of the state and region took notice of the settlement's year of living dangerously.[5]

The *Topeka Commonwealth*, with one of the largest circulations in

Kansas, gave the September 1872 shooting of Jack Reynolds front-page headlines well above the fold.

HOMICIDE AT DODGE CITY.
A NOTORIOUS DESPERADO KILLED.

The deaths of Hennessy and Charley Morehouse in early December also merited *Commonwealth* headlines.

SHOOTING SCRAPE AT FORT DODGE.
ONE MAN KILLED AND ANOTHER FATALLY WOUNDED.

At the end of the month came the killing of Matt Sullivan.

SHOT DEAD.
ANOTHER TRAGEDY AT DODGE CITY.

In January 1873 another *Commonwealth* headline announced the fatality of Ed Hurley and presumed death of Barney Cullen.

TWO MEN KILLED.

The demise of McDermott later that month yielded only a subhead.

MORE SHOOTING AT DODGE CITY.

The *Commonwealth*'s headline-writers went back to work, however, when the town's vigilantes executed Charley Hill and Ed Williams.

FROM THE FRONTIER.
ETERNAL VIGILANCE IS THE PRICE OF EVERYTHING.
TWO MEN KILLED IN A DANCE HOUSE AT DODGE CITY.

And they expressed outrage over William Taylor's vicious killing, which a Newton editor smugly labeled a "SPECIMEN OF DODGE CITY." The *Commonwealth*'s headline described the atrocity as

KILLING AN UNARMED NEGRO AND THE FUN OF IT.
CIVILIZATION A FAILURE.[6]

It fell to the *Leavenworth Commercial* and the *Wichita Eagle* to publicize the last violent incident in Dodge's perilous year. Both papers headlined the murderous confrontation between David Burrell and William Ellis.

One called readers' attention to "THE DODGE CITY TRAGEDY," the other to "MORE SHOOTING."[7]

With recycled stories bouncing from paper to paper, editors throughout Kansas eagerly publicized the image of Dodge City "making herself notorious," as the *Newton Kansan* declared. The *Wichita Eagle* reproduced the *Oxford Press*'s account of Brooks shooting Brown the yardmaster. Newspapers in Abilene, Emporia, Lawrence, and no doubt elsewhere carried the *Leavenworth Commercial*'s elaborate description of the Hill and Williams killings. Marion Center's paper did the same for the *Atchison Patriot* story on the vigilante murder of McGill. In this manner shared headlines such as "ANOTHER SHOOTING SCRAPE AT DODGE CITY" made the rounds of the Kansas press.[8]

Sensational story headlines also crossed the border to newspapers in neighboring Kansas City, Missouri, a major urban center.

The *Kansas City Times* ran an eye-catching heading above its account of the fatal brawl at Kelley and Hunt's dance house.

BORDER PASTIMES.
THREE MEN BORED WITH BULLETS AND THROWN INTO THE STREET.

Five days later it reprinted the *Wichita Beacon*'s report on that same homicidal row. The paper next headlined the killing of Matt Sullivan.

MURDER.
A DESPERADO SHOT IN HIS OWN SALOON.

A follow-up story was titled simply

MORE BORDER PASTIMES.

The vigilante action at Dodge merited the most elaborate—and shamelessly exaggerated—Kansas City headlines yet.

FROLICS ON THE FRONTIER.
VIGILANTES AMUSING THEMSELVES IN THE SOUTHWEST.
HOW CHRIS GILSON WIPED OUT A GANG OF
DESPERADOES AT SERGEANT—SIXTEEN
BODIES TO START A GRAVEYARD AT
DODGE CITY—RIFLES AND ROPES
THINNING OUT THE ROUGHS.

Above its own front-page story on the affair the *Kansas City Journal of Commerce* weighed in, less imaginatively, with

TERRIBLE TIMES ON THE BORDER.
HOW THINGS ARE DONE OUT WEST.[9]

Dodge City's notoriety even spread to the East Coast. A Saint Louis editor picked up the vigilante story from the *Journal of Commerce* and forwarded it, probably as an Associated Press dispatch, to the *New York Times*. On February 17, 1873, the bad news out of Dodge made its eastern metropolitan debut under a rather subdued heading.

BORDER RUFFIANISM IN KANSAS—SUMMARY
MEASURES WITH IT.

Within four months the *New York Tribune*, by all accounts the nation's most prestigious news outlet, introduced readers by the thousands to a place they likely had not yet heard of. Adapting information on the Taylor murder from the *Topeka Commonwealth*, the *Tribune* gave over almost ten column inches to the story.

THE DIVERSIONS OF DODGE CITY.

In Kansas there is a settlement called and known as Dodge City. . . .
In other parts of the far West youth are usually content to hunt wild beasts or possibly Indians; but in Dodge City, it seems, they have a passion for hunting negroes, and the more defenseless they are, the greater is the gusto of the sport. . . .
It does not appear that any functionary, military or civil, thought of interfering with the piquant games of these rough roysterers. The fact is that in charming Dodge City there is no law. There are no sheriffs and no constables. . . . Consequently there are a dozen well-developed murderers walking unmolested about Dodge City doing as they please.[10]

While the *Tribune*'s sarcastic headline and scathing editorial typified much of the Taylor coverage, it also reflected the journalistic banter, ranging from humor to ridicule, that frequently characterized reportage during the town's *annus horribilis*. Both the *Kansas City Times* and *Kansas City Journal of Commerce*, as mentioned, mocked Dodge's vigilantism—"border pastimes," "frolics on the frontier," "how things are done out West." A Topeka correspondent visiting Dodge early in 1873 similarly remarked that the town, "which is scarcely four months old ... has in that time attained considerable notoriety for liveliness, especially in the lively extinguishment of disputes and disputers at point of arms." An Atchison editor likewise found humor in Dodge City's predicament:

> The Kansas papers are inclined to make mouths at Dodge, because she has existed only one month or thereabouts and already has a cemetery started without the importation of corpses. Her enterprise in furnishing her material for interment is the cause of envy from her sister towns.

Quipped an Ellsworth editor: "Only two men killed at Dodge City last week." And a lively joke circulated: "A gentleman wishing to go from Wichita to Dodge City, applied to a friend for a letter of introduction. He was handed a double-barreled shot-gun and a Colt's revolver."[11]

It became easy to imagine Twain-like recreational homicide at Dodge City, whose very name lent itself to images of trigger-happy desperados weaving and ducking while citizens cowered behind closed doors. Within that context the *Kansas City News* announced that Wild Bill Hickok was dead, having been "RIDDLED WITH BULLETS AT FORT DODGE." Much editorial chuckling ensued when it became clear that the famous plainsman was very much alive and had never even visited Dodge.[12]

Yet the violence was serious and seemed to portend continued bloodshed as the *New York Tribune*'s damning editorial on the loathsome gunning down of Taylor darkly predicted.

> Dear, delightful Dodge City! If these things are done in its nonage [its youth], what a homicidal sort of maturity is before it.[13]

---

Determined to avert that prophesy, Dodge City had already taken steps toward the rule of law. The men chosen in the special election of June 5, 1873, and in the regular election of November 4 brandished a mandate to establish civil society within Ford County, as a report from Dodge made perfectly clear.

> Since the outrageous murder of Taylor by "Scotty" and his friends, the better class of citizens have determined to not only have law, but

to enforce it to the bitterest extremity. [They] have fully resolved that their town shall not be disgraced by any more such scenes of violence and bloodshed.

Almost all of the elected officials came from the town's business and professional elite, including ten of the eleven founding entrepreneurs. In the special county election four founders moved into elective positions: Frederick Zimmerman, one of three county commissioners; Herman Fringer, county clerk and district court clerk; George Cox, probate judge; and Morris Collar, township trustee. Five months later in the regular election Zimmerman and Cox retained their positions, Fringer remained as county clerk, Collar switched to superintendent of public instruction, and two other founding businessmen joined county government—Alfred Peacock, commissioner, and Alonzo Webster, treasurer.

Over the next ten years some strategic reshuffling took place, reflecting a long frontier tradition of sharing available tax-supported jobs, but the town's founding entrepreneurs remained prominent. At the Ford County level, Cox and George Hoover took commissioners' seats, Fringer succeeded Cox as probate judge, Zimmerman and Richard Evans—like Webster before them—served as treasurer, while Robert Wright won the top political position, representative to the state legislature. And from Dodge's elevation to a municipality of the third class in autumn 1875 and its first town election on December 1 to the end of its frontier days in 1886, four founders governed as mayor: George Hoover, James Kelley, Alonzo Webster, and Robert Wright.[14] Yet for the all-important role of county sheriff there would be no Jacksonian rotation in office, no spreading around of the available jobs. In both June and November 1873 and again in November 1875 voters elected a man who stayed in place until forced by term limits to vacate the post. (The Kansas constitution prohibited county sheriffs from running for successive third terms.)

Charley Bassett is still virtually unknown, having left few traces of his life. The fourth of five children, he was born in 1846 in the old whaling town of New Bedford, Massachusetts, where his father was a sail maker. By his teens Bassett was clerking in Philadelphia. Lying about his age, he enlisted in the Union army, serving in two short-time infantry regiments that performed various garrison duties from mid-1864 to late 1865. He then spent three years in the postwar regular army, mustering out at the end of 1868 probably at Fort Sill in Indian Territory.[15]

By late 1872, after supposedly "drifting about the mining camps and frontier towns for a time," Bassett turned up in Dodge. He was twenty-seven years old, five feet four inches tall, and (to judge from a later photo) displayed an unfashionably clean-shaven face.[16]

In July 1873 Sheriff Bassett was on the job, also doubling that winter as a township constable. Early in 1874 the county commissioners added a deputy sheriff, Jerome Hackett. A few months later the more experienced Edward Hogue, a cattle-town peace officer at Ellsworth in 1872–1873, replaced Hackett. Bassett and Hogue, the latter variously designated undersheriff or deputy sheriff, served as the county's top law-enforcement officers through mid-1876.[17]

Meanwhile, hide hunters were rapidly wiping out the buffalo, forcing many of those plainsmen and their groupies to get out of Dodge in search of other locales. The vacuum created by the dispersion of that disruptive population had not yet been filled by significant numbers of Texas cowboys.

With Bassett taking charge and the troublemakers moving on, Dodge quieted down. In October 1873 a correspondent from Topeka described the new civic demeanor: "The town of Dodge is quiet compared to last winter. The desperadoes have all taken their departure, leaving the peace-loving citizens in possession." Four months later the editor of the short-lived *Dodge City Messenger*, admitting that "the city has gained an unenviable name, far and near," concluded that "now, instead of those terrible scenes that we read of, being re-enacted, quietude reigns supreme."[18]

The sheriff's office intended to keep it that way. From summer 1873 until spring 1876 no documented homicides occurred in Dodge City. In December 1873 a newspaper up the railroad line made passing note of a shooting: "Harry Lovett, one of the early citizens of Newton, was shot through the left breast at Dodge City, Monday night [December 1–2], and is not expected to live." Lack of any follow-up suggests Lovett recovered. More than a year and a half later, in August 1875, the *Topeka Commonwealth* printed a Dodge Citian's half-whimsical account of a gunfight.

[William] Sweeney, the County Clerk, went on a spree last night [August 4–5] and entered the dance house of Tom Sherman, and while there, got into a row with Sherman, who shot him. It is supposed the wound will be fatal. It is not necessary for the county to go into mourning, as there are plenty of better men left.

Sweeney did not die. His shooter faced a felony charge, but *State v. Thomas Sherman* was inexplicably dropped in December 1875. As for Sweeney, he returned to work six weeks later and within a few months validated the local report's low opinion of him by skipping town with $125 of the taxpayers' money.[19]

---

Texas "herders"—as Kansas journalists of the time referred to cowboys—had occasionally appeared at Dodge City. Normally well armed, they could be dangerous sojourners. But recurrent Indian troubles tended to keep the Texas cattle trade from spreading as far west as Dodge. From 1867 through 1875 most cattle driven to the cattle towns followed the old Chisholm Trail to eastern and central Kansas.

Dodge's cowboy era actually began when the army decisively suppressed the Comanches, Kiowas, and Southern Cheyennes in the Red River War of 1874–1875, opening west Texas and the Texas Panhandle to large-scale ranching. By then the Santa Fe Railroad had provided a stockyard at Dodge, giving the town a decided market advantage. Southern cattle could be sold there, then either shipped east by rail to urban packing houses or trailed north to Wyoming or Montana for fattening into pricier beef.[20]

---

On November 2, 1875, with 819 official residents, some 300 more than the requisite number of 501, Dodge became a city of the third class, a status the community's entrepreneurs had thought necessary in preparation for its emergence as a full-fledged cattle-trading center. Among other benefits, this meant a new set of peacekeepers to bolster Charley Bassett's efforts. Beginning in 1876 law officers headquartered at Dodge included a county sheriff, an undersheriff, as many deputy sheriffs as needed, a city marshal, an assistant marshal, as many policemen as required, two township constables, and even a deputy US marshal.[21]

This formidable deployment of lawmen plus enforcement of gun control paid off in a relatively modest body count even as Dodge City's summer population swelled by an estimated 250 cattlemen and 1,300 mostly young cowboys, probably a third black and Hispanic, who visited town during each cattle trading season: June through October.

Back in 1873 the coroner's jury in the Ellis-Burrell double homicide had concluded that the violent episode was caused by the carrying of handguns. And the single surviving Bassett anecdote has the sheriff disarming participants and observers at all district court sessions convened at Dodge.

> In those days men appeared always well armed, but he astonished the natives by taking post at the court house door, when the district court was in session, and disarming all persons desiring to enter. Of the small party that attended court [on one occasion] he gathered forty-two six-shooters and only killed one man [sic].

A scrupulous New York editor added the term sic—"as written"—to clarify that the remark about killing was intended as a joke, although most readers may have taken it literally.[22]

By early 1874 Ford County's commissioners began the process of effectively banning both concealed and openly carried handguns in town. On March 9 they resolved that "any person or persons found carrying concealed weapons in the city of Dodge ... shall be dealt with according to law." Two months later they banned "within the limits of this Town of Dodge City" all but those involved in "legitimate business" from "carrying on his person a pistol." This time the commissioners added a definite local penalty—a fine of up to $100, three months in jail, or both, "at the Discretion of the Court."

As soon as Dodge became a formal municipality in late 1875, the city council reemphasized gun control by decreeing that nobody except federal, state, or local officers "Shall in the City of Dodge City Carry Concealed [weapons] about his or her persons." Violations would cost $3 to $25 for each offense. And Dodge's editorial corps assumed as one of its many civic duties detecting, exposing, and severely admonishing lapses in gun-control enforcement.

The anti-carry ordinance, as shown in a photograph taken some time between late autumn 1878 and early spring 1879, had been posted on an out-of-use well located at Second Avenue and Front Streets, precisely where incoming cowboys and cattlemen—having crossed the Arkansas River bridge—entered downtown Dodge. The notice warned: "THE CARRYING OF FIREARMS strictly PROHIBITED." When the city council removed all obsolete wells in April 1879, it straight away hired a local sign-painter to inscribe and post notices "to warn parties against carrying fire arms."[23]

The throngs of cowboys entering town during the summer and fall trail season were expected to leave their six-shooters at the first place they stopped—livery stable, saloon, or business house. Robert Wright's brick store became a convenient point to check weapons, and for a time the city marshal designated it as the town's official repository. As Wright later recalled, "A receipt was given for them. And my! what piles there were of them. At times they were piled up by the hundred."[24]

---

Although Wyatt Earp supposedly told his biographer that in 1876, Dodge City's first full cattle-shipping season, "there were some killings in personal quarrels, but none by peace officers," only one documented homicide actually occurred that year.[25]

In April 1876 a visiting correspondent wrote that "not long since [on January 14] a cold blooded murder was perpetrated here." John Tyler, like William Taylor, was a black entrepreneur, proprietor of a prosperous Front Street barbershop, the Tonsorial Palace, located next-door to Frederick Zimmerman's gun and hardware store. Tyler vowed to kill his wife's suspected lover if he so much as came near the couple's residence.

> It happened . . . that a harmless and good German citizen was passing through the alley in the rear of the negro's premises, on account of its being a little nearer route home. The negro thinking it was the paramour of his strumpet wife, fired and killed the unfortunate German.

A core of influential town merchants backed Tyler as a valued member of the business community. Henry Sitler and three founding businessmen—George Hoover, George Cox, Jacob Collar—numbered among Tyler's eight prominent bondsmen. And when Tyler's case finally came before the district court in January 1877, eight unnamed Dodge Citians (most likely the selfsame bondsmen) expressed concern that the pool of eligible jurors in and around Dodge might prove prejudiced against Tyler. They filed affidavits arguing that "the bias & prejudice existing in the minds of the people of Ford Co." would not allow Tyler to have "a fair and impartial trial" at Dodge.

The judge agreed, moving the proceedings east to Larned, where the case came before the June term of the district court. Larned's *Pawnee County Herald* summarized the outcome: "In the case of State vs. Tyler . . . the proceedings were quashed on the grounds of a defect in the information," apparently the misspelling of the victim's last name. Technical error indeed. But Ford County's district attorney, who then inherited the case, decided against refiling, since its prosecution had already cost more than $350 and, according to the *Dodge City Times,* the "tardy working of the machinery of the law had induced a forgetfulness of this pitiless spilling of innocent blood."[26]

That no deaths by gun violence occurred in 1877 is almost certain, since beginning in March of that year virtually complete files of Dodge City's pioneer newspapers are extant. However enthusiastically frontier journalists might conspire in cover-ups and damage control about local social conflict, they seemed no more able to resist a good homicide story than any circulation-chasing New York or Chicago city editor.

---

Eighteen-seventy-eight proved a different story. In March the editor of the *Ford County Globe*, Dodge City's second newspaper, complained of laxity in the enforcement of gun control against civilian pals of the city marshal, Edward Masterson, and his assistant marshal, Nate Haywood.

The council and mayor had appointed Ed as assistant marshal in June 1877. In its new officer, according to the biographer of his younger brother Bat, the town got a brave but "genial, easygoing, generous" young man who "found the free-and-easy, happy-go-lucky spirit of the typical cowpuncher to his liking and regarded the antics of the Texas youths tolerantly."[27] That December, following Ed's recovery from a bullet wound in the right breast while attempting to arrest a cowboy flourishing a pistol in the Lone Star Dance Hall, the admiring mayor and council elevated him to the city marshal's job and appointed Charley Bassett as assistant marshal. Since in the November 1877 county election Bat had won the office of sheriff (and promptly appointed Bassett undersheriff), by January 1878 the Masterson brothers held the two most important law-enforcement jobs in Dodge.[28]

The *Globe* editor's complaint came rather early in Marshal Ed Masterson's tenure. "Some of the 'boys' in direct violation of City Ordinances," he warned,

> carry firearms on our streets, without being called to account for the same. . . . There is something rotten with a man's conscience when he parades the streets with an exposed six-shooter, knowing that he is violating [the] law with impunity, simply because he is a friend of the marshal or policeman.[29]

The sight of men without officers' badges wearing sidearms clearly suggested to visiting Texans that they need not concern themselves overmuch with the anti-carry ordinance. That laxity in the system had tragic results.

On the evening of April 9, 1878, the first documented shooting fatality in Dodge since the death of John Tyler's victim two years earlier was a double homicide. Ed Masterson and Haywood, on patrol, had taken note of a noisy group drinking in the Lady Gay Dance Hall. One of them, Jack Wagner, wore a gun in violation of the no-carry law. Masterson demanded the gun, Wagner complied. But instead of confiscating it the marshal unwisely gave it to the group's trail boss, Alfred Walker, asking him to check it with the bartender, and he and Haywood stepped outside. Shortly thereafter Wagner, again wearing his gun, and the other cowboys exited the Lady Gay.

All hell broke loose. When Masterson attempted to take Wagner's gun from its shoulder holster, Wagner resisted, and a scuffle ensued. Haywood moved forward to assist Masterson; Walker shoved a gun in Haywood's face and pulled the trigger, but the cartridge misfired. Wagner meanwhile managed to maneuver his gun against Masterson's side and fired, blasting a wound channel through the marshal's abdomen. Sheriff Bat Masterson appeared on the scene, shooting Wagner once in the bowels and emptying his gun into Walker, who fled, shot through the lungs and holding his shattered arm. Both cowboys made it to Alfred Peacock's saloon, and were later moved to Robert Wright's brick store. Meanwhile, Ed Masterson staggered to George Hoover's saloon and collapsed. He died a half-hour later, Wagner the following afternoon. Walker survived his wounds, was removed to Kansas City for treatment, and disappeared. Four other cowboys faced an inquest that failed to produce sufficient evidence to try them as accomplices in the killing.

Local press accounts had it that Ed Masterson reflexively shot both his assailants. But in an 1886 court hearing Bat certified that "I shot those parties who killed my brother in 1878," having "killed one of those, as well as shot the other."[30]

Mayor James Kelley and his council reaffirmed their dedication to vigorous law enforcement, elevating the veteran Bassett to city marshal, a position he held simultaneously with that of county undersheriff until, after more than six years as a Dodge City peacekeeper, relinquishing both in the winter of 1879–1880. The assertion that during his law enforcement career Bassett had accumulated "several notches on his revolver, each of which stood for a human life," is unfounded. At Dodge, where Bassett never killed anyone, he was remembered as a "cool and fearless officer [but] a peaceable man." The administration also replaced the ineffective Haywood with the intimidating Wyatt Earp, who had served as assistant marshal of Dodge in 1876–1877. It also beefed up the force by adding two new policemen.[31]

But by the summer of 1878 Dodge faced a fiscal emergency, with police salaries totaling $3,900 per year, or 42.8 percent of all municipal expenditures, and city scrip (short-term promissory notes) changing hands at fifty cents on the dollar. Front Street businessmen convened and forced the administration to follow precedent from other Kansas cattle towns and impose a tax on professional gamblers and prostitutes, those (legally nonexistent) agents of disorder. Such assessments, disguised as monthly police court fines, funded Dodge City's costly law-enforcement budget thereafter. Municipal data for 1884–1885 certify that the tax on gamblers and prostitutes continued to cover police salaries, still the town's largest expenditure, accounting for 42.4 percent of the total budget.[32]

Despite the renewed commitment to a tough police force robustly enforcing gun control, another law officer and two other transients died that season from gunshot wounds. But none of those deaths could be blamed on lax law enforcement or violations of the carry law.

At 4:00 a.m. on the morning of July 13, 1878, came the fatal shooting of Harry McCarty, Ford County's new deputy US marshal. A professional surveyor rather than an experienced lawman, McCarty happened to be leaning on the bar in the newly refurbished Long Branch Saloon when a drunken cook from a nearby cow camp, being teased by other patrons, snatched the marshal's .45 Colt from its holster, accidentally discharging it into his groin. McCarty's femoral artery severed, he bled to death within minutes. The killer, tried in district court, pleaded guilty to manslaughter and received a penitentiary sentence of twelve years and three months.[33]

Two weeks later, on July 26, a row at the Lady Gay ended with the death of a young Texas cowboy, George Hoy. After a fuss with policeman Earp, Hoy and his pals retrieved their six-shooters at about 3:00 a.m., mounted up, and on their way out of town fired into the hall. Earp and James Masterson (Bat's younger brother) ran into the street and a couple of shots came in their direction. Returning fire, one or both of them shot Hoy from his saddle, and he fell at the entrance to the Arkansas River bridge, an arm broken in two places. Although under a physician's care, Hoy's shattered limb became infected. He lingered in agony for about a month and died on August 21, 1878.[34]

Finally, in early October, Dora Hand, a theater performer, was shot dead in her sleep during a failed attempt to kill James Kelley, as detailed in chapter 4.[35]

--- ⌁ ---

The editor of the *Dodge City Times* proved right on the mark in 1876 when he repeated assurances offered in 1873 and 1874 that "the rough days of Dodge City are now things of the past," while acknowledging that "the heretofore rough name that the city has borne abroad has prejudiced many against the locality."

Some travelers prepared for the worst "under the impression," complained Dodge City's *Ford County Globe* in January 1878, that "life and limb is unsafe." Wrote a young wayfarer camped east of town: "Dear Father. . . . Have laid over here to wait for a larger crowd, so as to be perfectly safe going through Dodge. There are nine teams now and will be three more in the morning, so we will be safe." Testified another overland emigrant: "When I was at Larned I was told not to go near Dodge City [as] I would be robbed of all I had besides standing a good chance to have my throat cut and my dead body thrown into the river." A year later the *Globe* reprinted an eastern Kansas reporter's similar observation: "Before going to Dodge, I was told to stay away; that it was not safe to be on the streets after night; and that it was run by robbers, pick-pockets and rowdies."[36]

Other visitors seemed less terrorized than fascinated by the town's violent reputation, which the editor of the *Globe* attributed to dime novels, with their "blood curdling stories and hair breadth escapes" and to local yarn-spinners' accounts of "the number, accomplishments and glorious ends of those who rest on 'Boot Hill.'" That grubby pioneer cemetery had become a tourist attraction as early as April 1873, when a Topekan escorting a tour group from Syracuse, New York recorded an apparently typical itinerary:

> We arrived at Dodge City on time, 11 A.M. We got a very good dinner at the only hotel in the place. After we had dinner we went around to view the stores, saloons, dance houses, and then upon the western hill, where lie six men that have "died in their boots," killed in some affray about the town.

Interviewed four years later while gathering souvenir pebbles from the site, a Pennsylvanian remarked that where he came from near Philadelphia, "Dodge City has a very hard name," and Boot Hill "is considered almost as great a curiosity as the grave of Shakespeare."

The next year another easterner provided his upstate New York newspaper with a fanciful description of Boot Hill.

> On a lonely side hill near by this modern Sodom there are twenty-eight tolerably new graves, and all but three of the occupants are reported to have "died with their boots on"—victims [of] the sweet music of the pistol or the pleasant toyings of the bowie knife.[37]

Newspapers around Kansas likewise confirmed that the local image had not improved. An Atchison reporter described Dodge as a place "where killing a man is no sin . . . and law but a terrible hoax." The newspaper at nearby Hays City offered particularly acerbic comments. One of its reporters wrote that

> the town of Dodge still holds her own as a hard, bad town. . . . Even the decent portion of the community have become so accustomed to the

fearful state of affairs that they regard a good stand up [fist] fight—no striking below the belt or when your adversary's down—a joke rather than a disgrace.

After deciding to see for himself, one of the paper's editors concluded that

Dodge is the Deadwood of Kansas. . . . Here rowdyism has taken its most aggravated form, and was it not for the exceedingly stringent or-dinances [against carrying guns] and a fair attempt to enforce them, the town would be suddenly depopulated. . . . Rowdyism elsewhere would pass as a modified form of respectability in this benighted city.

In the spring of 1878 an Illinois newspaper seemed to capture the prevailing out-of-town sentiment: "Without question Dodge City is the worst place of its size on this earth."[38]

---

Dodge's gaudy saloon-and-dance-hall culture also figured in its reputa-tion as a "modern Sodom." Through the cattle-trading years the number of saloons and dance halls waxed and waned and their names and man-agers regularly changed, but their character persisted.[39]

In 1878 Dodge's three dance halls, or houses, each featured a bar, gaming tables, orchestra music, and dancing (for a fee) with young women, some of whom could also be hired for sex. Former dance hall owner Hamilton Bell claimed that dance hall women conventionally were "prostitutes, who belonged to the house." A vaudeville performer who played Dodge in the late 1870s disagreed: "Many of those dance hall girls . . . were merely hired entertainers; their job was to dance with the men, talk to them, perhaps flirt with them a little bit and induce them to buy drinks—no more." In an 1883 newspaper interview an unnamed Dodge dance hall proprietor emphasized their mixed character. Two years later a visitor agreed: "The women were house entertainers, mem-bers of the local demimonde and girls who worked on nearby ranches as servants."[40]

As for saloons, a Kansas City correspondent reported that Dodge contained almost two dozen in 1877, some quite substantial affairs. "No little 10 × 12s," he wrote, "but 75 to 100 feet long, glittering with paint and mirrors, and some [managers] paying $100 per month as rent," with fancy improvements installed at their own expense. And at least eight of them featured gambling, the game of choice being faro, with players placing bets on which cards a dealer would draw from the deck. All the saloons came to life each morning at about 11:00 a.m., started to get lively at 4:00 p.m., and from 10:00 p.m. to 5:00 a.m. really pulsated.[41]

In the 1880s a Dodge City reporter penned, and a local paper published, an unprecedented description of the town's late-night party culture, something wholly unexpected from Dodge's usually circumspect press. Titled "Dodge City by Lamp Light, from Midnight until Dawn," it portrayed "the six hours that our city may be seen in its character that has been heralded to the world, unembellished and unaided by the fiction writer's paint." Alarmingly indiscreet (the editor felt obliged to attach a virtual disclaimer), the piece depicted Dodge's raucously sexualized night life, describing it as a "regular routine" along Front Street after the dance halls closed.

"Under the present order of things," the writer explained, "the *demi-monde* are permitted to visit the saloons and gambling houses after midnight, and it is needless to add that they never permit an opportunity to slip by without embracing this golden privilege." At the stroke of twelve—when the dance halls closed and the cowboys dispersed—they burst in, ready to celebrate. "Each of the saloons spoken of contains a piano, and as the painted beauties that visit them have several piano players and singers among their number, sounds of sweet music, mingled with discordant strains from cracked voices, issue forth." The women attract "a crowd of loungers, who are always to be found perambulating the streets at this time of night."

The merrymakers sing and dance, "and the bar does a thriving business." Night after night the same regulars appear: George Masterson, Bat's youngest brother, together with a crowd mainly identified by their colorful or demeaning nicknames, among them the Rincon Kid, Eat-'Em-Up Jake, Konk, the Stuttering Kid, and Barney the Dude, escorting Little Dot, Hop Fiend Nell, Emporia Belle, Scar-Faced Lillie, Miss One Fin, and other women.

On the assembling of this motley crew in one saloon, the fun then begins and to a stranger unaccustomed to the scenes that follow, it must appear extremely fantastical. It is no wonder that the youth who comes here is so soon estranged from the path of virtue and rectitude and falls an easy victim to the seductive ways of the unique and only Dodge.

An occasional fight takes place, brought on perchance by the over indulgence of one girl to another girl's best man; then pet names and sweet sayings are the order of the hour, and should too strong a reflection be made on some one else's personal habits and tastes . . . the "battle royal commences" and rages with unabated fury till some recognized leader of the crowd interferes and restores peace, when all take a drink and the fun again begins and continues unmarred till the rising orb of the day makes his appearance in the east, when all disperse and sleep off their night's debauch until the lamps are lighted for the next night's orgy.[42]

"Everybody is supposed and expected to visit" the dance halls and after-hours saloons, noted a reporter, and "everybody does." One morally offended visitor told his New York readers that "there was more concentrated hell in Dodge City than in any other place of equal size on the American continent." A traveler from the nation's capital agreed: "Dodge City is a wicked little town. Indeed its character is so clearly and egregiously bad that one might conclude—were the evidence in these latter times positive of its possibility—that it was marked for special Providential punishment." While projecting a certain metropolitan sophistication, even the New York Times took note of streets "thronged with swaggering, swearing cow-boys" and "billiard halls, concert saloons, and keno dens" flourishing past midnight.

Conventional wisdom had it that Dodge was "THE WICKEDEST CITY IN AMERICA," the wry title of an Indiana dispatch whose author "had expected from the descriptions I had read of it to find it a perfect Bedlam, a sort of Hogarthian 'Gin Alley,' where rum ran down the street gutters, and loud profanity and vile stenches contended for the mastery of the atmosphere."[43] But he found the place not that bad after all.

The town's editorial defenders agreed, retorting that Dodge simply made no attempt to disguise its sinfulness and illegalities. Visiting members of the press, therefore, could (and did) "do the city of Dodge by gaslight," fumed a local editor, and then go home and write about "the

*Deadly Prose* : 63

bad character of this town." Revisiting Dodge's touted transparency in such matters, the same editor presented it as almost a civic virtue: "The gross things that happen here happen in older communities. [But] there is no concealment, and that is why loose things and unruly acts appear so flagrant."[44]

As for Dodge City's law officers, they properly understood their main task to be insuring the absence of homicide rather than sin. The local commercial elite could live with intemperance, gambling, and prostitution as a necessary adjunct to the Texas cattle trade. Gun violence, however, continued to stir its entrepreneurial anxieties.

---

In contrast to its dreadful reputation, by the winter of 1879–1880 Dodge City had attained many of the earmarks of a conventional American county seat. With fewer than a thousand residents, it was a city only by self-definition. Like those of most other midwestern and western communities, Dodge's population inhabited a rectangular grid of streets and avenues that made for uncomplicated real estate sales. But its uneven topography encoded a distinctive social architecture, a north-to-south sequence of three micro-climates in which altitude coincided with respectability.[45]

To the north, the town's major emblems of civic virtue crowned two gentle bluffs. On the left a new red-brick public school had supplanted the old Boot Hill cemetery, the school committee chaired by Frederick Zimmerman having purchased the knoll from Herman Fringer. In the center an imposing brick and limestone Ford County courthouse fronted what would soon become Gospel Ridge, with its Methodist, Presbyterian, and Roman Catholic churches; meanwhile worshippers made do with a clapboard nondenominational Union chapel located catty-corner to the courthouse. To the east new middle-class family housing extended out along Military Avenue toward the fort. Several founding businessmen— Richard Evans, Alonzo Webster, Frederick Zimmerman, and Morris and Jacob Collar—had established country estates on the eastern and western outskirts. This northern sector of town betokened the Dodge City of propriety and moral modernization.[46]

Just below these modest heights on an east–west axis lay the town's elongated commercial district. Reflecting a strictly secular profit-and-

loss ethos, its business and professional men, literally as well as figura-
tively, held the middle ground between the reputable and the notorious
Dodge City. Their stores, offices, hotels, upscale saloons, and a new
opera house (a public auditorium) arrayed themselves along the northern curb of Front Street. On the southern side of the street lay the tracks
of the Atchison, Topeka & Santa Fe Railroad, representing what locals
referred to as the "deadline"—a term coined during the Civil War to de-
marcate the edge of a danger zone within which any prisoner-of-war
could be shot.[47]

Dodge City's deadline marked the boundary of its south side, the
town's transient district. Here, between the railroad tracks and the
low mud-flats of the Arkansas River, stood the livery stables, blacksmith shops, cheaper hotels and rooming houses and rental cottages,
the noisier, more disreputable saloons, and the notorious dance halls.
While all resident and visiting males might cross to the south side without misgiving—indeed, some perfectly respectable businesses, such as
the Elephant Livery Stable and the Great Western Hotel, stood there—
the railroad tracks delimited the movement of its females. Middle-class
"ladies" normally did not venture south of the tracks, while the south
side's "sporting women" were not to appear north of them except to visit
the Front Street saloons after midnight, when "reputable" citizens had
cleared the business district.[48]

This trifurcated spatial configuration of Dodge City circumscribed
the role and visibility of women and framed the town's adventures
through the rest of the cattle-trading era.

# CASE HISTORIES

4

Four adults died violently in Dodge City between October 1878 and November 1880. Together their stories offer a remarkable view of how the criminal justice system functioned on the Kansas frontier.

The legal proceedings never varied. After a suspect's arrest, a coroner's jury, mandated for any fatality by violence or under suspicious circumstances, determined the cause and manner of death. Next came a magistrate's hearing, where, if it appeared to the local justice of the peace, upon all the evidence, that a felony had been committed and there was probable cause for charging the prisoner with the felony, the individual was bound over to the district court. Should the evidence prove insufficient, the prisoner was discharged, ending the legal process. If bound over, the circuit judge of the Ninth Judicial District of Kansas then presided at Dodge over a Ford County district court trial.[1]

Both newspapers of the late 1870s, the *Dodge City Times*, edited by the dour and moralistic Nicholas Klaine, and the *Ford County Globe*, edited by the far less earnest Lloyd Shinn, document the lethal and legal particulars of the four cases more lavishly than usual: from location to context and motive, from killer to victim and fatal wounds, from coroner's jury and magistrate's hearing to district court proceedings.

The first homicide occurred around four o'clock on the humid and misty morning of October 4, 1878, when Dora Hand, a variety-show singer, stage name Fannie Keenan, died instantly from a .44 caliber bullet that tore through her heart. It was the single deadly round of four fired into Mayor James Kelley's two-bedroom cottage on the south side of town. One struck the bed of Hand's colleague, Fannie Garrettson; another—the slug that went on to kill Hand—pierced Garrettson's bedclothes. Badly shaken, Garrettson wrote friends the next day that if Kelley, hospitalized at Fort Dodge, had been sleeping at home that night "the probability is there would have been three or four assassinated."[2]

As a writer put it in the *Dodge City Times*, the thirty-four-year-old Dora Hand possessed an "eventful history." In later years Dodge City old-timers, especially dentist O. H. Simpson, who did not arrive in Dodge until 1884 but had a "nose for history as hobby," peddled the yarn that Hand came from a prominent Boston family, obtained a musical education in Germany, and then toured America with a grand opera company. Actually, she first appears in the 1870 federal census as Dora Crews, born in New York, residing in Sedalia, Missouri, and working as a prostitute. The following year she married a Saint Louis musician (fifer and drummer during the Civil War, not the dashing cavalry captain of legend), who probably helped her get a start in show business.

By the time Hand arrived in Dodge City from Saint Louis in the summer of 1878 she was a seasoned variety performer. A few weeks before her death she filed for divorce from her husband. Her petition to the district court alleged that over a year earlier Theodore Hand had deserted her and "did then and has ever since lived in open and notorious adultery" and "on several occasions by threatening the plaintiff with bodily harm compelled her to give and relinquish to him money and property the fruits of her labor."[3]

The suspected shooter, James Kenedy, twenty-three, an arrogant and volatile college dropout, came from one of the wealthiest and most respected ranching families in Texas. His parents, Mifflin Kenedy and Petra Vela, owned a south Texas spread amounting to well over 200,000 acres, from which large herds had been driven north to Dodge City and the other Kansas cattle towns.

While still in his teens Kenedy earned a reputation as a hotheaded troublemaker. Awaiting the sale of one of his family's herds at Ellsworth, Kansas, in 1872, the seventeen-year-old drank, played cards, and instigated a fuss with an older Texas cattleman, the ornery and well-known Isom "Print" Olive. Kenedy audaciously accused Olive of cheating, Olive replied with profane invective, and Kenedy left in a huff. Later that day, finding Olive in another saloon card game, Kenedy grabbed a pistol from the gun rack behind the bar and shot the startled Olive three times. Suffering a superficial wound from a bullet then fired by an Olive trail hand, Kenedy was arrested. Olive survived his wounds. Kenedy, with the help of friends, escaped custody and hightailed it out of town.

Six years later on another trail drive from Texas, Kenedy turned up in Dodge City, where his arrest by Assistant City Marshal Wyatt Earp for carrying a handgun, and later by City Marshal Charley Bassett for disorderly conduct, set him off. He complained to Mayor Kelley about police harassment. When Kelley brushed him off, Kenedy flew at the mayor, who in turn gave the young cattleman a thrashing, adding a bruised ego to his explosive temperament. Kenedy left town but came back six weeks later, presumably intent on revenge.[4]

The morning of the murder Earp and Officer Jim Masterson (another of Bat's brothers) discovered that shortly after the shooting Kenedy and a companion had been lounging in an all-night saloon, and the bartender claimed he saw a horseman he recognized as Kenedy galloping out of town. Then Kenedy's companion, who remained behind, admitted he believed Kenedy had intended to kill Mayor Kelley that night.

Following Earp and Jim Masterson's investigation, a coroner's jury, under Rufus Cook, Dodge Township justice of the peace and acting county coroner, immediately convened. The jurors concluded that "Fannie Keenan came to her death by a gunshot wound, and that in their opinion the said gunshot wound was produced by a bullet discharged from a gun in the hands of one James Kennedy [sic]."

By that afternoon, wrote Klaine of the Times, Ford County's Sheriff Bat Masterson had organized "as intrepid a posse as ever pulled a trigger"—Bat, Bassett, Earp, Deputy Sheriff William Duffey, and a deputized William Tilghman, a future Dodge City lawman. After settling on the fugitive's probable course into the Texas Panhandle, the men rode a circular route through hail and sheeting rain to arrive the next day, October 5, at a spot 35 miles southwest of town, certain that Kenedy had not made it there before them.

The gamble paid off. Kenedy arrived, spotted the posse, turned his horse, and ignored a command to stop. The posse men fired a volley, dropping the horse and pinning Kenedy under it, his left arm shattered by a .50 caliber bullet from Bat Masterson's buffalo gun.

Posse and prisoner returned the next day to Dodge, where the local doctor attempted to treat the critically wounded Kenedy, who then lay near death in the Ford County jail for several days. In late October, still too badly injured to be moved, Kenedy again appeared before Judge Cook, this time in a magistrate's hearing held in the sheriff's office adjoining Kenedy's cell. In a closed session, Cook brought the legal process to an end by releasing Kenedy for lack of sufficient incriminating evidence. Since the "sheriff's office was too small to admit spectators," reported the editor of the *Globe*, "we do not know what the evidence was, or upon what grounds he was acquitted."

In December, Mifflin Kenedy arrived from Texas with Major Blencowe Fryer of Fort Leavenworth, one of the army's most eminent surgeons. They moved young Kenedy from the Dodge House, where he had been confined since the magistrate's hearing, to the hospital at Fort Dodge. There Fryer successfully extracted damaged bones, one over 4 inches long, from Kenedy's mutilated upper arm.

Neither of Dodge's two newspapers nor any of its public officials criticized the outcome, although years later Earp supposedly told his biographer that after his capture Kenedy had confessed, asking, "Did I get that bastard Kelley?" When Wyatt answered that he had taken the life not of Kelley but of Dora Hand, Kenedy, evidently preferring death to dishonor, berated Masterson for failing to make a kill shot. "You damn son-of-a-bitch!" he gasped, "You ought to have made a better shot than you did." Astounded, Masterson snarled, "You damn murdering son-of-a-bitch, I did the best I could."[5]

Undoubtedly, the Kenedy family enjoyed considerable influence in Dodge. And Mifflin could well afford the most expensive legal talent from Kansas City or Saint Louis, so that a district court proceeding would have been time-consuming, expensive, and very possibly unsuccessful; no one had witnessed the shooting, for example. But there is no evidence to support the rumor that Mifflin, along with a group of his rancher friends, spent time in Dodge in October lobbying for his son's release and paying off the posse members to keep their mouths shut.[6]

The widely shared belief that James Kenedy would either die of his wound or never recover fully, keeping him off the trail and therefore out of Dodge City, proved correct. While still in critical condition he was returned to his parents' ranch, remaining in Texas with a permanently damaged arm until his death, most likely from pneumonia, in 1884.[7]

—◦◦◦—

Six months after the Hand murder another shooting occurred, as Bat Masterson's biographer incisively put it, "in the western tradition of angry men settling a personal dispute face to face with six-guns." Like nearly half the homicides at Dodge in the cattle-trading years that killing involved a woman.[8]

A prickly character with a dangerous reputation, Levi Richardson, age about thirty-seven, a buffalo hunter turned freighter, originally from a southern Wisconsin farm, had been in and out of Dodge at least since 1877. Wyatt Earp purportedly told his biographer that Richardson was an accomplished marksman who had abandoned "his plain, unvarnished style of shooting [and] took up gun-fanning"—a rapid-fire technique requiring the use of both hands, one to hold the handle of the gun and to keep the trigger depressed, the other to employ a chopping motion by which the lower edge of the palm repeatedly cocked and released the hammer.[9]

A young professional gambler, Frank "Cockeyed Frank" Loving, age nineteen, had spent his childhood in Texas and then in Kansas City, where his mother ran a boarding house. Claiming to know little about the teenager, the editor of the *Globe* thought he was "not much of a ro[w]dy, but more of the cool and desperate order when he has a killing on hand." Indeed, "gamblers as a class are desperate men. They consider it necessary in their business that they keep up their fighting reputation, and never take a bluff."[10]

April 5, 1879, started out cool, but had turned warm and muggy by that evening when Richardson and Loving, nurturing an enmity over an unnamed woman (who lived with an abusive Loving while welcoming attention from Richardson), met by chance at the door of Front Street's most popular bar, the Long Branch Saloon. Richardson, leaving the Long Branch, turned and followed Loving back into the saloon. One after the other they made their way through the gathering Saturday night crowd past the bar and the piano to the rear of the handsomely decorated, wallpapered, and gaslit establishment. Here a cast-iron heating stove, apparently a bulky 6-foot model, stood surrounded by gaming tables, a billiard table, and a number of chairs.[11]

Eyewitnesses later told what happened. Loving sat down on the edge of a table but as Richardson sat down next to him jumped to his feet, squaring off for a fight. "If you have anything to say about me why don't you come and say it to my face like a gentleman," he said, "and not to my back, you damned son-of-a-bitch?" Richardson then rose and sneeringly replied, "You won't fight." Shouted Loving, "You just try me and see."

Both pulled six-shooters from their jackets, and the close-quarters gunfight consumed at least a minute as each man maneuvered for a decisive shot. As deafened patrons scrambled for cover, the shooters crouched and dodged around the stove and billiard table, their exploding pistols at times almost touching. Until both revolvers clicked on empty, nine to eleven rounds—depending on whether Loving's .44 caliber Remington misfired only once or twice—had zipped and ricocheted through the smoke-drenched room. Marshal Bassett, having heard the first shots, dashed the 75 yards from Mayor Kelley's saloon in time to see the last round fired and to help Deputy Sheriff Duffey confiscate both weapons.

While one of Richardson's bullets had creased Loving's hand, three of Loving's own rounds took lethal effect. Richardson, his coat aflame from a close-range muzzle blast, tumbled against some chairs in a scuffle with Duffey, who was trying to disarm him. Wounded in the left breast, side, and right arm, Richardson rose, took a few steps, fell to his hands and knees, collapsed, and died. Later, "wondering how a man of Levi's skill with a pistol could have missed a man's body with five shots at a distance of twenty feet," Wyatt Earp chalked it up to "hurry-up-six-gun work." In Earp's opinion, Richardson, an expert shot, had hurriedly fanned; Loving, a fair shot, had deliberately fired plain and straight.[12]

County Coroner John Straughn convened a coroner's jury on Sunday and Monday. The evidence, including the testimony of two background witnesses and eight eyewitnesses, revealed that both men most likely anticipated violent action. They had traded words before, and Richardson had struck Loving, then told a friend that he would like to "shoot the guts out of the cockeyed son-of-a-bitch." Loving's pistol carried a round in every chamber instead of the standard practice of loading a weapon with only five cartridges. And shortly before the deadly encounter Richardson had left his papers with his landlady in case "anything happened to him." Richardson, by most accounts, fired first. And so the jurors, among them founding entrepreneur George Hoover, closed the case, declaring that "Levi Richardson came to his death by a bullet wound from a pistol fired by Frank Loving in self-defense."[13]

The local papers seized the opportunity to once again lecture Dodge City's lawmen about the necessity of strictly enforcing the gun-control ordinance. "Neither of these men had a right to carry such weapons," the *Globe* editorialized. Gamblers especially should "on no account . . . be allowed to carry deadly weapons." Indeed, the town had banned not only sidearms—openly carried, usually by visiting cowboys and cattlemen—but also concealed weapons like those secreted by Loving and Richardson in their jackets.

---

In early September a correspondent for a Kansas City newspaper noted that since the Richardson-Loving encounter Dodge had been so peaceful that "the police, under Marshal Bassett, are compelled to practice on cove oyster cans in order to keep their hands in."[14]

Exactly one week after that cheerful pronouncement, on the afternoon of September 8, lethal violence again erupted on Front Street. With a southern breeze having dispersed a persistent haze and temperatures in the seventies, Arista Webb and Barney Martin spent the late afternoon drinking at the Old House Saloon. They fell into a drunken dispute, Martin, as a reporter delicately phrased it, "charging Webb with concubinage with a black woman who has charge of Webb's house." Furious, Webb knocked Martin to the floor and began kicking him. Martin was heard to mumble an apology "for some of his strongest epithets." And the Old House bartender, Judge Rufus Cook, intervened, pushing both men out the door.

Martin plunked himself down on a bench outside, but Webb remained dangerously indignant. Immediately reentering the saloon, he asked Cook for the loan of a pistol, which the bartender denied. He said he would get one elsewhere "and kill the little son-of-a-bitch unless he retracted." Webb, according to the *Globe*'s account, then "walked up Main Street, threatening more vengeance at every step." At Zimmerman's gun and hardware store he again asked for the loan of a pistol. When refused, Webb hurried home, seized his Winchester rifle, saddled his horse, and rode back to Front Street. He dismounted, hitched his horse, walked up to where Martin sat on the bench talking to another man, raised the rifle with both hands, and brought the barrel down on Martin's head with great force.[15]

Barney Martin, about forty years old and Irish-born, had recently moved to Dodge from Hays City, setting up a tailor shop in a Front Street building sandwiched between the Occident and the Old House saloons. Described as a "remarkably small man" and an alcoholic who when sober "was quiet and industrious," Martin regularly patronized the adjacent taverns, where he frequently annoyed others with bouts of noisy and argumentative drunkenness.[16]

At nearly 6 feet tall and "powerfully built," thirty-two-year old Arista Webb came from a family of some prominence back in Tidewater Virginia. Referred to as "quite an extensive planter and slave owner," his father owned seventeen men, women, and children in 1850; ten years later the number had increased to twenty.[17]

Arista left home shortly after the Civil War, accompanied, it appears, by a native Virginian, a black woman named Christina, perhaps a former slave on the plantation. The two most likely made their way to Iowa, got married, had a child, and headed for Kansas. The legislatures of both states had passively nullified, rather than actively repealed, their antimiscegenation laws, enacted in 1840 and 1855 respectively. Following adoption of a new Iowa Constitution on August 3, 1857, and the ratification of the Kansas Wyandotte Constitution on January 29, 1861, the two legislatures simply omitted any mention of interracial marriage from their newly compiled laws.

By January 1879, if not earlier, the family had settled in Dodge City, where Arista found employment as a porter for two Front Street stores and Christina gave birth to the couple's second child.[18] While interracial marriage, unlike almost everywhere else in the 1870s, was not considered illegal, the law was one thing, popular attitudes another. Most white Dodge Citians joined their counterparts elsewhere in the nation in viewing matrimony across the color line as disgraceful, indecent, and morally repulsive, profaning the sacred institution of marriage. In a perfect illustration of such hostility, a week before the Webb-Martin confrontation, Deputy Sheriff Duffey, butcher Charley Hungerford, and lawyer Harry Gryden—the late Dora Hand's divorce attorney—organized a faux wedding ceremony for a black man and a white woman. The couple, said the *Globe* editor, "had applied to the officers for the settlement of a lovers' quarrel and were advised that the only way out of the difficulty was by the happy bond of wedlock." Possibly Barney Martin had numbered among the "stiffs" in attendance, and sniggered about it during his offensive remarks to Webb.[19]

Dodge City most certainly did not welcome the Webbs. Arista, admitted the *Globe* with a touch of irony, "had but few friends in this community, being ostracized by all who considered themselves decent and respectable, because he was married to a woman whom the Creator had seen fit to cover with a motley skin." Even the town's small black community more or less turned its back on the couple. A week after Webb brained Martin with his Winchester, the *Globe* reprinted a short notice about the city's blacks having "whipped and ducked" one of its number for "living with a white woman." Clearly, as elsewhere, Dodge City's African Americans frowned on racially mixed partnerships as likely to make trouble for all of them.[20]

Webb's status as an outsider inevitably informed the seemingly unanimous opinion on the street that his murderous behavior was not only outrageous but cowardly, and his punishment should be sure and harsh.

After fracturing Martin's skull, Webb attempted to remount, bystanders corralled him, and Marshal Bassett disarmed him, discovering the Winchester cocked and fully loaded. Bassett managed to hustle his prisoner across the railroad tracks to the city jail. When a crowd gathered outside the building, some intent on a lynching, Sheriff Bat Masterson whisked Webb off to the more defensible county lockup at the courthouse. The following morning Webb learned that after ten hours in a coma Martin had died, and the charge would be the capital crime of homicide.

A coroner's jury, assembled by John Straughn, examined Martin's body (lying in a nearby storeroom) and adjourned to the Long Branch to hear testimony. Among the sworn witnesses: the bartender Judge Cook, a clerk at Zimmerman's store, and an eyewitness to the fatal attack. The jury brought in a verdict that Martin "came to his death by a blow from a gun in the hands of A. H. Webb who struck said Martin with the intent to kill."

At a magistrate's hearing the next day *Globe* editor Lloyd Shinn, another justice of the peace, ordered Webb held without bail for the next term of the district court; the state's criminal procedure required that "persons charged with an offense punishable with death, shall not be admitted to bail, when the proof is evident or the presumption great." During his ensuing four-month confinement, it was said, Webb "possessed not the sympathy of a single individual except that of his Negro wife, who was a constant and patient laborer in his behalf."[21]

The Ford County District Court convened on January 7, 1880, with Circuit Judge Samuel Peters of Harvey County presiding and the same Harry Gryden who had helped arrange the recent mock interracial wedding serving as Webb's lead attorney. Webb's marriage surely affected the selection of a jury: over forty men had to be summoned before opposing attorneys could agree on "twelve good and lawful citizens of Ford county, Kansas."

Webb pleaded not guilty, and his three-day, otherwise open-and-shut trial hinged on attorney Gryden's insanity defense. Webb's father had written from Virginia that mental instability ran in the family. Arista's older brother was confined in the Eastern State Hospital for the Insane at Williamsburg, and his uncle had also been there for a time. Before leaving home, Arista himself had been judged by the family physician "unbalanced on many subjects, and was just one of those cases, in which a single slight debauch, would produce complete insanity for a time." The subtext: Arista's marriage to an African American woman had helped trigger his descent into madness.

In his charge to the jury, Judge Peters reviewed the two degrees of murder and four of manslaughter in Kansas, then clarified the legal meaning of criminal insanity. "A criminal intent," he explained, "is an essential element in every crime, and a person destitute of the mental capacity to entertain this intent cannot incur legal punishment." The jurors, therefore,

> must from the evidence be satisfied beyond a reasonable doubt that at the time the defendant struck the deceased he was not laboring under

mental delusion, hallucination or monomania that irresistibly and un-controllably forced him to commit the act. . . . If his reason and mental power are so affected by disease that he has no will, or controlling men-tal power, or if through a condition of mental disease his intellectual power is for the time so weakened that he at the time of the commission of the act could not resist an inclination to do the act, then he is not a responsible moral agent and is not punishable for the act.

Dividing on the first poll—seven for first-degree (or premeditated) murder, three for second-degree (or unpremeditated) murder, and two for manslaughter (or unintentional killing)—the jury finally made up its mind. Late in the evening of January 17 the foreman delivered a verdict of first-degree murder.

Webb's lawyers immediately moved that the court set aside and vacate the jury verdict and grant a new trial, citing seven alleged errors. Dodge Citians, for one thing, had made prejudicial comments about Webb in the presence of jurors during court recesses, in particular Ford County commissioner George Hoover's angry remark to Harry Gryden: "What are you going to do with your damn murderer?" More importantly, ar-gued Webb's attorneys,

It is a presumption of law "that insanity once proved to have existed is presumed to continue." Hence, if you find defendant to have been in-sane at any time prior to the commission of the offense with which he is charged, you must find, in the absence of evidence to the contrary, that the insanity existed at the time of the act complained of.

On January 21 Peters overruled the motion and sentenced Webb to hang in not less than one year, since a twelve-month confinement in the state penitentiary at Lansing was a legal preliminary to execution at the discretion of the governor. The Ninth Judicial District had never before issued a death sentence, and Webb's hanging, had it occurred on sched-ule, would have been the only legal execution in Kansas between 1870 and 1887.[22]

On January 23, 1880, when processed into the Kansas penitentiary, Webb described himself as married. Christina Webb followed him east, settling in Leavenworth, from where she could easily visit her husband in nearby Lansing. The city's Home for the Friendless, sheltering sick and destitute women and children and helping the former secure respectable and self-supporting employment, may have aided Christina. Within a short walking distance of the shelter the census taker recorded a Christina Webb, black, Virginia-born, age twenty-five, occupation servant, living in a stand-alone dwelling with a two-year-old son and an eight-month-old daughter.[23]

From Virginia, Arista Webb's family retained Harry Gryden to press for reconsideration of the sentence and a possible pardon. In May 1881 Gryden wrote Kansas governor George Glick that "the killing I believe and always shall believe to have been prompted by mental aberration." Like other governors of the time, uncomfortable at having the final say-so dumped in his lap, Glick on December 1, 1882, acknowledged the family's pressure by transferring Webb to the insane asylum at Osawatomie.

Three years later, Governor John Martin having replaced Glick, Webb's family tried again. On March 31, 1885, Gryden submitted a packet of papers to the Kansas Board of Pardons. All the documents testified to Webb's unstable mental health, including a petition from thirty Virginians "of the highest integrity and veracity" and a certification from the Webb family physician, as well as from the superintendent at Osawatomie. The last declared that while "now rarely manifesting the dangerous element of his disease," Webb's

> delusions are, however, the same in character as they have been all the time. . . . It is not probable that he will ever recover from his insanity, but it is probable that it will grow more simple and harmless in character, though it will be some time before it will be fully safe for him to be set at liberty, though he is easily controlled by an attendant. He could be safely moved to the home of his father, but would require confinement and care there as here.

In a separate letter Virginia governor William Cameron assured the Kansas board that "any conditions you may impose for the transfer of the Insane Convict from your state to ours, will, I am sure, be strictly complied with."

On May 19, 1885, the Kansas board recommended that Martin pardon Arista Webb. A new Dodge City journal, the *Kansas Cowboy*, on May 30 and June 7 printed notice of Webb's impending release. Receiving no objections from Dodge, on June 19 Governor Martin issued a pardon, stipulating that Webb's family take him home and never let him set foot in Kansas again.

Webb's family committed him to the Western State Hospital for the Insane at Staunton, Virginia, listing him as single. He was still there, age fifty-two, in 1900. Whether or not Christina and the children returned to Virginia is unknown.[24]

⸺◦⧼∽⧽◦⸺

Shortly before Thanksgiving of 1880, after more than a year without lethal violence, deadly gunshots once again broke the calm of Dodge City and disrupted the routine duties of its then resident law officers: Deputy US Marshal Hamilton Bell, Sheriff George Hinkle, Undersheriff Frederick Singer, Deputy Sheriff William Duffey, City Marshal Jim Masterson, and Assistant City Marshal Neil Brown.

Nicholas Klaine's *Times* broke the story on the killing, which occurred on the night of November 16–17.

MURDER IN DODGE CITY

On Tuesday night a murder was committed in this city, in that part of town south of the railroad track. . . . It has been some time since a murder has been committed in Dodge City, but the shooting Tuesday night offers no parallel to any of the crimes committed here. There was no provocation, and it is hinted that the unfortunate [Henry] Heck was the victim of a conspiracy, the facts of which may be developed upon the trial of the murderer.

Three days later the *Globe* printed a more forthcoming account that included the events leading up to the shooting. Like the report in the *Times,* the *Globe*'s lengthier commentary—from the breezy vernacular tone of the piece probably authored by Lloyd Shinn—began with an expression of considerable indignation.

HENRY C. HECK KILLED.<br>
JOHN GILL, ALIAS CONCHO, ESTABLISHES HIMSELF AS A KILLER

On last Wednesday morning the report that a killing had taken place in the city the night previous, was rife on the streets at an early hour.

The report was soon confirmed and everybod[y] felt that Dodge had still some of the bloody instinct for which she was so famous in the lawless days of her infancy, when money was as dross and whisky four bits a drink.[25]

Henry Heck, Ohio-born son of German immigrants, had arrived in Dodge City around 1876 at age twenty-five or so, and in fairly short order became a trusted employee and fast friend of Hamilton Bell, proprietor of the popular Elephant Livery Stable on the south side, as well as owner of a nearby dance house. In 1878 Bell closed the latter and built the Varieties Theatre and Dance Hall to accommodate floor shows and featured entertainers, such as the ill-fated Dora Hand. Its resident troupe, and with it the Varieties, folded in about six weeks, leaving what locals referred to as "Ham Bell's Dance Hall."

Henry Heck, Bell said, "kept the place," and was also, reported Lloyd Shinn, "left in charge of the extensive livery . . . whenever Mr. Bell was absent from the city." Heck's day-to-day dance hall responsibilities included keeping order, bringing him in close contact with Dodge's policemen, who always kept a watchful eye on Bell's establishment and its competitors.[26]

A Dodge City resident for not even a year, twenty-three-year-old John "Concho" Gill, cowboy turned professional gambler, had spent his early years in Texas. Almost 6 feet tall, Gill "was a quiet man," said editor Shinn, "and not considered quarrelsome or dangerous." When visited in June 1880 by the local census taker, Gill shared a Front Street building with four other single males, each in his own apartment: two sheep raisers, another ex-cowboy, and the manager of the local stockyard.[27]

In 1879 Heck and Caroline Moore, a young dance hall employee, cohabiting, Shinn wrote, "nearly ever since Mr. Heck has resided in this county," moved down to Mulberry Ranch a dozen miles below town on the Camp Supply trail near Mulberry Creek. Bell owned the place, having purchased the land and a small store thereon, which he turned into a more substantial operation. It was a "No. 1 location for keeping passers-by, and cattle or sheep," Bell later asserted. It had "good range, good water running by the place, a well of good water at the door, good corral 100 feet square, good house 22 x 35." Henry Heck either leased or managed the ranch. And for "nearly a year," said Shinn, while Heck "was raising a little stock which was being steadily accumulated by his industry and prudence," his "faithful companion [Moore] performed the duties which usually fall to the lot of a rural housewife."

But on a shopping trip to Dodge City in September 1880 Moore met, fell for, and soon moved in with Concho Gill. As Shinn tells it: Gill's "dark brown eyes, classic features, and complexion bronzed by a southern sun, together with the indolent life of a gambler's paramour, were too dazzling to be resisted, when compared with kitchen drudgery, and the society of her more homely lover."[28]

After some weeks of irate solitude, Heck issued an ultimatum. On November 13 he visited Moore and told her she had three days either to return to him or to get out of Dodge.

As an unseasonably early winter gripped the town, with temperatures hovering in the teens, Henry Heck, right on schedule, came to Dodge to separate Moore from Gill. Around midnight he made his way to the couple's apartment, where, according to Moore and Charley Milde, Gill's friend visiting from Texas, Heck kicked at the door but refused to identify himself. Roused from bed, Gill, who had been ill for over a week, grabbed a revolver, and, as the door flew open, fired twice. One bullet tore through Heck's right breast just below the nipple, perforating his lung. He turned and disappeared into the night, made his way to a nearby saloon, ordered a drink, announced he had been shot, left, returned a few minutes later, then dropped to the floor, expiring "without a groan."

Alerted by the shots, Assistant Marshal Brown hurried to Concho Gill's apartment, confiscated the fatal pistol, and arrested him.

Later that morning of November 17 a coroner's inquest convened. Law enforcement types characteristically impatient with troublemakers dominated the proceedings. Coroner John Straughn himself doubled as a deputy sheriff, while three of the six jurors had similar bona fides: Alonzo Webster, a Dodge City founder about to run for mayor on a law-and-order platform; US Marshal Bell, Heck's benefactor and friend; and Patrick Sughrue, a former Dodge Township constable and future Ford County sheriff. The jury heard testimony from a one A. J. Tuttle, from Officer Brown, from Charley Milde, and from Moore. The young woman had little to offer, claiming she was building a fire in the stove during the incident. But Milde testified that Gill "had said nothing . . . to indicate

[Heck's arrival] was expected by him." And Tuttle swore that Heck "had no weapon" when he saw him "one minute after he was shot." Tuttle also testified that Heck said "Concho had shot him." The jury's verdict: Heck "came to his death by a pistol fired by John Gill alias Concho . . . and the said shooting was done feloniously and without cause."[29]

At the early December 1880 magistrate's hearing, Justice of the Peace Lloyd Shinn bound Gill over to the district court "to answer to a charge of manslaughter in the first degree." In the words of the law Gill had killed Heck "without a design to effect death" at a moment when Heck was "engaged in the perpetration or attempt to perpetrate [a] crime or misdemeanor, not amounting to a felony."[30]

*State of Kansas v. John Gill, alias Concho,* opened at the Ford County courthouse on January 17, 1881, two months to the day since the shooting. As in the *Webb* case, Judge Samuel Peters presided. Charley Milde, City Marshal Jim Masterson, and saloonkeeper Alfred Peacock numbered among the handful of subpoenaed witnesses, which, oddly enough, did not include Caroline Moore. Peacock's presence strongly suggests that it was in his saloon that Heck had died. Neither the bare bones trial record nor the newspaper accounts contain witness testimony.

Gill pleaded not guilty. After a one-day trial the jury of twelve men— all from outside the corporate boundaries of Dodge—found him guilty not of first-degree manslaughter but of murder in the second degree, a killing "committed purposely and maliciously, but without deliberation and premeditation," punishable by "confinement and hard labor for not less than ten years."

On January 21, 1881, Peters, as was everywhere routinely done, denied the pro forma motion of Gill's attorney to dismiss on grounds that the verdict was "contrary to evidence." He then sentenced Gill to fifteen years' hard labor. Sheriff Hinkle and Undersheriff Singer assumed custody of the prisoner. The next day they conveyed him to Lansing, where Concho Gill joined Arista Webb at the Kansas State Penitentiary.[31]

Three years later James Young, Gill's stepfather, arrived in Dodge City from Texas. Interviewing the witnesses, he gathered new information and marshaled considerable community support for Concho Gill's pardon. By March 21, 1884, Young had persuaded thirty-six Dodge Citians to sign a petition to Governor Glick requesting him to commute Gill's sentence.

Members of the city's business, political, and legal elite numbered among the signatories. Robert Wright, Morris Collar, and George Cox represented the founding entrepreneurs. The mayor and city clerk joined other political signers. The new sheriff and deputy sheriff, Pat Sughrue and the sinister "Mysterious Dave" Mather, along with several well-known attorneys—Michael Sutton, who in 1880 had prosecuted Gill; Thomas Jones, Gill's 1880 attorney; and Harry Gryden, Webb's defense counsel—also signed. After penning his own signature, *Times* editor Nicholas Klaine noted that "time seems . . . to soften prejudices and produce sympathy." And Dodge City's police judge, admitting he "was not here at the time," appended a note: "From Statements of responsible citizens I believe this petition should be granted."[32]

In support of commutation, the petitioners first argued that "since incarceration [Gill's] health has failed, and there is strong probability that he will not live until the expiration of his term." Back when the 1880 census taker had come round in June, Gill reported that he was ill with scurvy. That November it was reported that for ten days before the killing, Gill had been "lying in bed sick." He obviously suffered from a chronic and debilitating condition, very possibly gonorrhea or secondary-stage syphilis (not uncommon among cowboys), some of whose symptoms—joint pain, skin blotches, depression, lassitude—mimicked those of scurvy.[33]

The second and more significant argument: "The crime for which said John Gill was convicted was committed by him under a misapprehension . . . that the man he killed was hunting him to kill him." That knowledge came from new testimony by Caroline Moore, now Caroline Lane, and Sallie Frazier, a black restaurant owner characterized by a local historian as "the strong-willed and litigious matriarch of Dodge City's minority community." In notarized statements the women testified that on the night of the killing Heck had told each of them separately that he "would kill said Gill before morning," and each in turn "told said Gill that . . . Heck had threatened to kill him."

Neither court records nor Attorney Jones's supporting letter to Governor Glick, which stated that Gill "would have been promptly acquitted had it not been for the evidence of a personal enemy [Hamilton Bell?]," even hint at why Moore and Frazier had not stepped forward earlier.[34]

Young, as legally required, posted notice in the *Dodge City Times* of his intention to file an official application on April 16 to commute his stepson's sentence. And so he did. But, for unknown reasons, Governor Glick refused to pardon Gill.

On August 19, 1891, his sentence having at last been commuted, Concho Gill emerged from the Kansas penitentiary after ten and one-half years of confinement for the murder of Henry Heck.[35]

————⚬∞⚬————

Four victims, four killers, four stories, each prominently featuring a woman, one of them as a victim, and each case revealing important aspects of Dodge City's criminal justice system during its earliest era. Importantly, in no case was vigilante action deemed an appropriate substitute for legal procedure. While Webb's despised interracial marriage and lack of friendships clearly laid him open to the harshest legal penalty, the constituted authorities had quickly put a stop to any talk of lynching. A few years later the editor of the *Dodge City Democrat* approvingly noted that "vigilantes may as well tumble to the fact that no Ford County sheriff ever had or ever will have a prisoner taken away by strangers." In Dodge there would be no headline-grabbing rough justice, no illegal execution sure to damage the community's always precarious reputation.

Frank Loving's exoneration proved to be the only "frontier" aspect of the four cases. The coroner's jury exposed the inclination to consider gunfights between two angry adults as having no innocent parties. Or, in the words of the *Globe,* "both [men] being willing to risk their lives . . . they fought because they wanted to fight." The rule of thumb suggested by the jurors' decision: a moral equivalence between killer and victim made little sense in carefully parsing the evidence. Finding that the dead combatant, Richardson, fired first, true or not, saved the public expense of a confinement and trial.[36]

The larger point of these narratives is that the people of Dodge City took violent death seriously and subjected alleged culprits to deliberate legal action dictated by conventions nurtured through centuries of Anglo judicial practice. All the cases followed a set of public rituals assuring villagers that although situated, as they saw it, on the geographic extremity of civilization, theirs was nevertheless a fully civil society, culturally located well within the larger American community.

# CIRCLE DOT COWBOYS

In the third week of June 1882, seven Texas cowboys from an outfit grazing cattle on Duck Creek in northern Ford County set out for nearby Dodge City. Like hundreds of cowhands and cattlemen before them, these Circle Dot men intended to "see the elephant."

Originally referring to the main attraction of any mid-nineteenth century circus, the elephant allusion was strictly metaphorical, meaning a unique sight or spectacle.[1] Here it specifically alluded to Dodge City, with its gaudy entertainments—the celebrated and widely condemned all-night bars, gaming tables, dance halls, and brothels.

In the 1870s and 1880s seemingly every cowboy ascending the Western Trail felt obliged to stop and ogle the excitement, if not actually participate in it. As one old Texan years later described his anticipation: "Dodge City enjoyed a reputation of being the fastest cowboy town on this side of the globe, and it was our joy and delight to know that ere long we would see that famous place."[2]

On the June day in question the Circle Dot cowboys rode into Dodge at approximately 9:00 a.m. Some fifteen hours later they galloped out again, six-shooters blazing, hostile bullets whining about their ears. They had indeed seen the elephant and congratulated themselves on having escaped unscathed.

Their story appeared in 1903 as chapter 13 of ex—trail hand Andy Adams's *The Log of a Cowboy*.[3] From the first a surprising number of readers and reviewers assumed it to be nonfiction. As recently as the mid-1990s nationally published authors continued to refer to the book as a cowboy memoir.[4] Western historians, however, have long recognized that the work, which is narrated not by Adams himself but by a Georgia-born twenty-six-year-old named Thomas Moore Quirk, is what its author intended: a novel.[5]

It seems fair to say that *The Log of a Cowboy* should be regarded as the first book-length "serious" or "adult" Western produced by an author who had actually made his living as a trail driver. The novel's literary qualities have been sharply disputed.[6] But specialists on the history and culture of the Old West have always awarded Adams's book high marks for its convincing fidelity to occupational detail. In the 1920s and 1930s the prestigious Texas scholars J. Frank Dobie and Walter Prescott Webb lavishly praised its effortless realism, pronouncing it an American masterpiece. "*The Log of a Cowboy* is the best book that has ever been written of cowboy life," Dobie said, "and it is the best book that ever can be written of cowboy life." Webb concurred: "Hitherto there has been written but one novel of the cattle country that is destined to become a classic— *The Log of a Cowboy*, by Andy Adams."[7]

The few who have commented specifically on the novel's Dodge City chapter, however, have disagreed as to its plausibility. Historians Joe B. Frantz and Julian Ernest Choate Jr. praised Adams for having contradicted "the sensational press and the romantic Western fiction [that] had made Dodge City . . . a sort of bloody angle of the plains. Adams stuck to the truth." But Don Graham, one of the book's literary critics, pooh-poohed the Dodge City chapter as less realistic than fatally clichéd. He found it an incongruous feature of "this most authentic of Western novels." In chapter 13, Graham said, "Adams would seem to be catering to popular tastes, to the stereotype of the cowboy as gunslinger."[8]

Separating fact from fiction in most literary works about the West is challenging at best. It is as problematic today as it was in 1872, for example, whether Mark Twain's description of recreational homicide at Virginia City is to be taken as serious reportage or as comic exaggeration. Twain and his "dime Western" contemporaries blurred the distinction between fact and literary invention, a mystification that Hollywood still magnifies, enhances, and widely disseminates.[9]

Almost all nonfiction treatments of Dodge City likewise bend and embroider the historical record. Two years after publication of *The Log of a Cowboy*, for instance, a novel set largely in frontier Dodge, *The Sunset*

*Trail*, mixed fact and fiction in a thoroughly puzzling manner. It offered odd distortions of many actual events, and rendered several of the town's pioneer business elite—including Alfred Peacock, Alonzo Webster, and James Kelley—as grammar-challenged rustics.[10]

Out of the ordinary, however, is Andy Adams's description of Dodge City in the third week of June 1882. A rare literary artifact, it is not only an accurate portrayal of "cowboy culture" and its association with guns and violence, something Dodge City attempted to regulate through ever more vigilant law enforcement. More importantly, for our purposes, it exposes a historical episode in the town's history that would otherwise have remained altogether mysterious.

---

Cattle-raiser Don Lovell and his employees are of course imaginary, as is their trip up the Western Trail, first to Dodge and then on to Montana Territory. But the novel is clearly based on Adams's own experience as a Texas cowboy. The author is known to have driven horses up the trail to Dodge City in the 1880s. In an autobiographical sketch, for instance, he certified that "Caldwell was the best horse market, but Dodge was a good point too." But as for memories of the cattle town, Adams was typically laconic. He notoriously resisted talking about his own life; a Texas historian who interviewed him remarked that "one was soon impressed with the futility of trying to dig an elaborated, factual story out of Andy Adams."[11] Yet Adams did tell J. Frank Dobie that he and Dobie's uncle, Frank Byler, used to hang out together in Dodge City, "trading horses and not neglecting other pastimes of what was then the cowboy capital of the world." On another occasion he denied having been involved in any of the town's legendary violence. While a cowboy "he was never in any real danger," he told an interviewer. "Nor," it was said of him, "did he have any adventures worth mentioning when he was in the tough Dodge City of the early days." Yet he retained a vivid recollection of the place. "I knew just where Boot Hill was," he said, "and how the trail went over the [Arkansas River] bottom and over the hill."[12]

Exactly when Adams visited Dodge City is not supplied by his various autobiographical snippets, but 1882 was the earliest possible date. In 1880 he was still at home on the farm in Indiana. Two years later, at age twenty-one, Adams headed for Texas, intent on working with horses. He reached San Antonio and landed a job at Smith & Redmon, dealers in horses and mules. Long afterward Adams mentioned that, like his fictional narrator Tom Quirk, his first trail drive occurred in 1882. One biographer says that Adams lived in Live Oak County south of San Antonio for "a year or two" before that first drive, but the record suggests otherwise. The drive itself, however, did start in Live Oak County, where Adams and other Smith & Redmon cowboys rounded up a horse herd and, as one old-timer remembered, ended with the herd's sale in Dodge City.[13]

Intriguing bits of independent information confirm that Adams's employment with Smith & Redmon took him to Dodge in June 1882. Dated June 7, 1882, a list of seventeen horse herds on the trail in northern Texas bound for Dodge City appeared in the town's *Ford County Globe*, including an entry for William Smith—almost certainly the William L. Smith of Smith & Redmon—owner of a herd of 500 animals.[14]

Then in chapter 13 of *The Log of a Cowboy* Adams quotes a complaint made by the famous Texas cattleman A. H. "Shanghai" Pierce, owner of 3,700 head that had just arrived near town—a sojourn documented by newspaper editor Lloyd Shinn on June 20:

> Shanghai Pierce the representative cattle man of Texas . . . is in the city amusing the boys, giving them old time reminiscences that many have long since forgotten. He can hold a Texas audience as level as any man we ever knew. It is useless to say that Pierce has many thousand head of cattle for sale on this market.

Adams has Pierce loudly complaining to an agent of some eastern livestock market:

> No, I'll not ship any more cattle to your town until you adjust your yardage charges. Listen! I can go right up into the heart of your city and get a room for myself, with a nice clean bed in it, plenty of soap, water, and towels, and I can occupy that room for twenty-four hours for two bits. And your stockyards, away out in the suburbs, want to charge me twenty cents a head and let my steer stand out in the weather.

Years later Adams said that he himself had heard Pierce utter these very remarks at Dodge City.[15] Since neither Pierce's private correspondence for 1882–1885 nor subsequent Dodge City newspapers of the period mention that the celebrated Texan ever revisited Dodge during its cattle-trading years, Adams would have had to have seen and heard him in the third week of June 1882.[16]

—⋅◦∞◦⋅—

Gauging the historical veracity of chapter 13 requires knowing something of the social and political context for the Circle Dot cowboys' visit.

By June 1882, the month Andy Adams (as well as his Circle Dot crowd) arrived, Dodge City housed about a thousand residents. Single males aged twenty to forty now shared their former hegemony with a virtually equal number of married men, and the proportion of wives and children had grown dramatically since the mid-1870s. And adult males from New England, the Middle Atlantic states, and the Midwest had gained a majority among the town's (exclusively male) voters, rising from 45 percent in 1875 to 58 percent in 1880. It was from these changing demographics that the "church element," as George Hoover termed it, the town's evangelical syndicate of Presbyterians, Methodists, and Baptists, recruited support for its main project: liquor prohibition.[17]

Back in the 1880 general election the people of Kansas had led the nation in altering their constitution to outlaw the manufacture, sale, and consumption of all intoxicating beverages, but transformative abstinence proved more easily legislated than enforced. Ford County had registered the smallest proportion (20 percent) of dry votes of any county in Kansas, and Dodge City's businessmen held to a hardened conviction that Texas cowboys and cattlemen might flat-out avoid any cattle market in which there were no saloons. Moreover, with Dodge over $3,000 in debt and liquor licenses an important source of municipal revenue, the town fathers simply decided to ignore the law and tough it out.[18]

Yet the new illegality of liquor complicated the three-tiered moral geography of Dodge City. No longer could any defensible distinction be made between Front Street's more upscale saloons and the casinos, dives, and brothels south of the tracks. All, as dispensers of beer, wine, and hard liquor, were now equally unlawful. Dodge City's pragmatic adjustment: a greater emphasis on "good order," more broadly defined than just the suppression of gun violence.

Pioneer businessman Alonzo Webster became the principal figure in this emerging response to the new challenge. Webster projected the air of an enforcer. Admiration persisted for his law-and-order leadership and lethal shooting in 1869 of an armed ruffian at Hays City. At Dodge he presumably numbered among the twenty vigilantes involved in the 1873 killings of Charles Hill and Ed Williams.

Now the business community looked to Webster's no-nonsense approach. Early in 1881, because of the illness of Ford County's sheriff and undersheriff, Webster temporarily filled in as chief law officer, using his position to lecture the police, as the *Globe* described it, "in unmistakable language that they were not only officers of the law . . . but also representatives of a community who expected them to enforce the laws and preserve the peace at all hazards." Along with his established reputation, that attitude propelled Webster into the mayor's office in early April 1881, with a mandate to ignore the three major illegalities—saloons, professional gambling, prostitution—but to eradicate violence, disorder, and petty criminality. In his first official act Webster warned that all "thieves, thugs, confidence men, and persons without visible means of support" would be tolerated no longer, and his city council promptly armed him with a new ordinance respecting vagrants.[19]

The first test of Webster's authority came just a few days later, on April 16, 1881, when he intervened decisively in the so-called Battle of the Plaza that briefly destabilized the commercial district, recklessly endangering midday shoppers and passers-by. The trouble rose from hard feelings between Jim Masterson and Alfred Peacock, partners in the ownership of the Lady Gay Dance Hall. As the feud became ever more bitter, some friend of the Mastersons wired Bat, then in Arizona, to "come at once." At high noon Bat stepped off the train and immediately precipitated a gun battle on Front Street. The sound of pistol shots emptied the saloons on both sides of the tracks, with partisans joining in the firefight, aiming at each other as much as at the original combatants. Nobody fell dead, but many rounds snapped indiscriminately through downtown.

A furious Mayor Webster grabbed a shotgun and drafted an impromptu posse that surrounded Bat, his brother Jim, and two saloon regulars. Tradition has it that Webster told Bat to drop his weapon, but Bat, his dander up, hesitated. "Put down that gun," said the mayor quietly, "or I'll kill you." Masterson obeyed.

In the end, Webster decided not to prosecute the Mastersons, both of them respected former law officers. But Bat had to pay an $8 fine for feloniously discharging his pistol, and the brothers and their friends were forced to get out of Dodge on the next train.[20]

Webster continued to demonstrate executive strength. His fiscal agenda included reinstituting the monthly fines on gamblers and prostitutes, which had been allowed to lapse, and introducing a "license tax" on owners of the now-illegal saloons. In an effort at further regularizing local law enforcement, Webster ordered the police into smart navy-blue uniforms, their ranks emblazoned on their hatbands. His 1881 tenure passed with only one killing, the police shooting on July 22–23 of a young railroader, Joseph McDonald, mistaken for a nighttime prowler.[21] Satisfied voters reelected Webster without opposition to a second term in April 1882.

Meanwhile, a small but growing number of Dodge City's religiously motivated activists had become increasingly impatient about their town's continuing noncompliance with the Kansas anti-liquor law. In his second term, and himself now turned prohibitionist, Governor John St. John, in December 1881, publicly singled out Dodge and several other Kansas communities for special legal attention by the state. Energized, Dodge's temperance activists came perilously close to gaining two seats on the five-man town council in the April 1882 city election.

Nicholas Klaine of the *Times* had bridled at St. John's December proclamation. "We assure the Governor that the law won't be enforced in Dodge City," he announced, "not by peaceable prosecutions . . . and not by spies, bribes or rewards." Then, on the eve of the 1882 spring election, he also issued an editorial directed at the evangelicals. "It is possible to overdo efforts at reform," he warned.

> There is no influence capable or powerful enough to make a sweeping change in the traffic of Dodge City. The power of the Governor is not strong enough to suppress whisky selling, gambling and the dance hall. . . . There can only be a modification or control of illegitimate traffic under the circumstances that now envelop us. We are satisfied and contented if these things are conducted properly, orderly and decently.

On May 23, six weeks after the election, nonetheless, reform enthusiasts formally organized themselves, gathering at a nondenominational site, the Odd Fellows Hall, and founding a local chapter of the Independent Order of Good Templars. This, the largest, most militant, and most evangelical society hostile to alcoholic drink, sought nothing less than the eradication of liquor usage throughout the United States and Europe.[22] By August 1882 the Dodge City Templars prided themselves on a membership of forty-five, both men and women.

The lodge itself proved short-lived, disappearing in 1883, and little is known of its members. Their makeup, however, is suggested by the sixteen men and women elected as officers. They included Robert Rice, manufacturer of upscale saddles, and Susan Rice, recently arrived Virginians; Anson Buzzell, Methodist clergyman, and Florence Buzzell, from New England; Philander Reynolds, stagecoach entrepreneur, and Lemira Reynolds, from Michigan; Louisa McAdams, from Illinois, married to a coal merchant; tailor R. R. Robbins, from Pennsylvania; and Irish-born wheelwright James Sullivan. Remarkably, five adolescents, average age seventeen, also served as lodge officers: a former Dodge House waitress, Ida Hustis; store clerk George Conrad; hotelier Samuel Galland's stepson, Charles Ramsey; and the Reynolds's niece and nephew visiting from Lawrence, Olin Hard and Inez Hard, a recent graduate of the University of Kansas. [23]

Yet back in early June 1882 the evangelicals—presumably including the local Templars—apparently agreeing with Klaine that local liquor prohibition could be achieved only at the price of extraordinary disturbance, struck a deal with Mayor Webster. They promised to refrain from collaborating with Governor St. John's impulse to interfere. In return Webster agreed to appoint a Good Templars' activist to the top law-enforcement job in Dodge, thereby guaranteeing that drinking and its associated indulgences would be closely supervised and excesses curtailed. The agreement clearly conformed to Klaine's prescription: "If these vices can be kept on stricter discipline, with a regard for the good sense and modesty of the community, they will be permitted to exist. . . . The moral sense of the community must be respected. It is time for violators of the law and the practices of immorality to have less of public gaze."[24]

On June 10, 1882, Mayor Webster accordingly discharged Dodge's law officers and hired an entirely fresh three-man force. Peter Beamer, the Good Templars' chapter secretary, became the new city marshal. A thirty-six-year-old plow and wagon maker, Beamer worked in Pat

Sughrue's blacksmith shop. Ohio-born, reared in Illinois, he enlisted in the Union army in 1861. Having fought as an infantryman from the early campaigns in Missouri to the sieges of Nashville and Chattanooga, the bloody Atlanta campaign, the famous March to the Sea, and the final battle at Bentonville, North Carolina, Beamer held the rank of regimental first sergeant at his discharge. He then tried gold prospecting, farming, and stock raising before settling at Dodge City in 1879. In 1881 he ran unsuccessfully for county coroner, but earned a slight majority in one of Dodge's two voting precincts. A persistent joiner, he served as secretary of Dodge City's Odd Fellows, chancellor commander of its Knights of Pythias, and worshipful master of its Masons.[25]

To aid Marshal Beamer the mayor appointed Clark Chipman as assistant marshal and Lee Harland (or Harlan) as policeman. Whether these officers, like the marshal, were Good Templars is unknown. Since February Chipman had been a low-level peace officer, a Dodge Township constable. Harland had never held a law-enforcement job in town. Following their confirmation by the city council, editor Lloyd Shinn cautiously endorsed all three: "Mr. Beamer is one of our best citizens—an earnest, unassuming citizen—temperate in his habits, and a person especially suited for the place. Lee Harland and Clark Chipman . . . are both nervy fellows and are, if we do not misjudge them, the proper men for the positions named." Editor Klaine briskly followed suit: "The appointment of the new police force will give general satisfaction. They are sober and honest men, and will no doubt discharge their duties faithfully and satisfactorily."[26]

Webster also instituted a code of conduct to govern police behavior, insisting, as Shinn reported, "that these rules must be observed or he will speedily remove any officer that violates them." The new police regulations consisted of fourteen items. For example, officers were to "wear the star or shield on the outside garment on the left breast," they could not drink on duty (if drink they did), leave town without permission, or get involved in private quarrels, and they were required to file appropriate paperwork with the city attorney after each arrest. Perhaps most important was rule three: "Each and every member [of the force] must be civil, quiet and orderly; he must maintain decorum, command of temper and discretion." Although the mayor took a risk by hiring beginners as officers, he must have felt that the accord with the evangelicals, his close personal supervision, and his new regulations would more than make up for a managerial gamble.[27]

The new police immediately went to work. On the very day of his appointment Assistant Marshal Chipman successfully pursued an escaped prisoner in an arduous round-trip journey of 55 miles by horseback. A few days later Marshal Beamer warned that "all dogs found without a license tag, after July 1st, will be shot," and that "all hogs found running at large will be impounded." Meanwhile, Dodge Township's justice of the peace and Dodge City's police judge busily processed human miscreants. They charged two with obtaining money under false pretenses, one with assault with intent to kill, several others with misdemeanors. The city attorney, reported Klaine, had ordered his new officers to arrest "the gamblers who do not hold tables"—those without regular venues, thus avoiding the monthly penalty on gamblers and prostitutes. "The result," Klaine added, "was a number of fines and a repletion of the city treasury."[28]

Then, quite abruptly, Beamer resigned. In September 1882, with Robert Wright as a silent partner, he bought out his employer and established the blacksmithing and wagon-making firm of Wright & Beamer.

As a lawman Beamer had lasted in office no more than twelve or fourteen days. "During the past week City Marshal P. W. Beamer handed to Mayor Webster his resignation . . . the same to take effect at once," reported Shinn on June 27. "Just what induced Mr. Beamer to take this step we were unable to learn. Mayor Webster assumes the duties of the office until such time as he may be enabled to fill the office." Two days later Nicholas Klaine proved even less forthcoming, revealing only that Webster had decided he could safely delegate the marshal's job, at least temporarily, to Beamer's second-in-command. "P. W. Beamer resigned the office of City Marshal," Klaine wrote. "Clark Chipman is acting Marshal." And with that, the editorial *omertà*, customarily governing all the news not fit to print, asserted itself. The evidently discreditable incident disappears entirely from the documentary record.[29]

Something had gone wrong, but no source explains what—except, almost certainly, chapter 13 of Andy Adams's *The Log of a Cowboy.*

<hr>

The fictional Circle Dot outfit's visit can be accurately dated because it coincided with the presence in Dodge City not only of Shanghai Pierce but of "Uncle Henry" Stevens, yet another well-known Texas rancher. The real-life Stevens—"looking as young, bright and cheerful as ever," reported Lloyd Shinn—arrived in Dodge on the evening of June 16, 1882, and he remained in and around town through the end of that month. The Circle Dot cowboys would visit Dodge shortly after Stevens's arrival.[30]

The novel's Don Lovell, owner of the Circle Dot herd, has traveled to Dodge by rail. Driving a livery rig, he greets his crew south of town. He is accompanied by a Texas cattle drover referred to as McNulta, "the old cowman," a character modeled on the well-known Richard McNulty (whose name, when pronounced with a western drawl, may have sounded as Adams spelled it). A native Texan in his mid-thirties, McNulty owned the Turkey Track Ranch in the Texas Panhandle from 1878 to 1881. He was remembered for once playing a peacemaker's role in Dodge City, persuading a belligerent Clay Allison to settle down and sleep off his drunk.[31]

Lovell and McNulta stay with the outfit overnight. The next day Lovell orders his men to take the herd across the Arkansas River and establish camp on Duck Creek north of Dodge. After that, half the cowboys might visit town.

Then McNulta issues some avuncular advice to Lovell's employees. "I've been in Dodge every summer since '77," he says, "and I can give you boys some points." First: "Don't ever get the impression that you can ride your horses into a saloon, or shoot out the lights in Dodge; it may go somewhere else, but it don't go there. So I want to warn you to behave yourselves." Second, they must obey the local gun-control ordinance. That means, says McNulta, that "you can wear your six-shooters into town, but you'd better leave them at the first place you stop, hotel, livery, or business house. And when you leave town, call for your pistols, but don't ride out shooting; omit that." He concedes that "most cowboys think it's an infringement on their rights to give up shooting in town"—a fatal attitude should the townsfolk retaliate, since "your six-shooters are no match for Winchesters and buckshot."

McNulta got it right. Only that spring editor Shinn had dutifully reminded transients that "the carrying of firearms is strictly prohibited by ordinance in Dodge City." The community's newspaper editors constantly demanded that officers lethally interdict any use of firearms in town. Of the eighteen adults who died violently in Dodge from 1876 through 1886, two happened to be cowboys brazenly challenging the taboo on "firing a parting salute," as Lloyd Shinn phrased it.[32] Western artist Frederic Remington would immortalize this defiant tradition in his famous 1902 bronze sculpture *Coming Through the Rye*.[33]

Following McNulta's speech, Tom Quirk, the *Log*'s narrator, pauses to meditate on Dodge City lawmen from the perspective of twenty years. "The puppets of no romance ever written can compare with these officers in fearlessness," he says. His listing of lawmen correctly embraces brothers Ed, Jim, and Bat Masterson, Wyatt Earp, Jack Bridges, Charley Bassett, Bill Tilghman, J. J. Webb, and Dave Mather. But it wrongly includes John "Doc" Holliday and John "Shotgun" Collins, neither of whom ever served as an officer at Dodge. And, presumably based on the mayor's 1881 duty as a substitute sheriff, Quirk includes Alonzo Webster on his list.

A body of popular nonfiction about Dodge and its lawmen had not yet accumulated when Adams wrote his novel; there is no evidence that he read through old Dodge City newspapers; and his misspelling of Tilghman's last name as "Tillman," the way it was pronounced, implies that Adams is consulting his memory of gossip rather than any printed source.[34] The same is suggested by the next three paragraphs, which relate an odd but recognizable version of the April 1878 killing of Marshal Ed Masterson and the fatal wounding of his murderer—most probably an around-the-campfire version distorted through many retellings.

> "Throw up your hands and surrender," said an officer to a Texas cowboy, who had spurred an excitable horse until it was rearing and plunging in the street, leveling meanwhile a double-barreled shotgun at the horseman.
>
> "Not to you, you white-livered s— of a b—," was the instant reply, accompanied by a shot.
>
> The officer staggered back mortally wounded, but recovered himself, and the next instant the cowboy reeled from his saddle, a load of buckshot through his breast.

————◈————

Tom Quirk is among those men remaining behind to guard the herd that night as the first cohort of Circle Dot cowboys leaves for Dodge. The next morning those who had been in town relate a true story about an elabo-rate practical joke played on a visiting lecturer, a self-professed medical expert on "private diseases" (presumably gonorrhea and syphilis). The tale is told as if it had happened the previous evening. Actually, the in-cident had occurred back in February 1880. Although reported at that time in the *Ford County Globe*, it would not be described in print again until publication of Robert Wright's memoir in 1913. Thus Adams's re-telling depends on oral tradition, a presumption supported by his hav-ing had to supply a name for the visiting speaker, something not likely to have been remembered by raconteurs. And in the interests of propriety he changes the visitor's occupation to "professor in the occult sciences."

Otherwise Adams's account agrees with the documentation: Bat Masterson solemnly chairs the meeting. By design, hecklers periodi-cally interrupt the lecturer. Finally Masterson draws a pistol allegedly intending to silence the critics, the lights go out, gunfire illuminates the room, the terrified speaker is hustled out of town the next day suppos-edly for his own safety, and the conspirators have a good laugh.[35]

---

Following a chuckwagon breakfast, the balance of the Circle Dot crew takes its turn in Dodge. The second group of seven includes the three most important of the novel's characters: Tom Quirk; Paul "The Rebel" Priest, a thirty-something ex-Confederate; and Quince Forrest, ten years Priest's junior, an incurable teller of tall tales and self-professed expert gambler.

During the ride into town Forrest, who had been in Dodge the pre-vious year, regales his companions with his plan to hunt up the Long Branch Saloon faro dealer who took his money in 1881, buy the man a drink, then win back every dollar. "There's something in this northern air," he exclaims, "that tells me that this is my lucky day. You other kids had better let the games alone and save your money."

Reaching Front Street, the seven rendezvous with their trail boss, James Flood, on the steps of the real-life Wright House, where owner Don Lovell is staying. Robert Wright had built this hotel on Second Ave-nue, catty-corner from his store, as a convenience for his more affluent patrons. Now "Renovated and Refitted," as a newspaper advertisement announced, it offered "Superior Accommodations to the traveling public" and a dining room "supplied with the choicest and best the market affords." Financially, however, the hotel was a losing proposition for Wright, who simply wrote it off as an expense of doing business as the biggest merchant in Dodge.[36]

Flood directs his men across the railroad tracks to a south-side livery stable. Here, says Quirk, "we unsaddled and turned our horses into a large corral, and while we were in the office of the livery, surrendering our artillery, Flood . . . handed each of us $25 in gold" as an advance on wages. Then, says Quirk, "we scattered like partridges before a gunner." Within an hour or so they get hot-towel shaves and haircuts and make small purchases—sewing kits to pistol cartridges—that they carry back to the stable and stow in their saddle bags. Quirk and Priest then visit the famous Long Branch. In June 1882 its managerial partnership boasted of having "refitted their enterprise in elegant style." They also had laid in "a fine stock" of brandy, gin, port, sherry, claret, and Bass Ale, drinkable only "for medicinal, scientific and mechanical purposes"—a sly reference to the prohibition law's short list of approved alcohol usages.[37]

After watching Forrest play faro at the Long Branch, Quirk and Priest move on to another saloon, where Priest meets an old friend, Ben Thompson, a wartime comrade and now a professional gambler. "The two cronied around for over an hour like long lost brothers," says Quirk, "pledging anew their friendship over several social glasses, in which I was always included." Here, as with the incident of the visiting lecturer, Andy Adams shifts the chronology of a documented occurrence. The reputed killer of several men, Thompson was an actual Texas character, a man "well known in Dodge," as editor Klaine put it, who had spent the 1880 cattle season domiciled there with his wife and children. Since 1881, however, Thompson had been serving as city marshal of Austin, Texas, and would continue to do so until late summer 1882.[38]

At noon Lovell rounds up his men, pays for a few drinks, and takes them for lunch ("dinner") at the Wright House, where, joined by Flood and McNulta, they occupy a ten-chair table in the dining room. At another table sit Uncle Henry Stevens and several other cattlemen, the most spirited being Shanghai Pierce, whom Quirk describes as "possibly the most widely known cowman between the Rio Grande and the British possessions . . . and the possessor of a voice which, even in ordinary conversation, could be distinctly heard across the street." Here his foghorn voice and endless supply of "yarns and cattle talk" dominate until well into the afternoon. Eventually, most of the Circle Dot cowboys get up and leave, but Quirk stays on—as the young Andy Adams can easily be imagined doing—completely enraptured by the cattlemen's gossip, including Pierce's complaint to an eastern livestock buyer, previously quoted, about inflated yardage charges.

Early that evening Flood urges his men to return with him to the herd, but, says Quirk, "all the crowd wanted to stay in town and see the sights. Lovell interceded in our behalf, and promised to see that we left town in good time to be in camp before the herd was ready to move the next morning." Exacting a promise that the cowboys would indeed leave for camp before midnight, Lovell retires to the Wright House.

Returning to the livery corral to saddle and tie up their horses, since they "fully expected to leave town by ten o'clock," the Circle Dot cowboys began making the rounds of the theaters, dance houses, "and other resorts which, like the wicked, flourish best under darkness." Their evening unexpectedly climaxes in what the narrator identifies as the Lone Star Dance Hall.

To appeal to Texans arriving by the hundreds, "Lone Star" proved a popular name for the frequently indistinguishable saloons and dance halls that came and went during Dodge City's cattle-trading years. In 1882 Charles Heinz operated the Lone Star Saloon & Restaurant, which most likely included a dance floor, since even the town's venerable Lady Gay Dance Hall had been rechristened in 1881 as Bond & Nixon's Old Stand Restaurant & Saloon (but still usually referred to as the Lady Gay). Whether frequenting the Lone Star, the Old Stand, or another such venue, a Circle Dot cowboy with only $25 in his pocket would find that participating in the fun could be expensive: $1 might buy two draft beers—the favored cowboy beverage—and a ten-minute set on the dance floor.[39]

Toward midnight the hilarity inside the hall escalates. "Quince Forrest was spending his winnings as well as drinking freely," says the narrator, "and at the end of a quadrille gave vent to his hilarity in an old-fashioned Comanche yell." Forrest's noisy behavior is observed by a man Quirk terms "the bouncer of the dance hall," who is armed and wearing a police officer's star. At the real Dodge City that man would have been Marshal Beamer, Assistant Marshal Chipman, or Officer Harland.

The presence of at least one of them would have been expected, since all cattle town dance halls were considered the most likely evening trouble spots, and officers singled them out for special surveillance. Thus Beamer, Chipman, or Harland normally would have checked the Lone Star more or less regularly each night.

In the novel, in any event, the officer confronts Forrest. "He was a surly brute," recalls Quirk, "and instead of couching his request in appropriate language, threatened to throw him out of the house. Forrest stood like one absent-minded and took the abuse, for physically he was no match for the bouncer." Quirk himself had been dancing with "a red-headed, freckled-faced girl, who clutched my arm and wished to know if my friend was armed. I assured her that he was not, or we would have had notice of it before the bouncer's invective was ended."

Forrest and Priest leave the hall, Priest returning a half-hour later and telling the others to leave quietly one at a time and rendezvous at the livery stable. "I remained until the last," says Quirk, "and noticed [Priest] and the bouncer taking a drink together at the bar,—the former apparently in a most amiable mood." If the bouncer was Marshal Beamer his drink would have been nonalcoholic: the local options, according to a newspaper advertisement, included "soda pop in lemon, strawberry, vanilla, raspberry, and ginger ale."[40]

At the stable the men retrieve their six-shooters, mount their horses, and start to return to camp, but on the outskirts of town Forrest calls a halt. "I'm going back to that dance hall and have one round at least with that whore-herder. No man who walks this earth can insult me, as he did, not if he has a hundred stars on him." When all agree to go back with him, Forrest issues a simple directive: "When I take his measure it will be the signal to the rest of you to put out the lights."

In a vacant lot behind the Lone Star they dismount and leave one man as horse-holder while the other six hide their guns in their clothing and return to the dance floor. Forrest and Priest exchange hats to give the former a different look. Then, says the narrator,

> as the bouncer circulated around, Quince stepped squarely in front of him. There was no waste of words, but a gun-barrel flashed in the lamplight, and the bouncer, struck with the six-shooter, fell like a beef. Before the bewildered spectators could raise a hand, five

six-shooters were turned into the ceiling. The lights went out at the first fire, and amidst the rush of men and the screaming of women, we reached the outside, and within a minute were in our saddles.

It should be emphasized that Forrest does not shoot the officer, as the scene is sometimes interpreted.[41] Instead, he uses his gun to club the man to the floor.

"All would have gone well," testifies Tom Quirk, "had we returned by the same route [taken into Dodge]; but after crossing the railroad track, anger and pride having not been properly satisfied, we must ride through the town"—that is, through respectable Dodge City above the deadline—in Texas cowboy style. Spurring their horses north on Second Avenue, passing the post office and the brick store and the Wright House, they fire their pistols in the traditional parting salute. Exactly as old McNulta had predicted, citizens fire back, aiming to kill. Finally Priest empties his weapon in the general direction of one very active shooter, and the Circle Dot crew escapes down a side street and out of town.

The cowboys had avenged their honor. Not only did Forrest severely punish the officer who had humiliated him. He and his comrades were gettin' outta Dodge with guns flaming. The Circle Dot cowboys had offended Dodge City's civic dignity in a thoroughly gratifying way.

———— ✤ ————

The ultimate affront to a cattle town's self-esteem was violence of a higher order than just a parting salute. However deplorable from the locals' viewpoint, rowdy exits seem to have occurred at Dodge at least a few times each year. Another matter entirely was the killing of a citizen or—even more of a civic catastrophe—the fatal shooting of an officer. In Dodge the gunning down of a lawman had happened twice.[42] If Quince Forrest had *killed* Beamer or Chipman or Harland and then escaped, the town would consider itself to have been "taken" by guests whose behavior it could not control.

At just this moment in real-life Dodge City, news reports from Caldwell, Kansas, revealed that two cowboys had fatally shot that cattle town's marshal and had eluded capture.[43] Editor Klaine took the opportunity on June 29 to remind Dodge Citians of the critical importance of transient management, the intensity of his discourse implying that he might have had a near-disaster at his own town in mind. A community that "suffers with the odium of having once been 'taken' [has] lost the prestige of self-government," he wrote.

> Once the ribald or dissipated class are allowed the least freedom, soon the condition of the town becomes chaotic. . . . We know what rigid, strict discipline is required to check the lawless element that sometimes gives Dodge a visit. There is the utmost vigilance on the part of officers to guard against riot, and to check the least intimation of rudeness. . . . The city is in constant police surveillance.[44]

The same issue of Klaine's newspaper included notice of Marshal Beamer's resignation.

⸺⟨∞⟩⸺

It is sensible to conclude that the dance hall incident novelized by Andy Adams actually happened, and that the big, well-muscled bouncer wearing a star and gun was Dodge City's blacksmith/marshal—the only newly appointed officer to resign from the force in June 1882. Peter Beamer must have had to convalesce from a serious concussion, during which time an angry Mayor Webster demanded his resignation for violating the dictum that officers always be civil, even-tempered, and politic. Beamer's careless handling of the noisy cowboy and his friends might easily have led to someone's death, very probably his own. The larger result, as at Caldwell, would have been a public-relations disaster. Within that context, Nicholas Klaine's editorial can be read as a community endorsement of Webster's remedial actions.

Mayor Webster reflexively responded to the crisis by jettisoning the theory that any husky male citizen of good character and the requisite nerve, pluck, and familiarity with firearms could handle a cattle town law-enforcement job. Shrewdly, in replacing Beamer he chose no stranger. "Jack Bridges, well-known by old timers, will receive the appointment of City Marshal of this city," Klaine announced. "He is now in Colorado, and has telegraphed Mayor Webster that he will accept the appointment, and will be in Dodge City about July 10th."[45]

Jack Bridges had been involved in law enforcement since at least 1869, when he began work as a deputy US marshal operating throughout southwest Kansas, earning a reputation as an officer of demonstrated bravery and competence.[46] Webster knew Bridges since the time both had lived in Hays City and from the marshal's stay in Dodge during the winter of 1872–1873. Not surprisingly, given what must have been a special mandate from the mayor, Bridges's only brush with homicide as Dodge's marshal was his involvement in the fatal 1883 shooting of Texas cowboy John Ballard, discussed in a later chapter.[47]

···◦∞◦···

Even readers with some knowledge of Dodge City in the cowboy era might mistake chapter 13 for part of a memoir, since the narrative speaks with unusual authority about the town. The evidence is good that Adams himself was in Dodge in June 1882. It is in that month that the imaginary Circle Dot cowboys play their parts in real period settings—in the Wright House dining room, at the Long Branch gaming tables, on the street leading north from the Arkansas River bridge. Likewise, the novel has such real personalities as Shanghai Pierce and Uncle Henry Stevens on the scene in Dodge at the very moment local newspapers say they were there, again in June 1882.

A plot that so decisively acknowledges the imperatives of Dodge City's gun-control ordinance is particularly striking. This aspect of cattle town law enforcement would fade rapidly from sight in the shoot-'em-up characterizations popularized by Hollywood. It would not, indeed, be recognized in the historical literature on the Old West until sixty-five years after the novel's publication.[48]

Adams also displays an impressive knowledge of events occurring when he himself could not have been present at Dodge: the fatal shooting of Ed Masterson in 1878, the terrorizing of an itinerant lecturer in early 1880, Ben Thompson's sojourn later that year. And, as already mentioned, there is Adams's list of Dodge City's better-known law officers, whose various tenures spanned the entire eleven years, 1876 onward, in which the town served the Texas cattle trade. He could only have gleaned this information from his own experience and from recollecting other men's Dodge City stories.

The unpleasantness at the Lone Star, as novelized by Adams, unquestionably corresponds in time with the real resignation (for otherwise unexplained reasons) of Dodge City's marshal—a remarkable coincidence. Marshal Beamer's premature retirement brought an abrupt end to a moderately progressive mayor's experiment in what could be termed "reform law-enforcement," an attempt to involve the evangelical community in sharing supervision of the town's sinful amenities. That failure resulted in renewed civic polarization, which in turn contributed, as will be seen, to the nationally publicized "Dodge City War" of 1883, to the anti-liquor mobilization of 1884, and to the frightening social violence of 1885.

# DODGE CITY'S SENSATIONS

In August 1878 a small notice appeared in New York City's weekly *National Police Gazette* under the "To Correspondents" column, where its editor regularly addressed out-of-town contributors.

> CITIZEN, Dodge City, Kansas.—Article published, but it arrived too late to illustrate it in this issue; thanks for the attention. Let us hear from you again and send address.[1]

Founded in the 1840s to publicize fugitives from the law, the *Police Gazette* was a lackluster publication until Richard Kyle Fox took over in 1876. Conforming its prose style to the then popular adventure novels, and printing it on pink stock, Fox added to its staple crime reportage illustrations, sports, and sex: "Vice's Varities" became a salacious regular feature. Almost overnight the so-called barbershop bible, the venue in which so many of its patrons paged through it, approached a circulation of half a million and established itself as easily the most notorious men's magazine of the Gilded Age.[2]

In gamely responding to Fox's call for more regional material, "particularly from the west and southwest," the Dodge City writer calling himself Citizen exposed his frontier town to a formidable mass readership for the first time.[3] Under the byline "Special Correspondent of Police Gazette," common to most hinterland dispatches, Citizen began the process by which Dodge City would one day reach parity with the notorious mining camp at Deadwood, South Dakota, a *Police Gazette* favorite, as symbolic of the Wild West.

Complying with the *Gazette*'s insistence on timeliness, the Dodge City contributor telegraphed his item—"LIVELY SCENE AT A VARIETY PERFORMANCE"—on the very night it occurred. Earnestly innocent compared to the usual *Police Gazette* exposé, the piece nevertheless adhered nicely to the standards required by tabloid journalism, combining as it did violence, men and women in close proximity, and popular theater.[4]

It described the shooting on July 26, 1878, of cowboy George Hoy by Assistant Marshal Wyatt Earp and Officer Jim Masterson as Hoy and his Texas companions retreated across the Arkansas River bridge, an event, wrote Citizen, that "is not an unusual one here. This city is a great cattle centre, and bears a pretty bad reputation abroad." On the night in question, he explained, the Lady Gay Dance Hall

> was beautifully perforated with bullets. At the time of the firing a banjoist was giving his performance on the stage, and a number of girls and men were seated in front and in the boxes. The audience was thrown into considerable consternation at this unexpected episode in the performance, but numerous six-shooters were promptly drawn and the fire of the "cow-boys" was vigorously returned from the windows. . . . There were some narrow escapes from death or injury.

Portraying the gunplay as a cowboy's revenge for having been worsted in an altercation with Wyatt Earp, the piece introduced that "good fellow and brave officer" to the American public at large. Citizen's conclusion—"the only reason for the attack on [the] hall was a reckless whim on the part of the 'cow-boys'"—echoed that of the *Dodge City Times*. According to its editor, Nicholas Klaine, the herder and his friends had simply staged yet another tiresome, if dangerous, parting salute as they galloped out of town.[5]

Years later the magazine identified the author of "LIVELY SCENE" as Harry Gryden.[6]

---

A Swedish immigrant, and by all accounts, as someone remarked, "one of the most genial and companionable fellows that has ever resided in our midst," Harry Gryden pioneered Dodge City's collaboration with its own notoriety.[7]

Born in Stockholm in 1843, Henry Eric Gryden, known as Harry, claimed his mother's family had connections to the court of Sweden's King Charles XIV, but his journalist father's growing disgust with the monarchy led him to move the family to America in 1856. Local records reveal that in 1860 the Grydens owned a farm in southeast Indiana and Harry boarded in nearby Cincinnati, Ohio, where he attended high school.[8]

While the Swedish saga seems plausible enough, Gryden's narrative of his Civil War years is semifictional. He neither joined the Union army in 1861, as he said, nor participated in the bloody 1863 Union attacks on Confederate-held James and Morris islands and Fort Sumter. Gryden's military record certifies that he received his father's permission to enlist at Columbus, Ohio, on January 21, 1864 (age twenty, occupation student), obtained signals instruction at Georgetown, D.C., and was stationed at Hilton Head, South Carolina, from February 1864 until his discharge in September 1865.

From Hilton Head, a Union bastion, Gryden accompanied some of the navy's amphibious raids into the Confederate interior. He probably participated in the reconnaissance up the Ogeechee River in December 1864 that made initial contact with the vanguard of Sherman's army as it advanced on the final leg of its famous march from Atlanta to the sea. Since his signals unit led the military reception, Gryden could have been, as he claimed, the flagman who wigwagged the first message from the tugboat *Dandelion* to Sherman's troops on shore. But the highest rank Gryden attained was the Civil War equivalent of private first class, not, as he claimed, sergeant and then second lieutenant.[9]

———·◄∞►·———

On his discharge Gryden roomed with his parents and read law in nearby Greensburg, Indiana, joining the state's bar in 1867. His subsequent appointment as federal inspector of distilled spirits for southern Indiana brought him to Leavenworth, a Hoosier town on the Ohio River, where he also practiced law. He married and became a father sometime after the 1870 census, which lists his occupation as "steamboat clerk," and he sold his allotted portion of the family farm in 1872 and 1873.

In 1876 Gryden, by then divorced, appeared in Dodge City, gained admission to the Kansas bar, and hung out his shingle.[10] A gifted courtroom attorney, Gryden maintained a busy and varied, although hardly lucrative, law practice. In the January 1878 session of the district court, for example, he argued thirty-nine of the forty-four cases on the docket. Civil suits, involving small sums of money and modest fees, comprised most of his workload. On the criminal side, Gryden represented primarily the city's demimonde and the black community in run-of-the-mill actions. For instance, he defended the town's prostitutes in their losing fight against the 1878 ordinance suppressing gambling and prostitution. (As discussed in chapter 3, the city council intended not to close down either business but rather to tax them as a means of financing the town's police force.) From time to time Gryden also served as counsel in a highly visible murder trial, representing, among others, the drunken cowboys held as possible accessories in the murder of Ed Masterson, and Arista Webb, the accused killer of Barney Martin.[11]

A strenuous Democrat, active at the regional and state levels in his party's affairs (earning him a courtesy appointment by Democratic governor George Glick as major in the Kansas militia), Gryden took a keen interest in local politics. Named city attorney not long after his arrival in Dodge, he enjoyed reappointment to that part-time job in 1880, 1882, and 1884. He also ran for election as city police judge three times, trounced in 1878 and again in 1881, losing by only two votes in 1880.

Beginning in 1877, Gryden also served a three-year stint as Ford County's assistant superintendent of public instruction, his reputed "high intellectual qualities and high attainments" winning him that paying position. In a community whose founding business leaders possessed no formal education beyond grammar school and whose only college graduates were the West Pointers at Fort Dodge, Gryden's Swedish lyceum schooling and urban high school diploma set him up, more or less, as the town's resident intellectual.[12]

Yet Gryden's reputation and finances suffered from his "dissolute habits," as an editor phrased it. He spent freely whatever he made from his law practice, from his public offices, and from his appointment as in-house counsel for the Western Kansas Cattle Growers' Association, on alcohol and gambling. Gryden's closest friends numbered among the town's leading members of its "sporting" subculture: ex-sheriff Bat Masterson, ex-mayor James Kelley, dance hall owner Nate Hudson, sometime police officer "Prairie Dog Dave" Morrow, and other south-side regulars.

Gryden's lifestyle and precarious finances lent some credence to ho-telman Samuel Galland's published report in Dodge City's *Ford County Globe* that as city attorney in 1880, Gryden was "making brags that he gets $50.00 per week for not prosecuting the gamblers." Gryden actu-ally implicated himself when he offered a riposte, then "surreptitiously purloined" it from the newspaper's office.[13]

Relishing the frontier ambience of Dodge City, Harry Gryden not only shrugged off criticism of his indulgent habits and rough associations but used them to inform the tone of his dispatches to the *Police Gazette*.

———— ·◦∞◦· ————

Putting a shine on Dodge City's violent reputation with his Lady Gay story, Gryden followed up with a lurid account of Dora Hand's demise in 1878. The *Gazette* article, a word-for-word news item first published in Nicholas Klaine's *Dodge City Times*, displayed the New York tabloid's quintessential mix of sex and violence; the unattributed reprinting so displeased Klaine that he never published Gryden again. Telegraphed the day of the killing, "MYSTERIOUS MURDER OF A WOMAN" gained an artist's rendition, making for a two-week delay in publication.

Disclosing the identity of neither the suspect, James Kenedy, nor the intended target, James Kelley, the story spotlighted the deceased. As a female entertainer, whom Gryden himself had been representing in a divorce proceeding, Dora Hand proved exquisitely vulnerable to thinly veiled suggestions of sexual promiscuity. "She was a prepossess-ing woman," wrote Gryden, "and her artful, winning ways brought many admirers within her smiles and blandishments. If we mistake not, Dora Hand had an eventful history." Violence ended her "varied life," cutting her down "in the full bloom of gayety and womanhood." The subtext: an "innocent victim" who, nevertheless, paid an existential penalty for her lifestyle.[14]

Then came Gryden's story on the Loving-Richardson encounter. Headlined "FATAL FIGHT ABOUT A WOMAN," the *Gazette* dispatch graphically summarized the April 1879 incident.

> Levi Richardson, a well-known freighter, was shot through the kid-neys, bowels and groin, by Frank Loving, a gambler, at Dodge City, Kan., last night. The trouble originated about a woman. The shooting

occurred at the Long Branch saloon. Richardson is dying. Loving is in jail.[15]

As Arista Webb's attorney, Gryden apparently felt obliged to give a pass to Dodge's next homicide—the Barney Miller murder in September 1879. Neither the *National Police Gazette* nor other major urban newspapers seem to have covered that tragic interracial story.

Later in the year Gryden penned for the *Ford County Globe*, now edited by Daniel Frost, a colorful rendition of a train robbery in New Mexico, allegedly committed by a gang of former Dodge City denizens. Gryden accompanied the expedition, led by ex-sheriff (now undersheriff) Charley Bassett, to investigate the daring raid. Years later a reminiscence praised a revision of the article, titled "THE DODGE CITY GANG" and printed in an unidentified eastern newspaper, as one of Gryden's finest pieces.[16]

In a May 1880 special to the *Kansas City Times*, titled "SHOCKING CASE OF INCEST," Gryden reported that according to "street talk" a local teenager had confessed that her own father had fathered her baby, who died shortly after birth. Denying the rumor, the parent "called at the *Globe* office . . . and requested that a reporter be sent to his home to ascertain and give the public the truth." After speaking with family members, neighbors, and the teenager, who denied having made such a confession, the reporter concluded that the father, a disabled Civil War veteran, had a "good reputation." Gryden retracted his story.[17]

About six months later, when John "Concho" Gill killed Henry Heck, Gryden, on a pre-Thanksgiving hunting trip in Texas with friends, missed out on a tabloid-worthy Dodge City yarn.[18]

Two probable Gryden descriptions of Dodge City violence came out in the spring and summer of 1881.

In May, Boston's *Illustrated Police News* featured—"very prominently," it was said—a flamboyant account of the nonlethal gunfight between the Mastersons and Alfred Peacock's partisans back in April. A portrait of Bat Masterson accompanying the piece initiated the national publicity that would in time make him, like his friend Earp, a popular-culture celebrity.

In July, "SHOT DEAD" appeared as a wire service report about a July 22–23 homicide.

Joseph McDonald, a railway employe[e], was killed by the marshal of Dodge City last night. The marshal [Fred Singer] had been called to arrest two men seen prowling around the house of a citizen, when he discovered McDonald in the grass with a revolver in his hand, and on his making a motion as if to shoot, the marshal shot him dead.[19]

In November 1881, Gryden revisited Bat Masterson's persona in re-sponse to a highly embellished account of the ex-sheriff's supposed exploits in the *New York Sun* titled "A MILD-EYED MAN, WHO HAS KILLED TWENTY-SIX PERSONS." Calling on the exiled Masterson in Kansas City, Gryden introduced him to a scrivener for the *Kansas City Journal*. Since Bat himself proved reluctant to verify the New York paper's fantasies, it fell to Harry to give the Gryden touch to the ex-sheriff's record. Under a shouted title—"BAT'S BULLETS. A TALK WITH THE FRONTIERSMAN WHO IS 'ON HIS THIRD DOZEN,' OR AT LEAST IS SAID TO BE"—Gryden, as an Atchison editor put it, "greatly renovated, repaired, and generally beautified" the *Sun*'s story. In recounting the Battle of the Plaza, for example, he had Master-son fatally wounding two opponents. Like other Gryden exaggerations, this one would enjoy wide circulation.

The same Atchison editor, highly amused, described Harry as "the celebrated romancist"—thus coining a bona fide neologism. Klaine of the *Dodge City Times*, not even slightly amused, furiously censured Gryden for transforming April's near-disaster on Front Street into very bad press.[20]

Gryden's professional life hit bottom in December 1881 when cred-itors attached his law office for a debt of $40; he also owed $200 in property tax and held a $50 mortgage on a building worth about $75. In mid-March he decamped for Colorado, where the sympathetic editor of the *Globe* hoped Gryden would not prove, "as is too often the case, he is his own worst enemy." Within a month Gryden came up stranded in Pueblo "on the rock of impecuniosity," as Klaine phrased it. He returned to Dodge in April 1882 claiming "the altitude [had been] too high for him," and in less than two weeks he reestablished his law practice. That, along with reappointment as city attorney, resuscitated the Gryden en-ergies. By early December he had added a law partner and moved the practice to the rear of the Old House Saloon.[21]

Over the next several months the journalistic reach of "Harry E.

Gryden, the able Dodge city reporter of the Associated Press, and an occasional correspondent of the POLICE GAZETTE," as that magazine identified him, expanded dramatically, with regional and national press references to "the correspondent of the Chicago *Times*" and "the correspondent of the Associated Press." Gryden's entry into the AP most likely resulted from his work as a writer for the staunchly Democratic Chicago paper, whose politics he admired.[22]

--------◆◇◆--------

On May 10, 1883, a Thursday, Americans all across the land opened their favorite newspapers to an AP dispatch—all but a few dated May 10, most on the front page, and all carrying either a Kansas City or Saint Louis dateline—that had gone out on the wire after initial publication as a story in the *Kansas City Star* titled "RUFFIAN REGIME. A STARTLING STATE OF THINGS AT DODGE CITY."

Editors everywhere substituted more sensational headlines. "A REIGN OF TERROR INAUGURATED BY VIGILANTES AT DODGE CITY, KANSAS" screamed Harry Gryden's regular Chicago outlet, and "PEOPLE OBNOXIOUS TO THE GANG IN POWER ORDERED TO LEAVE OR BE LYNCHED." Not to be outdone, the *Chicago Tribune*, the *Times*'s cross-town rival, also ran with dual headings: "IN THE HANDS OF A MOB" and "DODGE CITY, KAS., THE TOUGHEST TOWN OF THE BORDER, TERRORIZED BY THE LAWLESS ELEMENT—MARTIAL LAW ASKED."

In New York City the *New York Sun* reported "SERIOUS TROUBLE IN DODGE CITY. THE PLACE IN THE HANDS OF DESPERADOES, WITH THE MAYOR AT THEIR HEAD." The *New York Tribune* characterized Dodge as "A CITY CONTROLLED BY VIGILANTES." Even the *New York Times*—front page, above the fold—daringly proclaimed "A CITY IN THE HANDS OF A MOB" before rescuing itself from unseemly eloquence with a subhead: "REMARKABLE STATE OF AFFAIRS IN DODGE CITY, KAN.—SERIOUS TROUBLE FEARED." Out in Chautauqua County the *Dunkirk Observer* indulged in a little snobbery. "A MODEL CITY," its headline sniggered, recent events having illustrated "THE LATEST APPROVED METHODS OF RUNNING A WESTERN CITY." The headline's parting quip: "FUN IN THE WEST."

In Washington, D.C., the city's major news outlet, the *Washington Post*, announced: "AT THE MERCY OF A MOB. DODGE CITY, KAN., TERRORIZED BY AN ARMED BAND OF VIGILANTES." And the capital city's *Evening Critic* lived up to its name with an unheadlined but ominous bulletin:

*Dodge City's Sensations* : 111

DODGE CITY, KANSAS, must be a nice place to live in—the town in the hands of desperadoes and the Governor asked to proclaim martial law. Some blood-letting is needed.

Elsewhere much of the same:

"MOB RULE IN KANSAS" (*Helena Independent*)

"LAWLESS DODGE CITY. A KANSAS TOWN WHERE RUM RULES AND RIOT PRE-VAILS" (*Atlanta Constitution*)

"A LOCAL REBELLION. THE TOWN OF DODGE CITY, KANSAS, CAPTURED BY DES-PERADOES. THE LIVES AND PROPERTY OF CITIZENS IN THE HANDS OF GAMBLERS AND THUGS" (*Omaha Bee*)

"RULED BY VIGILANTES. DODGE CITY, KAN., IN THE HANDS OF A MOB" (*Evening Bulletin* of Maysville, Kentucky, and Ohio's *Newark Advocate*)

"BAD STATE OF AFFAIRS IN A KANSAS TOWN" (*Sacramento Record Union*)

"THE TROUBLES IN DODGE CITY" (*Richmond Dispatch*)

"MARTIAL LAW WANTED. THE TOWN OF DODGE CITY, KAN., IN THE HANDS OF DESPERADOES" (Indiana's *Albion New Era*)

"MOB LAW IN KANSAS. DODGE CITY IN THE HANDS OF DESPERADOES" (*San Antonio Light*)

"A REIGN OF TERROR" (*Dallas Herald*)

"KANSAS THUGS. A REIGN OF LAWLESSNESS AT DODGE CITY, KANSAS" (Iowa's *Chariton Patriot*)

And—uniquely succinct—"A ROUGH OLD TOWN" (*Butte Miner*). The *Saint Paul Globe* had a little trouble with the geography: "DODGE CITY, MO., IN THE HANDS OF A GANG OF DESPERADOES—A CONTEST BETWEEN RIVAL BANDS OF LAW BREAKERS."

··<∞>··

Dodge Citians agreed that a business rivalry between owners of the two most prominent, and adjacent, saloons in town, the Long Branch and the Stock Exchange, had spilled over into politics in the municipal election of April 1883, then morphed into the so-called Dodge City War.

Wealthy cattleman and banker William Harris, owner of the Long Branch in partnership with Luke Short, a gambler with a notorious past, lost his bid for mayor to freight agent and prohibitionist Lawrence Deger, backed by the politically influential Alonzo Webster, owner of the Stock

Exchange. Three weeks later Deger and his council—a majority (three of five) on hand to ensure that saloons would remain unmolested—passed two reform ordinances, one to "define and punish vagrancy," containing provisions that could apply to gamblers, the other for the "suppression of vice and immorality," targeting prostitution. While the second simply reenacted routine assessments of dance hall owners and their employ-ees in place since 1878, it also added something new: an additional fine of $5 to $50 for any prostitute found guilty of "plying or advertising [her] calling or business" on "the streets or any public place."

On the evening of April 28, 1883, the Saturday night following pas-sage of the new measures, Mayor Deger, alleging they were prostitutes, ordered Marshal Jack Bridges to arrest three vocalists at the Harris and Short saloon, where a five-piece band featuring female singers had re-cently been installed. An angry Luke Short, claiming women were also present at Webster's saloon, made a bad mistake by exchanging gunshots with a special policeman, who in addition happened to be the city clerk. No blood flowed, but Short and five other alleged ne'er-do-wells, four gamblers and a liquor peddler, suffered arrest as vagrants. A vigilance committee rallied by the mayor then ordered the six to get out of Dodge by May 1. To prevent any troublesome comings or goings, the committee placed armed guards at the railroad depot, Frederick Zimmerman's gun and hardware store serving as its provisional armory.[23]

The anger on Front Street had metastasized from Webster and Harris to their much less seasoned surrogates, the intransigent Deger and the bumptious Short, whose respective supporters lost little time in feeding alternative stories to the press and thrusting the town into the national news. Forty-four US papers are known to have printed Dodge City War stories; the actual number is in all likelihood higher, with Chicago's *Times* and *Tribune* and New York's *Times* and *Tribune* covering the turmoil for almost a month.

Luke Short, in Kansas City to mount a campaign against his expul-sion, clearly provided the *Kansas City Star* with the May 9, 1883, breaking story, which, with minor changes, became the original Associated Press dispatch that appeared the next day in newspapers around the country.

Short's account also appeared in a separate May 10 story published in the *Kansas City Times*—"BOTH VERSIONS OF THE TROUBLE OVER WHICH DODGE CITY HAS BEEN EXCITED FOR SOME DAYS PAST"—and in a *Chicago Times* addition to the AP dispatch that had been authored by Gryden. The Short narrative identified the wrongdoers as Deger and Webster. It cited a rigged election, selective enforcement of the prostitute ordinance, and the banishment of Short without due process of law. As two Montana papers put it, Webster "aspired to be the Boss Tweed of Dodge City."

The Deger supporters aired their version in the *Kansas City Times* piece, as well as in a second *Chicago Times* addition to the AP dispatch, picked up the next day by both the *New York Tribune* and the *New York Times*. Insisting they represented "the better class of the community determined to accomplish a reform," the Degerites argued that "the lawless element had become so obnoxious in the town that the authorities determined to drive them out." Since the "whole affair amounts to nothing more than a determination of lawful citizens to establish order," the action posed "no danger to life or property." The following day, May 11, the *Chicago Times* added that a "prominent cattle man who resides in Dodge City" referred to the exile of the Masterson brothers back in 1881, claiming "there is nothing especially remarkable in the present movement. The law cannot reach these cases, and consequently the people are obliged to a certain extent to take the law into their own hands."

Meanwhile Dodge City's reputation as a well-regulated cattle market suffered. Mayor Deger's vigilantes warned "the correspondent of the Chicago *Times* and other leading papers"—Harry Gryden—that he "must not be permitted to send any telegrams in reference to the situation." Indeed, turned aside when attempting to offer his legal services to the detainees, Gryden "was told that if he sent away as a correspondent anything unfavorable to the vigilance committee he would be 'bored.'"[24]

Taken aback, Governor George Glick wired Ford County's sheriff, George Hinkle, for an informed update. Hinkle's insouciant response—emergency over, all quiet at Dodge—infuriated the governor, who replied on May 12, 1883, that "the accounts of the way things have been going on there are simply monstrous," and have been "heralded all over the United States," and that "unless he exerts his official power to preserve order and protect the property of citizens of Dodge City he will be removed." As a Democrat, Glick was no friend to temperance reform, but he warned the sheriff that all the bad press might force his hand.

If this state of affairs is to continue, you can see what disgrace it will bring upon your city, upon your county, and upon the state of Kansas. The demand is made upon me, and is coming to me from all parts of the state, that it is a disgrace that must be wiped out. It is also demanded and charged by parties who are now demanding the enforcement of the liquor law, that every saloon and dance house in Dodge City must be suppressed, and there is coming up almost a universal demand over the state, that it shall be done, if I have to station a company of troops in the city of Dodge, and close up every saloon and every drinking place, and every dance house in that city.

Dueling memorials and delegations then besieged the governor's office. On May 13 a telegram signed by Dodge's prominent and more or less neutral businessmen, among them George Hoover, Robert Wright, Richard Evans, Jacob Collar, and George Cox, begged Governor Glick to "investigate before you act." On May 15 a petition from a dozen Short partisans, including James Kelley and Daniel Frost, urged the governor "to take such action in the matter as will afford Mr Short protection." The next day, Gryden (once again free to submit copy at the telegraph office) disclosed in the *Chicago Times* that Hoover and Wright numbered among a dozen Dodge Citians who met with Glick to dissuade him from intervening, with assurances that all remained calm in Dodge. Asked why Luke Short merited exile, one of the committee replied that Short "was a bad man generally; has a reputation of being a killer, and we don't want and won't have him there."

The day after the Hoover party's gubernatorial audience, a lengthy letter, penned on May 15 and signed by Mayor Deger and all twelve members of his administration—five councilmen, police judge, treasurer, clerk, marshal and assistant marshal, city attorney, and city physician—appeared in the *Topeka Capital.* Claiming Dodge is "quiet, orderly, and peaceable," the letter insisted that if the governor had stayed out of it the entire affair "would have passed by unnoticed."

The letter also opened the door to accusations of sexual impropriety. Its authors accused William Harris of "living in open adultery with a public prostitute." Replying a week later in the *Topeka Journal*, Luke Short went one better. Webster, he said, had "abandoned his family for a prostitute."

From start to finish, as the *Chicago Times* and *New York Tribune* re-ported, Governor Glick remained adamant that Luke Short be allowed to return unmolested to Dodge City.[25]

In the meantime, word spread that Bat Masterson had arrived in Kansas City on May 14, 1883, planning to end his exile and accompany Luke Short home. That prompted Hoover, Wright, and cattleman Chalk-ley Beeson to travel there for a meeting with the two men about how best to settle the matter. The upshot, revealed in the *Topeka Capital*: Short would be allowed to return safely to Dodge long enough to settle his business affairs, but no longer.

The Bat Masterson connection reignited journalistic interest. In a *Chicago Times* story Gryden declared that Dodge City was now "AT FEVER HEAT." Even more ominously, the *Kansas City Journal* reported that "Masterson precedes by twenty-four hours a few other pleasant gentle-men who are on their way to the tea party at Dodge." A special report in the *Chicago Times* of May 18, obviously another Gryden contribution, offered the stuff of Wild West legend. "The situation at Dodge City, Kan., is growing critical," it warned. Luke Short

> has telegraphed for his friends in Colorado and Arizona and secured [as bodyguards] five of the most famous killers and murderers in the country . . . Bat Masterson, marshal of Trinidad, Col.; Wyatt Earp, ex-marshal of Tombstone, Arizona; Doc Holliday, the slayer of Curley Bill in Arizona; "Rowdy" Joe Lowe, of Denver, and "Shot-Gun" Char-ley (Collins), of Colorado notoriety. Every one of these worthies has killed half a dozen men.

The Chicago editor, however, tacked on better news, which also ap-peared in the *New York Tribune*. The state's adjutant general, Thomas Moonlight, was in Dodge "trying to effect a compromise." He convinced Deger to allow Short's return for ten days to wind up his affairs and per-suaded the mayor to dismiss Assistant Marshal Clark Chipman, whom Short considered a key instigator of his troubles. The governor himself had earlier, on May 12, ordered Sheriff Hinkle to "dismiss that man" if, as reported, Chipman "was aiding in this mob." While Deger grudgingly demoted Chipman to policeman, Short announced his rejection of the ten-day option in Topeka's *Journal*, alleging his enemies would use the opportunity to assassinate him.[26]

Gryden's May 22, 1883, dispatch to the *Chicago Times* announced the arrival of Chipman's imminent replacement, newcomer Mysterious Dave Mather. Disinclined to talk much, hence the distinctive nom de guerre, Mather, as an officer in New Mexico, once killed a man in the line of duty. Gryden, as usual, offered an embroidered version.

> Dave Mather, better known as Mysterious Dave, the victor in many killings, is here. He never having broken the laws at this place, the authorities have not molested him. He is known as a dead game but a square man, with a wonderful facility of not missing his man or letting him linger long in agony.

In a later posting carried by the *Chicago Tribune*, Gryden added another layer of gilding to Mather's reputation. Announcing his swearing in as assistant marshal and deputy sheriff, Gryden dubbed Mather "one of the boldest and bravest men that ever stood up, and his reputation as a killer is awful to his opponents. . . . With such leaders as Jack Bridges, the City Marshal, and Dave the authorities have nothing to fear."[27]

As for Short, he certainly intended to return to Dodge but only when, he said, "they least expect me" and then only with his friends. Wyatt Earp, still warmly remembered in Dodge, was to arrive first and make initial contact with the enemy.

On May 31, 1883, Earp descended from the eastbound train at 10:00 a.m., he later recalled, escorted by four fearsome sidekicks, one of whom wore his hair waist-length, another with a face gruesomely disfigured by an old gunshot wound.

The first citizen to spot them exclaimed, "My God, Wyatt! Who are these people you've got with you?"

"Oh," Earp said, "they're just some bushwhackers I've brought over from Colorado to straighten you people out."

Earp's intimidating posse crossed Front Street. As it passed the Stock Exchange Saloon out came Webster, who, Earp said, "shook hands with me with an air of cordiality that the yellowish pallor of his cheeks belied." After filing into the Long Branch next door, Prairie Dog Dave Morrow, a Dodge Township constable, swore Earp and his associates in as deputy constables, legitimizing their bristling display of long guns and six-shooters.

"VISITING THUGS" read the title of Gryden's June 2, 1883, dispatch to the *Chicago Tribune*. It claimed that

> trouble has broken out afresh in this place, and considerable excite-
> ment is manifest, which it is feared by those best able to judge will
> result in an outbreak. This trouble arises from the fact that at least a
> dozen celebrated killers, headed by Wyatt Earp, and embracing such
> men as "Shotgun" Collins, "have been dropping into our city, one or
> two at a time, for several days."

As Earp recalled, the day he arrived the city council invited him to a hastily arranged meeting to "ask my intentions." Earp's response: Luke Short and Bat Masterson must both be allowed to return to Dodge, and he would be "better pleased" if this were "accomplished peacefully." If necessary, however, Earp said he was "prepared to fight." The council stood by its Moonlight compromise that Short could return temporar-ily. But Masterson would not be allowed back at all. Earp walked out. The council very shortly sent for him again. Earp assured its members "there could be no compromise."

Without waiting for a reply, Earp wired Luke Short to meet him in Kinsley, thirty miles northeast of Dodge. The pair decided to return to-gether by rail, dropping "off the rear platform of the sleeper as the train slowed up, each with a double-barreled shotgun in readiness," and were met by their friends. As the *Chicago Tribune* reported, Short and "Wyatt Earp, Shotgun Collins, Harris, and a number of others . . . marched up the street in a body—Short with a double-barreled shotgun on his arm."[28]

Short thought his troubles had ended on June 1, although June 3 seems more accurate. Gryden allowed in his June 4 special to the *Chicago Times* that "the arrival of Short yesterday occasioned no particular trouble."

But the end was not yet. A citizens' meeting had tasked Robert Wright with notifying William Harris that Short's visiting supporters must leave town immediately, or else all professional gambling would be shut down. As threatened, Gryden said in the same June 4 dispatch that gambling had been closed down because several of Short's friends, "notorious characters who had previously arrived, having been requested to leave," refused to comply. "It is not likely," maintained the *Chicago Tribune*, "they can be put out without a fight." A June 5 article in the *New York Times*, probably written by Gryden, reported that gambling had indeed been stopped, yet "the gamblers and desperadoes remain . . . and it is feared they will make their presence felt in some unlawful way. The city is sleeping upon its arms to-night." That same day the *Chicago Tribune*, under the headline "THE KILLERS ALL READY TO BEGIN FILLING THE GRAVE-YARD," reported that at Dodge "everything is quiet, but the air seems heavy with an impending calamity."

When Earp and Short's June 3 arrival had encountered no resistance, the former promptly wired Bat Masterson, "telling him to come on the next train." Accompanied by Charley Bassett, Masterson got to town on June 5, giving the "gamblers' party," said the *Chicago Tribune*, "two very important additions."

For Earp, Masterson's return signified something much larger. Once he had talked Masterson, still livid about being run out of Dodge, into shaking hands with Webster, "the trouble was over in a few minutes," he recalled. In Earp's opinion "we had conquered Dodge City without firing a shot. It was a great moral victory, for Bat and Luke were unmolested from that time forth." For his part, Masterson, in his 1907 narrative, had his nemesis Webster caving in immediately to Earp's demands.[29]

Still, on June 6, 1883, in view of the continuing presence of unwel-come sojourners, Robert Wright, the sheriff, the mayor, and others wired Governor Glick to activate a state militia unit as peacekeepers. In his capacity as a militia major Gryden breathlessly announced in both Chicago dailies that he had already sworn in forty-five volunteers. But by then Sheriff Hinkle had telegraphed the governor that "Short's fight-ers have left town. I am satisfied that we will not have any more trouble." Mobilization canceled.[30]

After that both Chicago papers gave up on the Dodge City War, but the two major New York dailies continued their coverage. The patience of the *Times* editors was fast running out, however. One of them devoted the better part of a June 8 column to a scathing review of the happenings at Dodge. At the frontier town, he observed, the

> stern vindication of law and order had the effect of rousing the Dodge Citizens to a burst of virtue in which they inflicted upon a select com-pany of law-breakers the unstatutory but condign punishment of shipping a car-load of them out of town, with a grim admonition not to come back.

[But] the boys of Dodge City refused to accept their banishment [and] other exiles are now returning to plague the virtuous. Prominent among these tenacious boys are Mr. BAT MASTERSON and Mr. CHARLES BASSETT, both of whom are ex-Sheriffs. . . . In fact, the latest state of Dodge City seems to be considerably worse than the first, if the correspondent of the Associated Press [Harry Gryden] is correct in saying that "there are more men in the city with a 'record' now than ever before," and if a "record" means . . . a transcript from the archives of courts of criminal jurisdiction.

The boys, it is to be noted, did not sneak back to the scenes of their boyhood. They debarked—at least MASTERSON and BASSETT did—from a regular train in the face of day, "accompanied by numerous friends" with records, and their landing was unopposed, though "heavily armed parties," both of their friends and of the champions of law and order, were present. A compromise has been arranged which is considered equally honorable to all parties, and under which "it is understood" that gambling will be publicly resumed to-day.

The editorial concluded on a genuinely disgusted note.

The effete inhabitant of the East will not consider this a triumphant result . . . especially as the dispatches indicate that the war and the compromise alike have concerned only two sects of boys, and not the decent citizens, if, indeed, the proportion of decent citizens is greater in Dodge City than it was in Sodom.

The following day both Manhattan dailies printed the same brief update, almost certainly from Gryden, stating that "the 'Short' faction is in the ascendancy, but is peaceably disposed. Some of our inveterate cranks are still a little sulky, and say that gambling shall not be resumed, but the better and more liberal class believes that its suppression will injure the business prospects of the town this Summer."

Gryden's afterthought incited the *Times* to additional editorial contempt.

It appears that the respectable citizens of Dodge City, Kan., for whom the public has been beguiled of some sympathy, are purely hypothetical. The assumption that there must be some respectable citizens in a town of several thousand inhabitants is purely gratuitous. . . . A town in which gambling is a leading industry, which must not be attacked by persons interested in the municipal prosperity, may as well be left to ex-Sheriffs and people "with a record."[31]

Although the stiff-necked Deger refused to budge, the city council did indeed lift the ban on gambling. Its members surely agreed with Adjutant General Moonlight's sage advice that the town, whose population actually numbered about twelve hundred, not several thousand, get on with it or the upcoming cattle-trading season would be ruined. Apparently proving decisive, however, was the likelihood that the resident gamblers would follow through on their threat to bring legal action against every saloon in town, in this way bringing liquor prohibition to Dodge. On June 11, 1883, all returned to the status quo ante.[32]

---

It remained Harry Gryden's rewarding task to give the bloodless war one last fling. He did so, appropriately, in the pages of the *National Police Gazette*, providing a wrap-up for thousands of readers who might have missed it in the mainstream press. The story, openly identified as his, surrounded a cut made from a collective studio portrait of Luke Short and some of his backers, taken just before Earp, Masterson, and Bassett cleared town on June 10, and titled "THE DODGE CITY 'PEACE COMMISSION.' A GROUP OF PROMINENT FRONTIERSMEN WHO RESTORED QUIET IN A TROUBLED COMMUNITY." The *Gazette*'s editor himself introduced the accompanying narrative, titled "DODGE CITY'S SENSATION," with a summary of events. Gryden then provided over-the-top vignettes about each member of the group, beginning with Masterson and Earp.

> Bat Masterson, of whom so much has been written, arrived from the West prepared for any emergency and with a shotgun under his arm. . . . He has been sheriff of Ford county, in which Dodge city is situated, and has occupied positions as marshal of a number of rough border towns. All his killings were done in the discharge of his official duties, and he has never even been tried for an offence.
>
> Wyatt Earp, of California, is the celebrity who about two years ago went on the war-path at Tombstone, Arizona, against a mob of desperadoes who had assassinated his brother, Morgan Earp. In the terrible encounter which ensued he killed not less than eight of the

assassins. Wyatt has been Marshal of Dodge city, Kan., and other frontier towns.[33]

<hr style="width:10%" />

No other big scoops followed Harry Gryden's *Police Gazette* story, but his pen kept busy.

Under the headline "DODGE CITY AGAIN. THE OFFICERS KILL A COWBOY AND THE COWBOYS SWEAR VENGEANCE," the *Chicago Tribune* published Gryden's piece about Marshal Jack Bridges and other lawmen picking off cowboy John Ballard as he and two friends, on the afternoon of July 9, 1883, gave the town a parting salute. The fatal bullet entered Ballard's right cheek and tore downward through his jaw and neck; he rapidly bled out at the Arkansas River bridge.

"The victim's colleagues threaten to kill every officer in the town before morning," Gryden wrote—then lamely had to admit that "no trouble is anticipated." Indeed, before the coroner's jury convened, Robert Wright, as he much later recalled, also assumed an officer had shot Ballard. Willing to risk a boycott by the cattlemen, Wright said "put me on the jury and I will be elected foreman and settle the question forever." He would tell his fellow jurors that "we must bring in a verdict of justifiable homicide . . . to protect our officers and save further killings." But, as two physicians testified to the coroner's jury, on which Robert Wright and Frederick Zimmerman sat, the bullet's trajectory indicated that Ballard had been carelessly shot by one of his companions, not by an officer. And that was that. Nobody in Dodge seemed interested in bringing a charge of manslaughter in the first degree against any of the other cowboys.[34]

The national press could not resist commenting on yet another Dodge City sensation. The *New York Commercial* responded that Dodge "must be a delightful place of residence, cowboys and six-shooters being as thick as huckle-berries in fly time." The *Chicago Press* hoped "that the inhabitants of that noted center of wickedness, Dodge City, will endeavor to reform it altogether. If they succeed, then there is every chance of a man dying a natural death there once in a while." In a different vein, a British newspaper confessed that it had had enough of Dodge City: "There was a period when it was [a] delight to hear of the ugly character of the city. But that time has passed."[35]

A year later, during the 1884 cattle season, Gryden brought two more fatal shootings to the notice of readers outside Kansas. The first merited only a one-sentence bulletin that made the rounds: "K. B. Schoat [*sic*], a cattle man of Goliad, Tex., was killed at Dodge City, Kan., in a quarrel with Dave St. Clair [*sic*], a gambler."[36]

At Dodge itself the papers documented the affair in detail. Outside Webster's saloon in the wee hours of Sunday, July 6, 1884, Kyle "Bing" Choate, age twenty-six and from a family of distinguished ranchers, overheard St. Claire complaining about cheaters at cards. Choate persuaded himself that the remarks were directed at him and his Texas pals. Following St. Claire into the saloon, Choate eyed the gambler and, just before handing his pistol over to the bartender, announced: "I am the fastest fighting son-of-a-bitch in Dodge."

Choate then left the saloon and returned with a six-shooter in one hand and a cane in the other. Stuffing the gun into his waistband he began poking St. Claire with the cane, challenging him to fight. The gambler finally said that if the cattleman were not surrounded by friends, "I'd take that six-shooter from you and stick it up your damned ass." At that, Choate fumbled at his gun while St. Claire pulled his own weapon from a hip pocket and fired once, sending a round into Choate that glanced off a rib, clipped the Texan's heart, and exited through his gut. Falling to the floor, Choate tried to get up again, but collapsed and died.

Legal proceedings commenced the next day. After over a dozen witnesses testified at the coroner's inquest, five of the six jurymen considered the shooting justifiable. At the subsequent magistrate's hearing the county attorney disagreed, but did conclude that the evidence "is not sufficient to convict him [St. Claire] before a jury," since it showed that "deceased gave the provocation, drew his revolver and gave defendant reason to fear he would be killed." On the heels of his dismissal the gambler got outta Dodge.[37]

Within weeks the second fatal shooting of 1884 occurred: Dave Mather killed Assistant Marshal Tom Nixon, and Gryden found himself acting as both city attorney and Associated Press correspondent.

The assistant marshal's death prompted a full version, datelined Dodge City, and what the AP managers termed a "pony report," a less expensive (to users) condensation wired from Kansas City. While readers in places such as Fort Wayne, Indiana, received the detailed account, those in Texas, Colorado, Minnesota, and New York got the short version:

> At Dodge City, late last night [around 10 p.m] on July 21, Deputy-Marshal Mather, notorious as Mysterious Dave, shot and killed Thomas Nixon, also a deputy marshal. The murder was the result of an old feud. Mathers fired four shots, any one of which would have been fatal. A cowboy standing near was also shot in the knee. Nixon had the reputation of being the best buffalo-hunter on the plains.[38]

What happened? The 1884 spring election had brought a new administration under George Hoover. The mayor and council replaced Mather (who remained a Ford County deputy sheriff) with Tom Nixon as assistant marshal. They also passed an ordinance outlawing dance halls just days after Mather's attempt to open one in Kelley's old opera house on Front Street. Mather saw Nixon's hand in this.[39]

A couple of months later, on a Friday evening, July 18, Mather and Nixon finally got into a public row on the steps of the opera house, ending with Nixon taking a shot at Mather. The magistrate's hearing allowed Nixon to post bond for his district court appearance on a charge of assault with intent to kill. As Nicholas Klaine revealed, Nixon "remarked that he had killed Mather and had no regrets." Actually he had inflicted only a slight facial wound.

Three evenings later, on July 21, Mather surprised Nixon in front of the opera house, firing four times before Nixon could get his own gun into action. One bullet lodged in Nixon's right arm and another in his right side; as he reflexively twisted away two more rounds struck him on the left side, the one that killed him passing through the heart, exiting at the left nipple, and wounding a cowboy bystander in the leg.

In the magistrate's hearing City Attorney Gryden got Mather bound over to the district court for trial. Eventually released on bail, and finally, at the end of December 1884, tried in a different venue (Edwards County), Mather won the day. No details surfaced, but the *Kinsley Mercury* reported that "the weight of the testimony showed that Nixon was the aggressor in the affray and that Mather was justified in shooting." Apparently the usual frontier extenuation prevailed: there are no innocent parties in a gunfight between two angry adults, even one with a three-day delay between gunshots.[40]

Harry Gryden ignored news of Dodge City's first two black-on-black killings. Although he certainly shared the racial attitudes of his time, as historian C. Robert Haywood put it, Gryden was a "favored counselor" of local blacks in criminal matters. As such, he may have wished to avoid offending his clientele through sensational accounts of violence within the small African American community.

On the evening of October 7, 1883, two African American men died violently in Dodge City's "negro dance hall," an establishment employing black women, catering to black cowboys, and, unsurprisingly, serving a racially mixed clientele. William Smith, one of the owners, took exception to the aggressive treatment of a dancer by Bill Hilton, a cowboy out on bail awaiting trial on the charge of murdering a black man elsewhere. Hilton immediately drew his pistol and killed Smith with a single round. Some of Smith's friends responded by mortally wounding Hilton, shooting him three times.[41]

Four months later, on February 18, 1884, Keziah Morris's abusive black boyfriend, Henry Chambers, a Robert Wright employee, smashed in her forehead with an iron stove lid. A district court trial convicted Chambers of second-degree murder. He died three years later of peritonitis while serving a fifteen-year sentence in the state penitentiary.[42]

The summer of 1884 found Gryden, still in his mid-forties, in declining health. Within six weeks of participating in Mysterious Dave's magistrate hearing he died, his final illness variously recorded as "consumption," "typhoid consumption," and "softening of the brain and hemorrhage." Nicholas Klaine, who had never warmed to Harry, conceded that if Gryden had "conformed to good habits he would have been an honored and useful citizen. But his talents and energies were frittered away. . . . May the lesson of his life be a warning to all."

Other obituaries proved kinder, but none grasped the importance of Harry's legacy. While the town's newspaper editors wrote the first draft of history—documenting the frontier Dodge of ordinary human experience, the passage of its collective youth, and its embrace of the American dream that tomorrow would be better than today—Harry Gryden introduced and carried forward a popular-culture conversation about Dodge, adding its colorful depravity and its occasional gun violence to the essence of Old West myth and legend.[43]

Fort Dodge in 1879, home to some 260 soldiers, a dozen officers, and about half
again that number of spouses, teamsters, and other civilians. Despite the occasional
Cheyenne raid on outside work parties, a protective stockade is deemed unnecessary;
the low board fence keeps out grazing cattle, as does the small enclosure in the
foreground protecting a wellhead. An angry inspecting general reported the fort as
unacceptably elegant for a frontier outpost, its two-storey commandant's quarters
(left center), hospital (long building on right), and other structures having been built
in beautifully dressed limestone when sun-dried mud bricks would have sufficed. A
court-martial was the reward for the lieutenant supervising construction. (Courtesy of
Kansas Heritage Center, Dodge City, Kansas)

Dodge City's first settler Henry Sitler in 1872, age thirty-five, stands in the doorway
of his sod house wearing a pioneer's working attire: dark shirt, jeans held up by
suspenders, and heavy boots. The adjacent telegraph pole has been erected in advance
of the approaching Santa Fe Railroad track-layers. The soon-to-be infamous Boot Hill
rises in the background. (Courtesy of Kansas State Historical Society, Topeka, Kansas)

*The view from Boot Hill in 1873. Just above the horizon a huge garrison flag marks the location of Fort Dodge 5 miles to the east. In the middle distance the Arkansas River wends its way; the nearer flag identifies Robert Wright's general outfitting store; on the far right Sitler's sod house sits near its telegraph pole. Note that the railroad tracks already separate Front Street's commercial district (on the left) from the jerry-built saloons, dance halls, and low-end businesses of the "south side." (From Deane Monahan,* The Arkansas Valley and Its Great Railway, *1873, facing page 18)*

*Three south-side enterprises in 1872. The one to the right is the settlement's first dance hall, the site of some of the town's early gun violence. In front stand two wagons stacked high with dried buffalo hides destined for shipment east. (Courtesy of Kansas State Historical Society, Topeka, Kansas)*

*Front Street in 1873, showing business houses operated by four of its pioneer entrepreneurs. From left to right: George Hoover's wholesale liquors and saloon; Frederick Zimmerman's guns and hardware (note the replica rifle looming over the sidewalk); Morris Collar's clothing store; and Alfred Peacock's billiards parlor and saloon. As seen here, photographers lining up camera shoots usually draw crowds. (Courtesy of Boot Hill Museum, Dodge City, Kansas)*

*Alonzo Webster, Dodge's modernizing mayor whose narrow-eyed gaze suggests a cold and confrontational side that masks an almost compulsive deference to the local evangelicals—until they turn on him. He would run Bat Masterson out of town in 1881. (Courtesy of Kansas Heritage Center, Dodge City, Kansas)*

*James Kelley, Dodge City's four-term political boss until unseated as mayor by Webster. Here he prepares to course his beloved hunting hounds in search of small game. His affection for these animals causes some to call him "Dog" Kelley, a nickname he understandably dislikes. (Courtesy of Kansas Heritage Center, Dodge City, Kansas)*

*Pioneer businessman Jacob Collar operates the Blue Front Store, which retails furniture and coffins, a standard frontier combination. He and his brother Morris, nonobservant Jews, are emigrants from the Habsburg Empire. Jacob's wife, Jennie, is noted for her local charity work. (Courtesy of Boot Hill Museum, Dodge City, Kansas)*

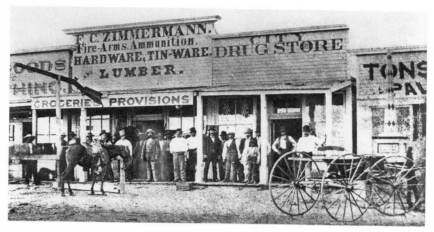

*Mutton-chop whiskers have declined in popularity since Appomattox, but Frederick Zimmerman, Dodge's "jolly gunsmith," delights in his eccentric facial hair. In 1876 he stands front and center in a wide-brimmed white hat. Since the buffalo are now virtually extinct, the arms and ammunition advertised above his head take second place to groceries, lumber, and other products. (He would soon drop the redundant final "n" from his name.) The building that once housed Morris Collar's store, the edge of which can just be seen, is now occupied by the Tonsorial Palace of John Tyler, Front Street's African American barber. (Courtesy of Kansas State Historical Society, Topeka, Kansas)*

*Bat Masterson (standing) and Wyatt Earp, the Old West's iconic duo, in about 1878. That year the former, age twenty-five, serves as Ford County sheriff, the latter, age thirty, as Dodge City assistant marshal. Five years later Earp would strong-arm the authorities into welcoming the exiled Masterson back to town. (Courtesy of Boot Hill Museum, Dodge City, Kansas)*

Nailed to an abandoned wellhead at the intersection of Front Street and Second Avenue, as pictured in the winter of 1878–1879, this sign warns incoming cowboys and cattlemen that "THE CARRYING OF FIRE ARMS strictly PROHIBITED." (Prickly Ash Bitters, manufactured in Saint Louis, is a popular tonic supposedly good for ailments of the internal organs.) (Courtesy of Kansas State Historical Society, Topeka, Kansas)

The only known photo (1875) of the exterior of the famous Long Branch Saloon, a popular gathering spot named for the posh New Jersey seaside resort frequented by President Grant. A steer's head glares down from a round plaque above the porch. The epic gun battle between Frank Loving and Levi Richardson would occur inside. (Courtesy of Boot Hill Museum, Dodge City, Kansas)

*The interior of the Saint James Saloon, a typical tavern layout. There are no barstools; once all tables are occupied, late-coming patrons must stand. At the lower right an insouciant young man, possibly a cowboy, parks his dirty boots on the tablecloth. (Courtesy of Kansas State Historical Society, Topeka, Kansas)*

*Sarah "Sadie" Ratzell, a Philadelphia-born prostitute reared on a Kansas farm. Rumor that she has considerable money stashed in her cottage would lead to the police killing of a suspected burglar in 1881. (Actually, in the absence of a bank, she deposits her savings with businessman George Hoover.) A few years later, fondly termed "an old citizen of Dodge," she survives a dangerous stab wound inflicted by another woman outside a saloon. (Courtesy of Kansas State Historical Society, Topeka, Kansas)*

*Popular variety-show singer Dora Hand, stage name Fannie Keenan, pictured here in a photo discovered in the 1920s. She would be inadvertently killed in an attempted assassination of Mayor James Kelley in 1878. (Courtesy of Kansas Heritage Center, Dodge City, Kansas)*

*A skilled leatherworker puts the finishing touches on a fancy hand-tooled California saddle of the type designed for the ranch trade. He may be an employee of the Gallup Saddlery Company of Pueblo, Colorado, which opened a Dodge City branch in 1878. (Courtesy of Kansas State Historical Society, Topeka, Kansas)*

A bird's eye-view of Dodge City in June 1882. On the upper left a grade school with fancy cupola now crowns Boot Hill. On the far right an incoming train passes the local stockyard. The Arkansas River is pictured at low ebb, but during its annual spring flood the swirling waters can threaten to overrun the five backyard latrines pictured on the lower left. (Courtesy of Kansas Heritage Center, Dodge City, Kansas)

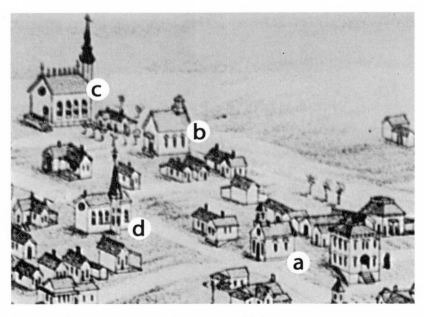

Close-up of Gospel Ridge and its four churches: (a) the nondenominational Union; (b) the Presbyterian; (c) the Catholic; and (d) the Methodist. The two-storey square building in the lower right is the Ford County courthouse. (Courtesy of Kansas Heritage Center, Dodge City, Kansas)

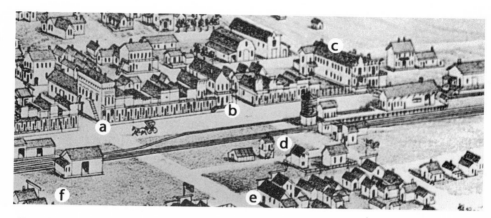

Front Street and the near south side: (a) Robert Wright's brick store; (b) James Kelley's opera house and saloon; (c) George Cox's Dodge House; (d) the city hall and jail (a lockup on the ground floor with an outside staircase to the city clerk's office and police court); (e) the notorious Lady Gay Dance Hall—adjoining gabled buildings linked behind a single facade; and (f) the former site of Henry Sitler's sod house. (Courtesy of Kansas Heritage Center, Dodge City, Kansas)

The bridge over the Arkansas River where most Texans just off the trail get their first view of Dodge. And here is where some cowboys leaving town fire off the "parting salutes" that so annoy residents and cost two cowboys their lives when officers return fire. Hamilton Bell's Elephant Stable lies straight ahead, while the large building rising against the horizon on the left is the redesigned courthouse.

*Dodge House hotelier George Cox, with daughter Clara Belle and wife, Amy, are dressed for a family portrait. How the ex-army sergeant from Georgia and the young woman off a New Jersey farm found each other is not recorded—an example of how little is known about the private lives of even the town's leading figures. (Courtesy of Boot Hill Museum, Dodge City, Kansas)*

*"Chuck time" for a dozen cowboys holding a herd south of Dodge City in 1884. One of them, standing at right, attends to the cooking and is traditionally exempt from other duties. Note that the men's work clothes differ remarkably from the ballyhooed "authentic" garb of the Cow-Boy Band members that same year. (Courtesy of Kansas State Historical Society, Topeka, Kansas)*

**THE DODGE CITY "PEACE COMMISSION"**

A GROUP OF PROMINENT FRONTIERSMEN WHO RESTORED QUIET IN A TROUBLED COMMUNITY.

No. 1 - LUKE SHORT. No. 2—BAT MASTERSON. No. 3.—WYATT EARP. No. 4.—M. F. McLEAN. No. 5.—CHARLES BASSETT. No. 6.—NEAL BROWN. No. 7.—W. H. HARRIS. No. 8.—W. F. PETILLON.

*A famous photograph that appears in its first published form as an engraving in New York's* National Police Gazette. *The caption, meant to be humorous, mimics the name of the delegation that sought to negotiate an end to the Civil War. Luke Short, Bat Masterson, Wyatt Earp, and long-serving officer Charley Bassett are pictured before heading out of Dodge. Local politico W. F. Petillon, not considered "one of the boys," is consigned to last place (no. 8); in some versions of the original photo his image has been entirely removed. (*National Police Gazette, *July 21, 1883, p. 5)*

Harper's Weekly *engraving showing Saint Louis school children presenting a drum to the celebrated Dodge City Cow-Boy Band. The elaborately costumed ensemble is attending a western cattlemen's convention. The $20,000,000 on its banner is the total value of livestock owned by its sponsors. (*Harper's Weekly*, December 6, 1884, p. 798)*

*David "Mysterious Dave" Mather, assistant marshal, sporting his official police officer's wide-brimmed fedora with a hatband that displays his rank. After being laid off by the mayor and council in 1884, he quarrels with his successor and shoots him dead. (Courtesy of Kansas Heritage Center, Dodge City, Kansas)*

*Swedish immigrant Harry Gryden, lawyer and tabloid journalist, whose European lyceum and Cincinnati high school education, despite his alcoholism, lend him standing as Dodge City's resident intellectual. His colorful writings, first appearing in 1878, introduce millions of readers to the town's already notorious reputation. (Courtesy of Kansas State Historical Society, Topeka, Kansas)*

*Attorney Michael Sutton in his law office. Dodge City's most powerful lawyer, he becomes a prohibitionist leader, alienating many of his business-community associates. He gets out of Dodge, temporarily, after bullets are fired into his house. (Courtesy of Kansas State Historical Society, Topeka, Kansas)*

*In 1885 Dodge City saloon owners begin transforming their establishments into quasi drug stores to circumvent the Kansas prohibition law. Here a partition with swinging doors separates the pharmacy out front from the principal business in the rear—an elaborate counter presided over by a pair of longhorns, framed liquor ads and sports posters, and two bartenders. A well-dressed patron lounges at the side. Dodge's last saloon is not shut down until the first years of the twentieth century. (Courtesy of Kansas State Historical Society, Topeka, Kansas)*

# END GAMES

It was ex-mayor Alonzo Webster's idea for celebrating Independence Day 1884 at Dodge by hosting, in the words of a reporter, the first "genuine Spanish bull-fight" ever held on United States soil. In an interview for a Saint Louis newspaper, Webster said his check of the Kansas statutes revealed no legal obstacle, conveniently overlooking the law against maiming, beating, or torturing "any horse, ox, or other cattle." Two days later the business community had pledged $10,000 to cover costs.

In that same interview the ex-mayor claimed he just did not remember "how he came to think of such a thing." But the *how* of it is less interesting than the *why*.[1] It seemed distinctly out of character that this no-nonsense, rather humorless business owner, so devoted to law-and-order modernization, would come up with something calculated to dismay middle-class, churchgoing sensibilities all across the country.

An enigmatic and complex character, Alonzo Webster grew up in the wildly evangelical western New York, where anti-liquor activism, second in importance only to radical antislavery, had deep roots and played a central role in social and political life. "Though not a professed christian," it was said of Webster, "he had the utmost respect for the christian religion."[2]

As mayor, Webster certainly had treated the church element more deferentially than did most Dodge City leaders. In return, evangelicals as well as the business community supported Webster's moderate reform regime of 1881–1883: the campaign against vagrants and petty criminals, the regularization of law enforcement, the refusal to defer to an aggressive Bat Masterson, the desire to see some constraints on gambling and prostitution. And early in his second term Webster had struck an adroit bargain with the evangelicals. They would not intrude liquor prohibition into local politics, and he would launch the "reform law-enforcement" experiment discussed in a previous chapter.

Even before that deal, Webster had convinced himself that the temperance people could coexist with liquor consumption—a mainstay of the town's cattle-trading economy, after all—so long as drinking occurred within a sufficiently demure environment. In late 1881 Webster bought and richly refurbished a Front Street property, christening it the Stock Exchange Saloon. Described as a "neat, quiet and orderly house," its tony name and "fine pictures," purchased in a Kansas City art gallery, suggested the hushed ambience of a metropolitan gentlemen's club.[3]

Webster's pact with the church element held even after he stepped aside in the city election of 1883 and supported a confirmed temperance man, Lawrence Deger, as his mayoral successor. Interestingly, Deger found it necessary to publish a card in the *Dodge City Times* denying that he "pledged to Webster to do as he want[s] me to" and that "if elected I wont qualify," thus leaving the office to the former mayor. During his tenure, as assumed, Deger did not challenge the saloons, but did—clumsily and unsuccessfully—take on gambling and prostitution, thereby touching off 1883's Dodge City War.[4]

Not even mutterings by the Santa Fe Railroad's top brass about ending the town's status as a division terminus could force Dodge to resist moral relapse. In 1884 a dozen saloons still ornamented Front Street in the two blocks between Robert Wright's brick store and George Cox's hotel, and those on the south side prospered as usual.[5]

Fed up with the status quo and now believing they had strength enough to go it alone, the Gospel Ridge folks reneged on their accord with Webster, letting it be known they intended to field a slate of firm anti-liquor candidates in the upcoming 1884 city election.

To Webster, hoping to reinvigorate his health at a spa in Hot Springs, Arkansas, the news from Dodge came as an infuriating surprise. Terming his late allies "unprincipled, damned hypocrites," he viewed their betrayal as a declaration of war on him and all other bar owners. "Well," he wrote in a blistering letter to the newly launched *Dodge City Democrat*, "if the war is inevitable, let it come. We have more ways than one to defend ourselves."

In making the issue of the April 1884 election "whiskey or no whiskey," as another writer to the *Democrat* put it, the prohibitionists proved remarkably premature. The anti-temperance mayoral candidate was George Hoover, who also happened to be president of the group funding the new paper, edited by W. F. Petillon, a local politico. Hoover gained office with 81.9 percent of the popular vote and carried the rest of the ticket, including two other founding entrepreneurs, council candidates George Cox and James Kelley, with him.[6]

Two months later the prohibition stalwarts again misfired, having been encouraged to do so by two recent legal developments: a ruling that liquor cases could be commenced in district court and the decision of Jeremiah Strang, the district judge for southwest Kansas, to bar liquor vendors from jury duty. The first permitted complainants to bypass Dodge Township's justice of the peace. The second held out the possibility that when the district court next convened in Ford County it would give a more favorable hearing to whiskey cases.

So it was that on June 16, 1884, H. P. Drake, one of the losing prohibition candidates for city council, filed complaints against Dodge City's liquor suppliers, including Alonzo Webster and George Hoover. Taking seriously a threat of legal action to remove him from office if he failed to act, Ford County's Sheriff Pat Sughrue arrested the accused for an appearance before Judge Strang. The judge had to dismiss the cases at the October 1884 session because, as nine months later he explained to Governor Martin, the complaints lacked verification of probable cause by "oath or affirmation" as required by *State of Kansas v. Gleason*, decided by the Kansas Supreme Court in July 1884.[7]

Meanwhile, in May, shortly after the temperance activists had reneged on their promise to keep liquor out of politics, the embittered Webster unleashed his lurid proposal to host the nation's first Spanish bullfight with himself as general manager.

---

After 1883's Dodge City War had captured the attention of the nation—with nobody killed and no property destroyed—a taste for national exposure, whether praise or criticism, whether serious or tongue-in-cheek, had captured Front Street. Living in the toughest, wickedest town in the West seemed less a public-relations disaster than a source of pride. As an advertisement for the bullfight taunted out-of-towners: "Come on ye Eastern piggamies [pygmies] and see what Kansas can do under the management of the citizens of Dodge City."

A widely distributed circular, "GRAND SPANISH BULL FIGHT," publicized the three-day event (July 2 through 4), proclaiming "Reduced Rates on All Railroads, from Chicago and St. Louis." Prizes, it announced, would be awarded for ancillary sporting activities, including horse races, competitive roping, target shooting, and—it had finally reached southwest Kansas—baseball.

Local criticism did float down from Gospel Ridge. Its Methodist minister prayed that the bullfight, a "stench in the nostrils of civilization," would provoke a counterreaction that offered "a genuine word of encouragement to those . . . striving for a better state of morals."[8]

Other observations came from near and far. "Dodge City," remarked editor Nicholas Klaine, "is getting an extraordinary share of gratuitous advertising through the State newspapers, and considerable comment is extended outside of the State borders." On June 30, 1884, for example, a special correspondent for the *New York Herald* penned a lengthy piece on preparations for the event that "has attracted so much attention all over the country." He thought the "audacity of the place is wonderful. . . . Where is there another town in the country that would have the nerve to get up a genuine Spanish bull fight on American soil?" A *Cincinnati Enquirer* writer characterized the bullfight as the latest iniquity of "this sweet little village." Closer to home, the *Topeka Commonwealth* lamented that "such a brutal proceeding is to occur in Kansas." And the *Wichita Eagle* gave up hope that Dodge might yet become civilized.

The national president of the SPCA, the Society for the Prevention of Cruelty to Animals, telegraphed Governor George Glick from New York urging him to put a stop to the morally repugnant spectacle; the *New York Times* printed it in full. While the protest arrived too late, even had it been timely, there was little chance Glick, as in 1883 a reluctant interventionist, would have interfered.[9]

If any publicity is good publicity, then for about a month Alonzo Webster's suggested July novelty had splendidly filled the void created by the departure of sustained nationwide attention.

On Independence Day itself celebrants from all over the region filled to capacity Dodge City's specially built 3,500-seat "amphitheater" (covered bleachers) to see five brilliantly garbed matadors from Mexico go up against twelve fiercely horned bovines from Texas. Correspondents for New York, Chicago, Saint Louis, and other newspapers arrived to provide national coverage. Despite expectations, afterward many agreed with Governor Glick that on the whole it proved "rather a tame and insignificant affair," since just a single bull had enough fight in him to permit his dispatch according to the ceremonial thrust of the sword.

Organizers immediately scheduled another bullfight for the next day to accommodate disappointed visitors unable to reach Dodge on July 4 due to delays in railroad service. That fight proved "more interesting than the first," reported editor Frost. "A better selection of fighting bulls were introduced," and "the matadors showed . . . what bullfighting really was," although this time no animals died.

Still, the Independence Day festivities ended badly with the lethal shooting of Kyle Choate by Dave St. Clair in Webster's notionally sedate saloon an hour or two after midnight on July 6, 1884, as discussed in chapter 6. "The usual killing bee was indulged in and a man in the prime of life cut down prematur[e]lly," a Larned editor dryly noted. "Altogether the 4th at Dodge may be called a success, as they count success."[10]

The bullfight's notoriety touched off yet another round of Dodge City mythologizing. All sins forgiven, Bat Masterson had been back in town since winter. His outsized presence at the novel gala provoked comment in the *New York Herald*.

One celebrated character here, called Batt Matterson, is said to have killed thirty-two men; but he is a peaceable sort of man nevertheless. He might be considered a hard citizen by New Yorkers, but he is a sociable, good natured and kind hearted fellow, except when some one "treads on his corns."

A version that popped up later in media markets as distant as Fort Wayne, Indiana, and Reno, Nevada, read: "The most influential man in Dodge City is said to be Bart. Matterson, who has killed thirty-two persons, according to common fame, and is spoken of as a sociable, good fellow, when he isn't crossed."

The *New York Herald*'s colorful thumbnail sketch prompted an Ohio

editor to a bizarre retelling of the Battle of the Plaza, Masterson's bloodless 1881 encounter with Alfred Peacock's friends.

> Dodge City, Kan., the town which recently distinguished itself by in-
> troducing the Mexican "sport" of bull-fighting to American soil, was
> previously known to fame. . . . Some two years [ago] the town marshal
> was threatened with death. He telegraphed his brother at Tombstone,
> 1,000 miles away, who rushed to his aid by the first train. The two
> barricaded themselves on the public square, and with Winchester ri-
> fles deliberately picked off their enemies whenever they appeared.[11]

----- ∞ -----

More benign publicity followed later that year. The Kansas Cattle
Growers' Association, headquartered at Dodge, funded a November
1884 trip to the National Stockmen's Convention at Saint Louis for the
Dodge City Cow-Boy Band, a group that had already performed win-
ningly at the bullfight and the Topeka state fair. Organized in 1882 by
Chalkley Beeson, then owner of the Long Branch, to entertain evening
crowds on Front Street, the brass ensemble of eighteen professional
musicians, almost all recruited from the town's dance halls, assumed a
novel persona as strictly amateur, its members off-duty cowpunchers.
(Its press agent at one point admitted that the musicians were "mostly
cowboys in jest.")

In Saint Louis, booted and spurred, the Dodge City bandsmen
sported grey slouch hats, red and white bandannas, dark blue flan-
nel shirts, calfskin chaps, bullet-laden gun-belts, and ivory-handled
six-shooters. On the convention's opening day they marched flamboy-
antly down Olive Street, their leader keeping time with a nickel-plated
pistol, while one of them held aloft a pair of mounted longhorns hung
with a banner inscribed with the group's name. The delegates from
Kansas and the Indian Territory followed, trailed by a crowd of enthusiastic youngsters as cheering citizens thronged the sidewalks and
hung from windows.

But the conspicuous display of handguns displeased a number of the
convention attendees. "We are not responsible for this circus," a Texas
rancher told a reporter. This "revolver business," he added, "is out of
place." Explained a Colorado delegate:

It is painfully true that people in the East have been led to believe that a greater portion of cattlemen of [the] Southwest and West are as a rule desperate characters; and that we roam about over the prairies armed to the teeth with knives and revolvers. We want to dispel this idea as it places us in a false light before the world. Years ago when likely to meet a bunch of Indians, we were required to go heavily armed [but] times have changed and the necessity for revolvers no longer exists.

Yet the unique incongruity between appearance and performance made the Dodge City musicians public favorites. Astonished audiences heard polished renditions not only of popular marches and waltzes but of such light classics as the "Miserere" from Giuseppe Verdi's tragic opera *Il Trovatore*.

Two of the nation's most widely read family newsweeklies described the Cow-Boy Band at Saint Louis in both text and illustration. *Harper's Weekly* carried an engraving of local school children presenting a drum to the ensemble. *Frank Leslie's Illustrated* not only published a full-page group portrait, but gave over its entire cover to "ESTHETIC COWBOYS AT LARGE IN THE STREETS OF ST. LOUIS," showing bandsmen bedecked with flowers bought from young street vendors.

When the railroad offered the Saint Louis delegates a free trip to Chicago, the invitation included the Dodge musicians. On their November 23, 1884, arrival, mustered in a circle around their director in the rotunda of the Palmer House, they performed to gratifying applause. The next day they marched down the street, leading a procession of carriages carrying the western visitors toward the stockyards.[12]

Some 200 delegates and their Cow-Boy Band mascots accepted another free trip, this time to Minnesota. At the Minneapolis train depot on November 26 a reception committee gave the musicians a hearty welcome. "Come on boys and feel at home," a spokesman boomed. The band then "discoursed excellent music" as they led the visitors to the West Hotel. There they formed up and performed while the delegates registered for dinner.

The next day the excursionists briefly visited Saint Paul, with the band leading everyone to the Merchants Hotel and then performing there. "Their unique uniforms made them objects of curiosity at once," wrote an awed reporter, "and they were surrounded by a large crowd of people until they subsequently escaped to their [railroad] car at the depot" and accompanied the cattlemen back to Chicago.

Samuel Prouty, editor of the *Kansas Cowboy*, Dodge City's newest weekly paper, hoped that the public response to the musical group could ease a dozen years of bad publicity. The Cow-Boy Band, he crowed, "is giving Dodge City such an advertisement as she has never had before."[13]

Yet national media exposure brought some unusual results. A love-struck teenager from Saint Joseph arrived in search of a boyfriend who had told her "he was going out to Dodge City [to] join a band, wear leather breeches, carry a six shooter and live . . . where cowboys ride through the streets every day, discharging their revolvers, killing enough people so as to keep the preachers busy delivering funeral sermons." (A private detective quickly caught up with the young woman and escorted her home.) Then, according to editor Prouty, "a squad of green-looking galoots stepped off the train . . . all armed with heavy revolvers and in plain sight. One of our councilmen noticed them and had them disarmed. They were from the east and had patterned [themselves] from a picture of the Cowboy band."[14]

---

News out of Dodge during what turned out to be its final cattle-trading season continued to stir outrage. A female traveler seemed to capture the essence of the town's bad reputation when an excursion train carrying a party of wealthy New Englanders paused at Dodge on its way west. The woman, testified a witness, "jumped off saying she wanted to set foot on the soil where stood the worst town in America."

A report claimed that despite the Kansas law against prizefighting, the town planned to host a match between the renowned John L. Sullivan and his latest challenger. An angry Kansan sent a copy of the item to Governor John Martin, who, unlike his dithering predecessor, immediately ordered the attorney general to put a stop to it, activating the militia if necessary. A later rumor had it that Dodge would sponsor another bullfight. Neither story proved true.

And on May 10, 1885, yet another homicide occurred. At the Junction Saloon Mysterious Dave Mather and his brother Josiah shot and killed David Barnes, a settler in town to prove up his land claim. The trouble arose from a card game, the two Daves disagreeing over who had won a final hand. Out came the concealed weapons. Barnes's bullet creased Mysterious Dave's forehead, and ricochets wounded two bystanders, one in the hip, one in the leg. Josiah Mather fired a lethal shot from behind the bar. Barnes, killed instantly, sank to the floor. Indicted for felonious homicide, the Mather brothers eventually jumped bail and got out of Dodge.[15]

But the town's most malignant notoriety stemmed from its continued defiance of liquor prohibition. In 1884 eight of Dodge's eleven founding entrepreneurs—both Collar brothers, George Cox, Richard Evans, Herman Fringer, George Hoover, Robert Wright, and Frederick Zimmerman—had joined "virtually every businessman" in town in signing an open letter urging temperance agitators to stay out of Dodge. "Our city is peaceable and prosperous and we do not desire any outside interference in regard to our local government," they stated, "nor will it be tolerated by us." And, complained a temperance activist, many other perfectly respectable citizens simply believed that the saloon presence "does not hurt me and I will let it alone."

Accordingly, in the spring 1885 election the majority of voters once again had turned to a respected pioneer, this time Robert Wright, to modify the pace of moral mobilization.

Under Mayor Wright's permissive eye, as an editor acknowledged, "the saloons, gambling halls, and dance halls are in full blast again." A visitor from Caldwell, where open liquor trafficking had been ruthlessly suppressed, "was not a little surprised to see half a dozen fine saloons with their front, side and back doors wide open to the public, and the 'ardent' being dished up over the counters in the most approved fashion."[16]

---

By then, June 1885, the reformers had worked up a head of steam. Back in late 1884, as Dodge's temperance movement was at a low point—the IOGT chapter had disappeared, prohibitionists had suffered a stunning defeat in the city election, and they had gotten nowhere in court with the so-called whiskey cases—the state's reigning Republican Party had saved the day. It nominated for governor the popular John Martin, an Atchison editor and admired Civil War veteran, laying on him the task of healing the GOP's four-year fracture over prohibition. Martin did so by firmly declaring the 1880 constitutional amendment a settled issue, a major component of the Republican program. Any figure who hoped to remain influential in party affairs, at any level, would simply have to toe the line. Martin's defeat of Democratic governor George Glick drove the message home.[17]

At Dodge, long a Democratic town, orthodox Republicans at last felt free to publicly declare themselves. Temperance advocates by definition if not religious conviction, this "best element of men and ladies of Dodge City," as one of them phrased it, included important opinion leaders like attorney Michael Sutton and editor Nicholas Klaine. And at least forty other women and men offered firm support. Some, like Emma Sitler, married to the town's original founder, Henry Sitler, were longtime residents. Some, like S. A. Bullard, a gentleman rancher from Boston, Massachusetts, who kept a residence in town, were newcomers.[18] And some, like Samuel Galland, having gained fame from his ferocious month-long campaign to keep a new dance hall from being built near his Great Western Hotel, were converts to the cause. Galland, who had once proclaimed himself a believer "in the unalienable right of a man to govern his own stomach," founded a "Temperance and Protective party" as an adjunct to the KSTU, the Kansas State Temperance Union, the powerful lobbying group that had penned the 1880 constitutional amendment.[19]

Significantly, on February 18, 1885, Kansas lawmakers had changed the legal architecture of the war against liquor. In places like Dodge City where local officials refused to act against saloons, any private citizen could now initiate "an action in the name of the state to abate and perpetually enjoin" any business that manufactured, sold, bartered, or gave away liquor. The reenergized KSTU announced its intention to help in decontaminating Dodge City once and for all.

Preparing the ground, a religious revival over the course of twenty-three nights at the Methodist church on Gospel Ridge attracted members of all three Protestant denominations. And a religious "praise meeting" at the opera house drew 550 persons, according to editor Klaine, who called it the largest crowd ever assembled in town.[20]

Now a solid coalition of evangelicals (Methodist, Baptist, and Presbyterian) with secular Republicans, the reformers welcomed KSTU president Albert Griffin to Dodge. On June 21, 1885, he gave a lecture—not, as editor Prouty conceded, "one of those old stereotyped temperance stories, but one of good sound sense." Griffin returned to Dodge and spoke again on June 24, then organized sixty men and women into a local chapter of the temperance union.

Four days later Griffin was back once more, this time to file injunction papers against the saloons. Forewarned, the bars had closed, moving a crowd of irrigation ditch diggers, idled by rain and finding nowhere to drink, to besiege Griffin and a companion in Samuel Galland's hotel. The redoubtable Bat Masterson, hastily deputized, stood off the mob and negotiated the visitors' exit on the next train east. "WHISKY REBELLION. CONTEMPTIBLE OUTRAGES OF A MOB OF 300 DODGE CITY RUFFIANS ARMED AND ORGANIZED FOR FIGHT," screamed the *Topeka Capital*'s headlines, and "TEMPERANCE PEOPLE COMPELLED TO FLEE FOR THEIR LIVES." Another overwrought report from Dodge materialized in a Saint Louis paper: "The feeling here is overwhelmingly against temperance, and some of the most dangerous desperadoes in the country live here. . . . If the prosecution is not dropped *there will be death and destruction in this community*, and no power on earth can prevent it."[21]

In his own newspaper Albert Griffin sketched an image of Dodge reminiscent of Mark Twain's colorful description of Virginia City in the 1860s:

> The fact is that the town is now and always has been controlled by a gang of cut throats. . . . The man who has "killed somebody" appears to have a magnetic attraction for some men and women, and, in addition to the long list of murderers already domiciled in Dodge, there are men constantly on the watch for a chance to "make a record" (this being the polite Dodge City way of describing murder) without endangering their [own] lives too much.

Without a doubt the February legislation allowing private citizens to sidestep local officials in initiating liquor enforcement was making a difference. For the first time since the 1880 enactment of the prohibition amendment, selling alcohol openly, seemed risky, at least to some Dodge City purveyors.

On March 8, 1885, two days before the new law went into effect, the town's most prominent liquor wholesalers had thrown in the towel.

George Hoover, whose sales in the past two years—April 1883 through February 1885—totaled almost $65,000 (around $1.65 million in 2015 dollars), laid off his three employees and disposed of inventory, mainly liquors but also cigars, citrus fruits, and bar supplies. Hoover's competitor, Henry Sturm, offered closeout prices on no less than eighty barrels of whiskey, fifteen cases of champagne, twelve of wine, three of gin, and miscellaneous quantities of peach brandy, apple brandy, rock and rye, rum, and other alcoholic drinkables. He then held open house, inviting townspeople to help themselves to what had not sold.[22]

Some retailers followed suit, especially after Sheriff Sughrue, anticipating prosecutions by the attorney general himself, posted notices around town that sale of intoxicating beverages must end by the first of May. Two or three saloons became restaurants. The owners of a few others, including Alonzo Webster, circumvented the law by applying for local pharmacy licenses allowing them to operate as druggists selling alcohol for legally exempt medicinal purposes.[23]

When on July 7, 1885, Attorney General Simon Bradford met with Dodge officials about the Griffin disturbance, Sheriff Sughrue assured him that of the town's seventeen saloons operating before the February law went into effect on March 10, only about ten remained open. Three days later in a newspaper interview Bradford engaged in some political puffery. "Out of forty saloons selling liquor [at Dodge] in violation of the law last March less than a dozen remain," he claimed, exaggerating the decline by inflating the earlier count. He also told the reporter that he believed "the backbone of the temperance element of [Dodge] city are the ladies and the Women's Christian Temperance Union." Before leaving town, and at their request, Bradford had indeed met with women intent on forming a female prohibition group. But they did not succeed in organizing Dodge's chapter until December 1885. Nationwide the Women's Christian Temperance Union attracted hundreds of female Good Templars resentful of the male monopoly on the IOGT's most prestigious offices.[24]

------

Yet Dodge City's reputation continued to shred. In October 1885 its number of saloons, based on monthly fees paid to the city, actually advanced to fourteen, one of which had been opened in Sturm's old building. That same month Bat Masterson and his buddies thwarted the attempts of an Edwards County officer to arrest a lawbreaker hiding out in Dodge. These occurrences confirmed Governor Martin's growing suspicion, which he expressed to Mayor Wright, that things at Dodge were going from bad to worse. Addressing the fugitive issue Martin demanded that "proper, prompt, and vigorous measures are taken to punish this outrageous violation of the law." He then turned to the town's moral decay.

> Visitors inform me that the saloons are increasing, not only in numbers, but in depravity; and thieves, desperadoes, gamblers and criminals generally, are multiplying. It is also alleged that these lawless characters dominate in the city; that they have terrorized all the better elements of society; that they openly and defiantly flaunt their viciousness and depravity; and that they appear to think there is no power or authority that can reach or punish them.

He then hectored Wright about the economic costs.

> You know that decent and peaceable people avoid Dodge because of its notoriously bad reputation. You know that capital will not come to Dodge because men of means regard property as unsafe there. You know that the A., T. & S. F. Railroad Co. wants to erect important and valuable industries there, and is deterred from doing so wholly by the fact that Dodge is the resort of so many depraved and vicious characters . . . and the fact that vice and crime are so wanton and brazen there.[25]

The news sped along Front Street. Communications flew back and forth between Topeka and Dodge. Governor Martin repeated his charges; the county attorney, the sheriff, and the mayor denied them. And fellow Republican Michael Sutton advised that the governor's strongly worded letter "has created no little rage and I'm receiving some very uncomplimentary and warlike messages."[26]

On November 5, Mayor Wright finally sent a lengthy reply. "Governor," he wrote, scarcely restraining his fury,

> you have been imposed upon by a lot of soreheads of this Town. This Gang only consists of about a dozen who breed all the trouble here & continually keep things in hot water. [They] pretend to be Moralists

but . . . are hypocrites of the deepest & darkest kind. Such even is M. W. Sutton[,] N. B. Klaine . . . & a few others of this kind.

The mayor concluded on a more reflective note, guaranteeing Martin that things would come right of themselves. Rural settlement now enclosing Dodge would interdict the Texas cattle trail and end the commercial need for saloons and other illegal enterprises.[27]

Even as Wright put pen to paper, the results of the autumn 1885 Ford County election had caused yet another outrage: fraudulent returns from Dodge City—something like 600 more ballots cast than the number of potential voters—kept temperance men from winning office. While the Kansas Supreme Court's order for a recount worked its way through the legal system (for another two years), the ballot-box insult brought local prohibitionists' anger to the boiling point.[28]

···◦∞◦···

On November 7, 1885, the governor censured the mayor in his most strongly worded message yet, directing Wright "to close up those places which are an offence to the State—the dance halls, the open gambling houses, the notorious places of prostitution—and to drive out the desperate, reckless, lawless desperadoes." Two days later "the city authorities," reported Daniel Frost, "closed all gambling in saloons, and also put a quietus on the music"—the after-hours crowd had danced its last waltz on Front Street. The south-side dance houses themselves would close on New Year's Day: "All dance halls in Dodge City will be closed. Now, and forever!" concluded editor Frost. "Amen."

Still too little for Martin, who was himself within months of converting to strict prohibition. Conspicuous noncompliance with the prohibitory law continued, offering the governor a perfect opportunity to order Attorney General Bradford, in his first big undertaking, to file suit against Dodge City's saloonkeepers. When Bradford arrived at Dodge on November 24 he found virtually all the bars closed, and at a meeting he received a solemn promise from the majority of the owners that they would permanently quit the business.[29]

This pledge the attorney general proved naive in accepting, since the liquor retailers (including Sturm, who had closed his wholesale liquor business nine months earlier) joined those who had already become licensed druggists. In early December the editor of the *Democrat* could wryly note that "twelve drug stores, in as healthy a town as Dodge City, shows that the druggists are looking well after the wants of our sick."

Bradford left town on November 26, Thanksgiving Day. What exactly happened afterward remains cloaked in mystery.[30]

---

In the predawn hours of November 28, 1885, as Nicholas Klaine reported, a "fire burned the buildings in which were the principal saloons." Breaking out at the Junction Saloon, it consumed the adjacent Opera House Saloon, then swept westward, leveling all the Front Street buildings between First and Second Avenues, including the Long Branch and the Stock Exchange saloons, and decimating the contents of Robert Wright's brick store.[31]

At four in the morning, accompanied by a tavern owner and his barman, the infuriated mayor surveyed the smoldering ruins, concluding that some fanatics among the temperance people had set the blaze. Wright immediately led the trio over to Railroad Avenue and the home of Michael Sutton, the town's most visible and influential prohibitionist. According to a written complaint to Governor Martin by eleven reformers, now including Frederick Zimmerman (whose own store had burned), Wright and his companions, "all drunk," had fired two pistols and a Winchester rifle at the house "with the purpose and intent of murdering him (Sutton)."

A couple of days later Wright beat Sutton in gaining an audience with Governor Martin. The mayor claimed that despite what others might say "he was simply attempting to protect Sutton's property" and had fired ineffectively at a prowler. In a skeptical report on Wright's views of the incident the editor at Medicine Lodge—where Sutton formerly lived—offered his own opinion: "Even putting the most favorable construction" on the mayor's story, he said, "it is not at all surprising that Mike should suppose that an attempt was being made upon his life." In any case, "if that is the way the Dodge City mayor has of guarding people, we don't want him for a body guard of ours."

Sutton then visited the governor on December 8, 1885, offering the reformers' complaint as proof of an assassination attempt and adding that he would reside in Larned "until assured of safety and protection" at Dodge. These accounts "of attempted assassination . . . startle us," reported the *Kansas City Journal*, and "until one party or the other can verify the statements made it would be unwise to publish them."

Martin tried to get at the "real facts," as he put it, by turning to a third party. First he confided to district court judge Jeremiah Strang that he was "very much impressed" with Wright's "apparent earnestness [in] telling his story." He asked Strang to look into the seven charges in the complaint against what its authors termed "the lawless mob misnamed a city government."[32]

None of the first six allegations, reported Strang, were true. As to the seventh, the "alleged attack on M. W. Sutton on Nov. 28 last by R. M. Wright," he had issued a warrant for Wright's arrest on the charge of felonious assault as well as a subpoena for Sutton and others to appear as witnesses at a hearing set for January 4, 1886. Arrest made, witnesses summoned. But less than two weeks before the hearing Strang wrote Martin that he had "lost all sympathy and patience with the extravagant, insincere and hypocritical methods of Sutton & two or three of his creatures at Dodge—& more than disquieted with their malicious misrepresentations in relation to men & matters." In turn, Sutton characterized Judge Strang as "a friend of the 'Gang' at Dodge." The hearing itself resulted in postponing the trial, apparently indefinitely.[33]

---

Arson, the word that dared not speak its name, proved something so poisonous to any community's good prospects as to demand the utmost secrecy and discretion.

It served the interests of neither the temperance people nor their opponents to put gossip into writing. Post-fire communication with the governor and attorney general focused not on the fire itself but on the gunplay at Sutton's house, the reformers' larger grievances against town officials, and the officials' exasperation with the reformers.

And while Dodge City's four editors freely discussed the extent of the conflagration's damage, they threw a blanket of silence over possible culprits and their motives. Nicholas Klaine's only comment—"The origin of the fire is unknown, and all theories are speculative"—stood as the town's final word on the subject until thirty years later when an elderly

Robert Wright smoothed over the incident by blaming the explosion of an oil lamp in the Junction Saloon.[34]

The editors proved equally unforthcoming when, in the wee hours of December 8, 1885, a destructive new blaze flared up, this time at the Chestnut Street apartment of two prostitutes, wiping out yet another downtown block that included the town's two or three "sporting houses." This time a news story blandly attributed the fire to a carelessly attended heating stove.

Yet local and state officials clearly shared an anxiety about the actions of anti-liquor extremists. Mayor Wright held arsonists among them responsible for decimating downtown Dodge. Governor Martin had confided to a friend his grave unease about "fanatical prohibitionists" around the state.

A lynching at Caldwell, the state's other remaining cattle town, confirmed the mayor's suspicions and the governor's apprehension. That town had finally shuttered its saloons, consigning the liquor business to a belligerent group of bootleggers who evaded prosecution. On the very night that Dodge City's second fire cleansed Chestnut Street a posse of frustrated Caldwell militants hauled the chief lawbreaker out of a warm bed, dragged him to the stockyard, and strung him up, a note attached to the body warning the others to close down.[35]

It would not have taken much to turn a fringe element of Ford County's prohibitionists, fed up with evasion and delay, into vigilantes willing to set Dodge City alight—twice—to rid it of morally obnoxious goods and services. First target: the saloons so conspicuously disfiguring its main commercial street. Second target: the prostitutes and sporting houses that were shifting base from the south side to Chestnut Street, thus encroaching on "respectable" Dodge City north of the railroad tracks.

From the mid-1880s into the new century, Kansans' violence against remaining liquor retailers—usually committed by women activists like the famous Carrie Nation—consisted of shattering windows, mirrors, bottles, and glassware. But dynamite, a violent alternative to fire, proved effective. In 1898, under cover of darkness, prohibition militants at the village of Woodbine in Dickinson County pushed dynamite through a basement window of a saloon and blew it to smithereens. And in 1905 a lone extremist dynamited three Allen County saloons in a single night. The number of "retail liquor dealers" in Kansas in 1906 was still 3,425.[36]

<hr />

In early March 1886, as businessmen made plans to rebuild in brick and granite, Governor Martin elevated Dodge to a city of the second class, a designation Mayor Wright's council, responding to a citizen petition, had requested. That at least sanitized the political system by requiring the registration of eligible voters: no more ballot boxes aggressively stuffed by transients.[37]

In the subsequent mayoral contest, wide-ranging disenchantment with Wright's pugnacious tenure led to a draft of former mayor Alonzo Webster by virtually every businessman, joined by "one-half of the saloon druggists" and a "united temperance faction," said editor Frost. Attempting to frustrate Webster's candidacy, "the boys," as Wright fondly called them, asserted themselves one last time. Bat Masterson, replaying the gambit that ended the Dodge City War in 1883, filed criminal complaints against the remaining saloons/drugstores, hoping to force them to contest Webster's moderate reform platform. This time the scheme fizzled; unopposed, Webster became mayor for the third time.[38]

By then the district court had disposed of several "whiskey cases," with only one guilty verdict, and continued all the others, since the complaining witness, Bat Masterson, had slipped out of Dodge in late March 1886, never to live there again.

Most of the saloonmen/druggists resumed business, with some actually running prominent advertisements in the local papers. Henry Sturm, for instance, announced (in German) that his Metropolitan Drug Store, opened after he closed his wholesale liquor business, stocked "imported Port, Claret, Rheinweine und Likore—Rum, Ale & Porter." Mayor Webster, as was his wont, offered a concession to Gospel Ridge by ordering all saloons closed, "front and back doors," on Sundays, then— having it both ways—advertised that his own outlet carried "Pure Wines and Fine Kentucky Whiskies."[39]

Days before the Sunday closing decree, the last known violent death of Dodge City's frontier era—its thirty-sixth—occurred on April 15, 1886, on a sidewalk south of the tracks. Restaurateur Ed Julian and saloonkeeper Ben Daniels owned adjacent establishments. Julian was a querulous troublemaker awaiting trial for a violent dustup with Sheriff Sughrue. Daniels had recently been replaced as assistant marshal of Dodge.

Commonly acknowledged, a long-standing feud existed between the two, which for Daniels reached the breaking point earlier in the day when Julian filed a complaint against him for violating the prohibition law. As an armed Julian walked by his saloon Daniels stepped out, pumped two rounds into his enemy's back, then administered the coup de grâce to the recumbent Julian with two more shots.

A district court jury acquitted Daniels, most likely because the old frontier rule of thumb about violent personal feuds once again dictated the survivor's exoneration. "No one could have prevented this tragedy," Daniel Frost editorialized. "The bitterness which existed between them was almost certain to bring them together sooner or later, and as many predicted, that one or the other, or perhaps both would be mortally wounded, if not killed outright."[40]

By then the demise of the Texas cattle trade had ended the commercial justification for brothels, gaming tables, and heroic quantities of booze. Gone were the "olden times," Frost editorialized, "when all of Ford County was in Dodge City and there was money and fun to spare. . . . Even the life of only a little over a year ago, will never be known here again."

With unfeigned regret, on April 17, 1886, Frost called on the *Kansas City News* to "please discontinue referring to Dodge City as the 'devils own,' we have reformed."[41]

# CONTESTING BOOT HILL

After 1886, liquor, gambling, prostitution, and gun violence, once so thoroughly open to the national gaze, no longer defined Dodge City. A *New York Times* headline, no less, offered a fitting epitaph: "THE WICK-EDEST PLACE OF THE 'WILD AND WOOLLY FRONTIER' NOW A PROSPEROUS CITY." The accompanying story admitted that some diehards still enjoyed pointing out "dark stains on the floors of deserted rooms which were caused by the life blood of some 'tough' or 'tenderfoot' who died with his boots on." But it assured readers that "people no longer go armed in Dodge City, and the stranger within her gates can walk the streets at all hours without being shot at."[1]

While most Dodge Citians greeted the post-frontier era with great hopes and expectations, no sooner had the business of small ranchers and farmers replaced that of the Texas cattle trade and overland freighting than the year 1887 ushered in a decade of drought, poor crops, foreclosures, and depopulation, followed by the national economic depression of the 1890s, second only to the 1930s debacle in its destructive effects. "For ten long years," Robert Wright recalled,

> Dodge City was suspended in reverses. . . . Property went down to five and ten cents on the dollar, in value. . . . People would not pay taxes. . . . Many of the business houses closed, and large numbers of residences were without tenants. Parties were invited to live in them rent free, so the insurance could be kept up. . . . Land around Dodge sold as low as fifty cents per acre.[2]

By the time the town got back on its feet, a variety of illnesses had claimed the lives of five of its eleven founding entrepreneurs. Herman Fringer, who had never married, died of edema in 1885 at his mother's house in Ohio, dismaying her with his deathbed refusal to be comforted by Christian doctrine. Alonzo Webster, plagued by rheumatic fever that he had contracted during the Civil War, followed in 1887. Frederick Zimmerman, the oldest of the group, died in 1888. Alfred Peacock, Dodge's breakaway Latter-Day Saint, relocated to Salt Lake City to care for his widowed mother. An alcoholic, he died there in 1891 from cirrhosis of the liver. After Jacob Collar's 1893 death his wife had his body reburied at the Jewish cemetery in Denver, where she had moved to be near relatives. Morris Collar, Jacob's brother, outlived all the others, dying in 1923 in Oklahoma, where for years he owned a prosperous hardware store.

The economic depression wrecked the lives of two others, James Kelley and George Cox. The former declared bankruptcy and drifted about for several years, working on a nearby ranch and, according to his obituary, "elsewhere as the spirit moved him." Estranged from family, Kelley gained admission to the Soldiers' Home at Fort Dodge by special resolution of the Kansas legislature, since residence was specifically denied to ex-Confederates. He died there in 1912. George Cox, after an ill-timed banking venture collapsed and a fire destroyed the Dodge House, retired to Saint Louis to live with a daughter. He was killed in a car crash during World War I.[3]

Robert Wright also struggled through the nineties, his financial reverses accompanied by alcoholism and a succession of disillusioned wives. In 1915, two years before his death, with the editorial assistance of Nicholas Klaine of the old *Dodge City Times*, Wright completed *Dodge City: The Cowboy Capital and the Great Southwest*. Without a major publisher the book's sales did not meet Wright's expectations, perhaps because it did little to satisfy readers' narrow fascination with celebrity gunmen and Boot Hill. But it stands today as one of the distinguished reminiscences of the trans-Missouri frontier.[4]

George Hoover, Dodge City's very first businessman, turns out to have been its most financially astute. He invested his profits from liquor wholesaling in a loan company specializing in good-value farm mortgages, which at the turn of the century morphed into a prosperous state bank. Before his death, incidentally, he still had not come to terms with Kansas prohibition. After business hours—"rain or shine," it was said—Hoover and fellow founding entrepreneur Richard Evans would meet a few friends in the back room of Jacob Bloom's ice cream parlor for a round or two of whiskey toddies. Evans died in 1912, Hoover in 1914.

Henry Sitler, the man who started it all, chose to raise cattle far from Dodge until his return to town in 1882. Sitler died in Dodge City in 1917.[5]

‒‒‒‧⦾‧‒‒‒

Most Dodge City residents, for whom the town's past had been a most extraordinary time, welcomed its retreat to the ordinary.

Ironically, just as everyone was adjusting to the end of all the excitement, Dodge City finally made its debut in yellow-back fiction in an 1888 novelette titled *The Dandy of Dodge; or, Rustling for Millions*. Writing under the pen-name "Lieutenant A. K. Sims," the author, a homesteader, had begun scripting stories for the popular Beadle publications before leaving Indiana. Sims opened his Kansas tale with a disclaimer. "I write of the days when Dodge City was the great cattle town of the West, with all that the name implies," he said. "Those days are passed."

Some of the story's action plays out at the 1884 bullfight, but otherwise all is imaginary. The plot, unexpectedly, is a faithful rendition of what sociologist Will Wright, applying the literary structuralism of Claude Lévi-Strauss to the movies, termed a Classical Western: "the story of the lone stranger who rides into a troubled town and cleans it up, winning the respect of the townsfolk and the love of the schoolmarm." But here the newcomer is a crooked gambler nicknamed "Dandy." At the price of only a few lives, our hero foils an attempt by Dodge's arrogant crime boss to steal ownership of a huge ranching operation from its rightful heir, a fragile young woman. Ultimately Dandy forces the bad guys to get out of Dodge, he gets the woman, and he finds respectable employment in Kansas City.[6]

In 1889 the Dodge City Cow-Boy Band represented the town at President Benjamin Harrison's inaugural parade in Washington, but a year later it disbanded. Its ranks thinned by musicians moving on to dance halls elsewhere and beset by internal conflict over scheduling, the members sold their instruments and distinctive outfits to a group in Denver.

In the following decade citizens' indifference to Boot Hill, the notorious promontory in their midst, allowed its topographical integrity to suffer dismemberment. Excavating the basements for successive school houses in 1880 and 1890 damaged its crest, and in 1899 the town's street commissioner ordered its southern slope dynamited to permit a westward extension of Walnut Street. Later the authorities permitted more of its sand and gravel to be carried away for use as filler at a new racetrack down by the river.[7]

In 1899 a local editor reflected the consensus of many when he boasted that Dodge was no longer the scene of "high carnival" where "rapturous lewdness and bawdiness held sway. . . . 'Clothed in her right mind,' Dodge . . . took her departure from sin and lewdness and the city is now a paragon of virtue, sobriety and industry."

In 1910, when a young journalist from Wichita came to town and purchased the *Ford County Globe*, he found that the newspaper's files generously documented Dodge's frontier days. Presuming them to be of great local interest, he reprinted a colorful news item, the first, he announced, of a series. Only after a committee of citizens paid him a visit and demanded he abandon the plan did he discover the local aversion to memorializing Dodge City's frontier past.

The state's newspapers broadcast that attitude. A headline over a 1910 Topeka story read, "STAID DODGE CITY REGRETS ITS PAST. PRESENT RESIDENTS DON'T LIKE TO HEAR OLD DAYS DISCUSSED." A few years later a Kansas City reporter assured readers that this effort at willful amnesia had succeeded. "Dodge City," he said, "has forgotten its past."

Well, not quite. The town's commercial club, issuing a recruitment brochure in 1911 aimed at "people desiring the right kind of town in which to live and do business," could not resist slyly referencing its notorious history. "No city in the United States of the same size has been so thoroughly advertised," it announced. "To say that one has never heard of Dodge City is to say that he does not read. No [consumer] of books, newspapers and magazines can make such an admission."[8]

By then Dodge's colorful story had attracted the attention of the nation's new mass-circulation magazines and their middle-class readers, initiating a national conversation about the town's character. Virtually without exception articles showcased Dodge's frontier peace officers, of whom Wyatt Earp and Bat Masterson had already achieved legendary distinction. Western fiction and cinema as they evolved in these same years also highlighted the confrontation of lawmen and desperadoes.

The climactic street duel, with its long walk and fast draw, originally appeared in Owen Wister's classic 1902 novel *The Virginian*, universally considered the first serious print western. The author happened to be a privileged Philadelphian whose friend Theodore Roosevelt had urged him to write the book in the interests of creating a distinctively American literary genre. Four years later Wister's ritualistic one-on-one duel made its film debut in the Edison Studio's *A Race for the Millions*, and soon it became an enduring movie cliché. With so many Americans now learning their frontier history in darkened theaters, such choreographed violence came to be recycled into the popular image of "the real West."[9]

Dodge City's first important appearance in periodical literature also came in 1902 with an article by a Kansas lawyer, E. C. Little. Published in *Everybody's Magazine*, "The Round Table of Dodge City" literally mythologized the town's frontier officers as "Knights-Errant Who Surpassed the Achievements of Heroes of Romance."

The author offered biographies of three officers who had served at one time or another at Dodge: Bat Masterson, Dave Mather, and Pat Sughrue. The last, the author's informant, still lived in town. His assistance helped frame an issue for the next thirty years: the extent to which post-frontier Dodge City would collaborate in the formation of its own narrative.[10]

Most spectacularly featured by author Little was the laconic Mysterious Dave. The article's main illustration, rendered by the renowned western artist Frederic Remington, depicts an exaggerated version of Mather's midnight encounter with a group of armed celebrants at Las Vegas, New Mexico, in 1880. Firing once, Dave had inflicted a mortal wound on the leading carouser. In Remington's more lethal reconfiguring Mather looks mysterious indeed. Ghostly and smoke-shrouded, he hovers in the background with several dead and dying victims sprawled across a murky foreground. And in the spirit of Mark Twain and Bret Harte, Remington employs rough humor in the picture's legend, describing Dave as "The Only Descendant of Cotton Mather who has Distinguished Himself." Indeed, Mather was a collateral descendant of that famous seventeenth-century clergyman.[11]

The following year Andy Adams's novelized but masterfully true-to-life view of Dodge appeared in print, as explored in chapter 5 above. Adams, too, extolled the town's frontier lawmen. And, like E. C. Little, he concluded that "the puppets of no romance ever written can compare with these officers in fearlessness."[12]

In 1904 popular magazines printed four Dodge City short stories written by Alfred Henry Lewis, the editor of *Human Life*, a Hearst publication headquartered in New York. Less wedded to historical veracity than Andy Adams, Lewis fashioned comic accounts of real events and personalities loosely based on information provided by his good friend Bat Masterson, now a sportswriter for the *New York Morning Telegram*. In one story, a barely recognizable account of Masterson's 1877 election as Ford County sheriff, Lewis puts words into the mouths of Robert Wright, Alfred Peacock, James Kelley, and Alonzo Webster, as well as thoughts into the heads of Luke Short and law officers Bill Tilghman and Al Updegraff. All but Wright and Masterson speak the backwoods patois popularized by Bret Harte.[13]

Notably missing from Lewis's cast of characters is Wyatt Earp, Masterson's old comrade from Dodge City days, his place taken by an imaginary chum named "Cimarron Bill." Probably Earp, obsessively protective of his dignity, objected to being fictionalized by Lewis, who had once described Wyatt, in print, as a "blackleg gambler—crooked as a dog's hind leg."

In 1905 these stories reappeared in Lewis's full-length novelization of Masterson's frontier adventures, published under an inexplicably bland title, *The Sunset Trail*. Of the book's sixteen chapters, ten proved to be fanciful versions of real events at Dodge: the killings of Ed Masterson and Dora Hand, the Dodge City War, and Bat Masterson's 1885 rescue of Albert Griffin from the mob. Although remarkable for its minimalist gun violence, the novel does elevate Masterson's lifetime shooting victims to five.[14]

In 1907 Bat himself, at editor Lewis's urging, penned a series for *Human Life* on "Famous Gunfighters of the Western Frontier." It consisted of essays on Luke Short, Ben Thompson, John "Doc" Holliday, Bill Tilghman, and Wyatt Earp. Lewis contributed a concluding sketch on Masterson himself.[15]

As the new century wore on, journalists writing in a wide variety of publications created ever more lurid portraits of the town. "In Dodge City . . . the revolver was the only sign of law and order that could command respect" (*Outing* magazine, 1904). "The reign of law at Dodge was enforced by the 6-shooter and . . . the court of last resort there was presided over by Judge Lynch" (*Kansas City Star*, 1918). "They were buried literally with their boots on . . . these victims of saloon, dance-hall, and gambling fights. When one was 'bumped off,' the authorities just hustled the body out to Boot Hill and speculated upon what else the day would bring forth in bloodshed" (*Literary Digest*, 1925). "Dodge . . . the Old Hell-Raising Trail's End Where Colt was King" (*Liberty*, 1928).[16]

Bat Masterson had long since achieved cultural stardom, being an occasional guest, for example, at President Theodore Roosevelt's White House. And as his old hometown's quintessential historical figure he attracted—as always—the gossip of raconteurs and fabulists. In 1910 an elderly Thomas Jones, once Concho Gill's inept defense counsel, told an awestruck Topeka journalist about the night in 1878 when Ed Masterson fell mortally wounded at the hands of Jack Wagner. Bat Masterson, "crazed with grief and rage," said Jones, ". . . ran with a pistol in each hand into Peacock's and began shooting at every cowboy he saw. The saloon was quickly emptied of its patrons. All told, four or five men were killed."

In his comments on Boot Hill, Jones also indulged in the sport of body-count inflation. Back in 1877 someone told cowboy Charlie Siringo that no less than eighty-one bodies rested on Boot Hill, all but one having died violently. Jones happily improved on that figure. "I suppose I would be safe in saying that from first to last more than two hundred men died with boots on at Dodge," he said.[17]

Never mind that when the graves on Boot Hill were relocated in 1879 to a special section of the new Prairie Grove Cemetery, to make way for a schoolhouse, lawyer Michael Sutton, in a public address, said they numbered "twenty-five or thirty." The local consensus somehow settled on thirty-three. Somebody viewing a photograph of Alonzo Webster's interment in the Prairie Grove Cemetery in 1887 said he counted the thirty-three Boot Hill graves. But a high-resolution examination of that photograph negates any systematic count. All it reveals is a long furrow of disturbed earth paralleling the cemetery fence, dotted here and there with some fifteen to twenty white stubs that might have been burial markers. During the 1890 construction of the second schoolhouse and the later sand-and-gravel operation at Boot Hill, workers unearthed nine more bodies, raising a plausible estimate to forty-two, but including men and women who had died by accident or from natural causes. Finally, in 1926, after Prairie Grove had been built over by residential housing, a reporter wrote that traces of the relocated Boot Hill graves could still be seen in the alley west of Avenue C.[18]

---

In the 1920s an eastern Kansan named Fred Sutton became the most commercially successful exploiter of Dodge City's story to date. Born in 1860 and living on the family farm in the 1870s, Sutton by 1885 worked as a bartender in Saint Joseph, Missouri. At the turn of the century an Oklahoma brewery hired him as a bookkeeper. The 1930s found him employed as an inspector for Kansas City's board of public works.[19]

Sutton scored a major coup when the *Saturday Evening Post* accepted for publication a pair of "as-told-to" memoirs written with Sutton by a Kansas City journalist. The magazine, which published serialized novels, novelettes, short stories, and articles on politics, travel, biography, and other nonfiction of interest to middle-class readers, enjoyed a weekly circulation approaching 3 million—outselling all other popular magazines of the twenties. Published in 1926, the Sutton pieces, the ghostwriter later said, resulted in "thousands of letters from all parts of the country" asking for more. So he and Sutton followed with *Hands Up! Stories of the Six-Gun Fighters of the Old Wild West* (1927), largely a reiteration of the *Post* articles.[20]

Fred Sutton presents himself as the world's expert on the Old West's most lethal characters. "In the last fifty years," he writes, "I have known most of the marshals, sheriffs and bad men who earned reputations." Making things up as he goes along, he says that he was living in Dodge in 1874 and that he was working as a cowboy on the nearby Triangle-Bar Ranch even earlier. Sutton's new pals at Dodge, Bat Masterson and Bill

Tilghman, tutor him in the mechanics of the fast draw. He even becomes intimate with Wyatt Earp and Ben Thompson, and has a ringside seat for Mysterious Dave Mather's antics.[21]

Sutton also hangs out a lot with Wild Bill Hickok. "I was with him often in Dodge City," Sutton writes of the celebrity plainsman. When Hickok fled Hays City after a controversial killing there, Sutton and Bat Masterson welcome him to Dodge, where the trio become fast friends. Pure fantasy. Hickok left Hays in 1870 when Dodge City had yet to be founded, when Masterson was still growing up in Illinois, and when Sutton himself was only ten years old.[22]

In an especially melodramatic passage Sutton intrudes himself into the aftermath of Ed Masterson's death with a report no more plausible than the bizarre version spun earlier by Thomas Jones. The wounded city marshal, Sutton says, literally died in his arms, while brother Bat, "who had killed twenty or thirty men up to that time," sits down and cries like a baby. "I put my arm around Bat's shoulders to try to comfort him," concludes Sutton.

He also boosts Bat's body count by inserting him into the Boot Hill saga. "As peace officer at Dodge City when it was the most lawless and disorderly town in America, [Bat] added thirty-seven to the graves at Boot Hill," he says. It so happens that Bat served as undersheriff, then sheriff, for thirty months. Killing more than a man per month seems a bit much even by Sutton's standards.

Years later, after Fred Sutton had become an ardent collector of Old West memorabilia, he bragged of having personally obtained from Masterson a revolver with twenty-two notches in the handle. "You killed twenty-two men with this gun, Bat?" Sutton asked. Bat, with a straight face, replied that the notches did not include Mexicans or Indians.

Actually, Masterson had tired of being pestered by Sutton, who had convinced himself that all bona fide shooters tallied their kills with jackknives. So, as Bat later told Wyatt Earp, he bought an old .45 Colt in a New York City pawnshop, cut the notches, and gave it to the awestruck collector just to get rid of him.[23]

---

Dodge City celebrated its semicentennial in 1922. A parade through the streets extended a mile and a half, with floats, marching bands, cowboys and cowgirls, a stagecoach, covered wagons, old-timers, and war veterans. An estimated 12–13,000 visitors, some arriving by special train, viewed this "Pageant of Progress," attended other events, and took in what remained of the old frontier town, Boot Hill capturing the most interest.[24]

Three years later the city council, perhaps moved at least in part by that well-populated event, passed an ordinance calling for an August 20 special election on whether or not to save Boot Hill from complete destruction by buying it from the board of education, removing the dilapidated school, and transforming what remained into a memorial park. Also included was a provision for issuing $10,000 in bonds to fund the purchase.

Reporting on the council's action, the *Dodge City Journal* noted that "there has been a great deal of agitation by local organizations for the purchasing of this historic site." Indeed, the Kiwanis and Rotary clubs, the chamber of commerce, the American Legion post, and the realtors' association all weighed in as strongly favoring the proposal. And eighty-four individual supporters offered their opinion that the promontory stood as "an old landmark of the pioneer days, reminding us of the heroic struggles of the early residents of Dodge City who did their part in laying the foundation of business and civilization [in] the Great Southwest."

Seeking support from outside the enthusiastic male business community, proponents suggested other possible uses for the Boot Hill site. Ideas included a soldier's memorial, a civic auditorium, a new city hall, and maybe even profitable sale to the Protestant Hospital Association, which according to rumor had already offered $40,000 for the property.[25]

Boot Hill Park opponents rolled their eyes. Over 400 of them signed petitions belittling the suggested reasons for purchase as "utterly absurd," and objecting to "being taxed to pay for a memorial to the class of people that are buried on Boot Hill" (as if their graves still dotted its slope). The site's only purpose, they argued, would be "to remind the coming generations of the wild and woolly days they care nothing about" (as if the younger generation cared nothing about things wild and woolly).

On election day the ballot question—"Shall the city buy Boot Hill"—lost badly, 197 to 368, failing in every precinct. About 80 percent of registered voters simply stayed home, while the opponents scored a solid turnout.

Six months later a new petition campaign, this time justifying municipal purchase of Boot Hill more openly as preservation of "the last historic spot of our city," was again met with naysaying petitions. Since a memorial park would only celebrate "the history of the prostitute, the gambler and the thug," the No petitioners strongly recommended that the hill's "identity be forgotten."

Lacking other options, the board of education sold Boot Hill to the hospital association, which came to regret its purchase: The old school building on the site proved too deteriorated to convert into usable space. The municipality gamely took the hill off the association's hands, and in 1929 let the contract for a much-needed modern city hall and jail to be built on its crest.[26]

--------◇◇-------

Astride a transcontinental railroad and now a paved, heavily traveled US Highway 50, Dodge City found itself in the late 1920s an object of fascination for growing numbers of tourists lured by the town's historical notoriety.

Those Dodge Citians against honoring their town's wicked past, although defeating the park proposition, seemed increasingly marginalized. A *New York Times* correspondent captured their dismay:

"Wild Dodge," famous for Boot Hill, where early-day bad actors were buried unceremoniously and with their boots on, is a black spot in its history that present-day Dodge City is trying to erase. Try as its citizens may to think of Dodge [as other than] the proving ground for the straight shots of 1872, horse thieves, cattle rustlers and the other hard-boiled gentry, visitors still insist on seeing Boot Hill . . . and the bullet holes in what is left of French Annie's redlight apartment instead of the $300,000 high school and athletic field and Wright Memorial Park.[27]

Undeniably, an ever-increasing tourism inspired renewed interest in preserving what remained of the centerpiece of the town's story. An elderly Hamilton Bell, now patriarch of Dodge's pioneer survivors, conceived of transforming the upcoming cornerstone-laying for the new city hall into a "Last Round-Up" of regional old-timers. He and several cronies mailed 200 invitations to Kansans and Texans who, as Bell's missive phrased it, "knew Boot Hill when there was some purpose in its name." It urged them to "come back and we'll make the old camp live again." More than 600 recipients pledged attendance. Wire services picked up the story and gave it national circulation.[28]

"Citizens who believe Dodge City's unsavory past should not be capitalized [on]," explained the *New York Times*, succeeded in forging a compromise: The commemoration would include religious observances presided over by the celebrated evangelist Billy Sunday. The critics, said the *Times* reporter, "see in the revival services a means of giving Boot Hill at least a semblance of decency. They hope it will be remembered as the place where Billy Sunday spoke rather than as a picturesque spot of the seamy West when Dodge City was the toughest town on the frontier."

So it was that a certain ambiguity surrounded the 1929 rendezvous. The Reverend Mr. Sunday kicked off the festivities on November 3, a Sabbath, holding forth from a wooden podium erected on Boot Hill. He "shouted against sin," reported *Time* magazine. His final words, said the *Kansas City Star*, were that he had "come to dig one more grave on Boot Hill—to bury the devil in." Secular ceremonies the following day featured a parade to the famous knoll. There, in "a re-dedication" of the long-gone cemetery, dignitaries unveiled a life-sized statue of a cowboy-as-gunfighter caught in the instant of yanking his pistol. It had been fashioned in cement by a local dentist, O. H. Simpson, known for his innovative gold-inlay technique but a sculptor by avocation.[29]

The crowd of some 20,000 then adjourned to Billy Sunday's podium for instrumental and vocal music, a poetry reading, prayers, and a keynote speech by Kansas City journalist A. B. Macdonald, apparently selected for this honor because of his recent coauthorship of Fred Sutton's fraudulent, if commercially successful, memoirs.

Macdonald reminded hearers that they stood or sat on almost sacred ground, perhaps the most historic spot in Kansas if not the entire region. It was, he said, a site that uniquely reflected the great transformation from Old West barbarism to modern civilization. Still it was clearly the notorious past, not the progressive present, that preoccupied both speaker and audience. Boot Hill would forever remind Americans, concluded Macdonald, that "Dodge was once the wildest, wickedest and woolliest town in the whole country."[30]

---

On hand that week to compose the *Saturday Evening Post*'s coverage of the gala was Stuart Lake, a writer from California. For Lake, like others before him, the history of Boot Hill served as an index to the old town's allegedly unrestrained gun violence. Most of his reportage reflected the tall tales or badly eroded memories of a few elderly conventioneers. One "Old Cowman," for example, told Lake that more than 100 shooting victims had been interred on Boot Hill; a moment later he revised himself, lowering his estimate to a "conservative" figure of ninety-two.[31]

Looking to support such hefty quantification, Lake poked around for evidence in the old files of the *Ford County Globe*. Finding none, he boldly fabricated. Correctly citing the issue of April 30, 1878, as stating that at nearby Hays City the cemetery contained sixty-four bodies, he then adds a supposed quip by the *Globe*'s editor—"Hays will soon be giving us a run"—that was nowhere to be found in the paper. The May 7 issue, says Lake, reported two more graves discovered on Boot Hill. There was no such report. The May 14 issue supposedly chronicled new burials resulting from "a half-dozen shootings." It did not. A quotation from that same issue referring philosophically to the planned Prairie Grove Cemetery—"Hurry up with that cemetery, for 'we know not the day nor the hour'"—is consciously misconstrued as evidence that space was running out at Boot Hill. "Additional Boot Hill burials were noted frequently during the fall of '78," writes the Californian. That is false. The February 4, 1879, issue, Lake says, reports that thirty-three bodies had been removed from Boot Hill to Prairie Grove. Although the figure, as already noted, reflected the local consensus, the *Globe* of that date printed no body count at all.

Three additional *Saturday Evening Post* articles by Stuart Lake followed in 1930 as a run-up to publication of the author's full-length Wyatt Earp biography. The final installment summarized Lake's unsourced version of his hero's law-enforcement career in southwest Kansas. "Trouble was Dodge's synonym," he wrote. "By the time Wyatt Earp reached the camp [in 1876] some seventy or eighty argumentative visitors had been buried with their footgear in place—Dodge had lost accurate count."[32]

Published in 1931, ten years after Bat Masterson's death and two after Wyatt Earp had died, Lake's book not only replaced Masterson with Earp as the Old West's iconic lawman, but was possibly the most important event in the evolution of Dodge City's image since the Dodge City War. *Wyatt Earp: Frontier Marshal*, which includes Lake's inflated body counts, became an instant best seller, and has provoked in excess of eighty years' controversy over its merits. Two Earp biographers writing in the late 1990s disagree sharply in their evaluations. "Lake was more right than wrong," asserts Casey Tefertiller. Rejoins Allen Barra, "Lake wrote a terrific novel." Andrew Isenberg, the most recent biographer, seems to side with Barra. Stuart Lake, Isenberg says, renders Earp "as a kind of dime-novel Western hero, or silent-film cowboy." Flaws and all, Lake's still widely read book solidified Earp's status as an American figure of international renown.[33]

Ongoing national publicity culminating in *Wyatt Earp*'s best-selling reception, together with the Great Depression's severe economic effect on southwest Kansas, seem to have collaborated in wiping out any remaining resistance to memorializing Dodge City's bygone days.

Many locals now lamented that Robert Wright's 1913 memoir was no longer available for purchase. In 1930 a special printing of 500 copies sought to satisfy this recent appreciation.[34]

At the same time townspeople began reshaping Boot Hill into a marketable commodity. In advance of a 1932 Kansas Rotary Club convention, Dr. Simpson, Dodge's artistic dentist, fashioned several supine faces and upturned toes, arranging them on the lawn below his cowboy statue as playful representations of eroded gravesites from pioneer days. Simpson's comic touch, much approved by viewers, prompted elaboration. Volunteers added more make-believe burials, erected clownish headboards supposedly identifying their inhabitants, and planted cacti and sunflowers among them. Later amplified with a "hanging tree," a small corral, and a chuckwagon, all proudly tended by municipal employees, this ambiguous exhibit—"half-shrine, half-stunt," one journalist called it—became a permanent display for tourists' perhaps somewhat puzzled contemplation.

In 1937 a transcontinental bus line added Boot Hill to its list of stops at points of historical importance, and in July of that year some 250 persons per day paused to view its attractions.[35]

---········◦∞◦········---

During the 1930s Hollywood cinema amplified its role as a staple of mass entertainment. By then references to frontier Dodge had occurred on film several times, a movie called *The Dodge City Trail* appearing as early as 1914. Coinciding with the town's refurbished importance to popular culture, a forgettable remake came out in 1936.[36]

The next film, *Dodge City* (1939), proved more than memorable. After Warner Brothers announced plans to produce it, the town's enthusiastic chamber of commerce dispatched a delegation, cochaired by Hamilton Bell and the Kansas lieutenant governor, to Hollywood to urge that the studio premiere the film at the real Dodge City. Movie executives ultimately agreed, and elevated the premiere into a national media event.

The presence of the film's principal actors—screen luminaries Errol Flynn, Olivia de Havilland, and Ann Sheridan—lent glamour to the occasion, while the governors of Kansas, New Mexico, and Colorado provided suitable gravitas. Special railroad sleeping cars sat on sidings to help house overflow crowds.[37]

Motion picture historians have considered *Dodge City* a classic, two of them praising it as among "the most elaborate and exciting films of the 'town-taming' school." Shot in sumptuous Technicolor, the movie relocates its namesake backward in time, portraying it as a flourishing cattle market four years prematurely. An on-screen preamble, titled "Dodge City, Kansas—1872," summarizes the town's civic infancy in a cascade of popular clichés: "Longhorn cattle center of the world and wide-open Babylon of the American frontier, packed with settlers, thieves and gunmen. Dodge City, rolling in wealth from the great Texas trail-herds, the town that knew no ethics but cash and killing."

Errol Flynn plays a Confederate veteran hired by Richard Dodge (here a wealthy businessman) to bring civil society to the settlement. He does so almost nonviolently, being forced to kill only two villains in pacifying Hollywood's Dodge.

Five other Westerns followed the 1939 blockbuster, but they did little more than capitalize on the town's very recognizable name. *King of Dodge City* (1941), *Vigilantes of Dodge City* (1944), *West of Dodge City* (1947), *Desperadoes of Dodge City* (1948), and *The Gunfight at Dodge City* (1959) proved no more than stock Western yarns. Several fictionalized films about Earp or Masterson featured their sojourns at Tombstone rather than at Dodge.[38]

Two unusual cinematic treatments of the 1960s proved more distinguished. The first, director John Ford's last Western film, *Cheyenne Autumn* (1964), includes a Dodge City interlude: a mean-spirited Wyatt Earp and a drunken Doc Holliday provide comic relief in this otherwise tragic fact-based story about Dull Knife's band of fugitive Cheyenne Indians. The second film, *A Big Hand for the Little Lady* (1966), retitled *Big Deal at Dodge City* for British release, is a gentle comedy about a homesteader and his spouse drawn into a high-stakes poker game at Dodge. Despite its all-star cast—Henry Fonda, Joanne Woodward, Jason Robards, and Burgess Meredith—this unpretentious film is almost unknown today.

A great deal more influential were three popular television serials that featured Dodge City: *The Life and Legend of Wyatt Earp* (1955–1961), *Bat Masterson* (1958–1961), and especially *Gunsmoke* (1955–1975), one of the longest-running prime time series in television history, airing 635 episodes. From 1957 to 1961 *Gunsmoke* topped the Nielsen ratings, with an average of nearly 18 million television sets tuned to the show for each of these seasons. Even in its final year, after ratings had finally slumped, *Gunsmoke* still appeared on some 14 million television sets.[39]

Perhaps paradoxically a "family" Western, a comfortably engaging soap opera (minus any love melodrama), *Gunsmoke* for twenty years followed the fortunes of Matt Dillon, Dodge City's marshal; Miss Kitty, a glamorous and kind-hearted saloon proprietor; Doc Adams, the town's philosophical sawbones; and Dillon's successive sidekicks, deputies Chester and Festus.

Beyond featuring the names of the Long Branch Saloon, the Dodge House, and a few other sites, *Gunsmoke* made no concessions to authenticity: its characters lived and interacted within the usual generic Western stage set. Each episode's opening scene, the so-called title card, showed Marshal Dillon engaging an opponent in formal single combat, dropping him at about 40 yards with a smooth draw-and-shoot. That recurring scene was, of course, a historical anomaly. Approved methods for suppressing violence and disorder in the real Dodge City—or in any Old West town—did not include officers challenging bad guys to street duels.

Otherwise, far from presenting the settlement as intrinsically violent and anarchic, *Gunsmoke*'s Dodge City represented an island of civic stability amid weekly onslaughts of outsiders: drunken cowpokes, pugnacious owlhoots, crazed nesters. Still many times more homicidal than its real-life counterpart, television's Dodge did accurately resemble the old frontier town in the sense that it was a dangerous place mainly because of those who did not live there.

———·‹∞›·———

In 1937 William "Dad" Rhodes, a retired cement contractor and eventually dubbed "a showman of the highest regard," established what he styled the Boot Hill Tourist Attraction, a tent containing souvenirs and a visitors' register. More than 12,000 curious tourists, Rhodes claimed, signed in during the occasion of the 1939 movie premiere.

After World War II Dodge City's junior chamber of commerce assumed control of the site and built a Boot Hill Museum at its base. Into it volunteers moved a large collection of pioneer memorabilia displayed since 1932 in the house of its amateur curator, the son of Chalkley Beeson, long-ago owner of the Long Branch Saloon and organizer of the Cow-Boy Band.

In 1950 citizens revamped the fake gravesites on Boot Hill, and members of the fire department contributed new inscriptions for the mock headboards. "It doesn't make a bit of difference if Boot Hill is a lot of baloney," quipped a local businessman. "People are going to keep right on coming anyway."

Television exposure only added to the town's already extraordinary draw for tourists. By 1957 Boot Hill was reckoned to be one of Kansas's most important attractions. In that one year alone more than 300,000 tourists pushed through the turnstiles at the Boot Hill Museum. Some 500 typically visited on Sundays, 200 on weekdays.[40]

Early the next year actor Hugh O'Brian, television's Wyatt Earp, arrived in Dodge to unveil the cornerstone of the Front Street replica, an elaborate stage-set reconstruction built on the street below Boot Hill. And that summer the wildly popular cast of *Gunsmoke* showed up for the dedication ceremonies.

At the close of the twentieth century, courtesy of Hollywood, countless millions thought of Dodge City as purely fictional, like Shangri-La or Camelot or Oz. "So, yes," a travel writer instructed readers of the *New York Times*, "I can confirm that there really is a Dodge City."[41]

# EPILOGUE:
## HOMICIDE, MORAL DISCOURSE, CULTURAL IDENTITY

In 1886 Dodge City's population of 2,000 meant it remained a village or, in the census definition, "rural-nonfarm," until around 1905, when it passed the 2,500 population threshold and became officially urban—a city in more than just name. By 2010 over 27,000 men, women, and children resided in Dodge. Hispanics, scarcely noticeable in the 1880s, accounted for 57.5 percent of the total, having been drawn north by meat-packing jobs at National Beef and Cargill Meat Solutions, Dodge City's largest employers.[1]

On the outskirts of today's Dodge the landscape, smoothly undulating, pale green or tan depending on the season, stretches toward the horizon on every hand, just as it did in the old days. The railroad tracks still lie where Irish workers spiked down the originals in 1872. A bridge still spans the Arkansas River where Texas cowboys and cattlemen crossed to Front Street from the Western Trail and the Panhandle ranges. But the waterway itself, a casualty of upstream irrigation draw-down, is now scarcely more than a knee-high grassy expanse.

Dodge Citians now tend lawns and rake leaves that drop from the occasional trees, mainly tough, wind-resistant American and Chinese elms subsisting at the very outside edge of their natural growth zone. Street by street low-rise cottages march north from the heart of the original settlement. Among a very small handful of surviving pioneer structures is the Mueller-Schmidt house, built in 1881 of honey-colored limestone, standing beautifully preserved on a leafy corner at what was once the eastern periphery of town. Above present-day Magnolia Street, the residences shift to modest ranch houses, extending north toward the landscaped suburban dwellings beyond.

The original Front Street is long gone. Its structures being largely built of wood, the arsonists of 1885 had virtually leveled it. What did not burn was subsequently torn down and rebuilt in brick and masonry, then leveled again by US Route 50 that overlaid the famous thoroughfare with concrete.

Yet reminders of the past reside in Dodge's downtown. Below what remains of Boot Hill the Front Street replica offers scrupulous reconstructions of several of the town's original business houses and saloons, together with the Boot Hill Museum that displays relics and artifacts as well as housing a historical archive. A startlingly assertive bronze statue of Wyatt Earp stands on a circular plinth on what was once Chestnut Street, now Wyatt Earp Boulevard. Coattails flying, the figure raises its long-barreled revolver and pirouettes to its right, as if just catching sight of the gun being drawn by Dr. Simpson's cement cowboy on Boot Hill. Since Earp's imposing status in popular fiction owes more to the O.K. Corral gunfight in Arizona than to his two-term sojourn as an assistant marshal in Dodge, perhaps a more apt memorial would have been a heroic image of the martyred Ed Masterson, or maybe that of his brother Bat, whose close association with the village both preceded and outlasted that of Earp by several years.

Dodge City's most famous native son is also nowhere commemorated. Born in 1936, Dennis Hopper grew up in various apartments around town while his father served overseas during World War II. At age twelve, harvesting wheat on his grandfather's farm a mile or two west of Boot Hill, he developed a taste for beer, he recalled, which initiated his legendary drinking and drug use.

Hopper studied art under Thomas Hart Benton in Kansas City before venturing to New York and then Hollywood, where, gifted and difficult, he began winning stage and movie roles. In 1969 he became an overnight celebrity by having coauthored, directed, and starred in *Easy Rider*, often considered the defining critical film of the countercultural 1960s.

Today's Dodge City continues to welcome maybe 100,000 tourists annually. And in a clever play on the ubiquitous catchphrase, posters and brochures urge potential visitors to

GET THE
HECK
~~OUT OF~~ into
DODGE!

In summer tourists view male actors fight blank-cartridge street battles and women dance the cancan in the reconstituted Long Branch Saloon. A wax museum and a penned herd of Texas longhorns also draw crowds. Trolley tours carry the curious out along the trace of the old Santa Fe Trail to Fort Dodge and back, to Gospel Ridge (no longer graced by its 1880s churches), and to other historic stops around town. West on Route 50 tourists can try their luck at a casino or take in events at the nearby conference center. If in town on a Tuesday evening in June or July they might attend a performance by the reborn Dodge City Cow-Boy Band, billed as "the oldest municipal band west of the Mississippi."

But all is not fluff. The Kansas Heritage Center, founded in 1966, stands at the northern boundary of the old town company's platted grid. It houses a research library in which staffers with a respect for scholarship welcome visitors and answer requests for information about the old frontier town. Inquiries have fallen off a good deal since first-run television versions of Dodge ended in the 1970s, but those in charge still field incoming questions, occasionally from as far away as England, Germany, and Australia.[2]

--------◆◆◆--------

As an item of popular culture Dodge City remains a commodity. Since 1872 its association with violence has made it a consumer product retailed to a primary market of tourists, and wholesaled to readers and viewers. But at another level imaginary Dodge is also a cultural production, a text that helps expose some of the nation's core values. As symbol and metaphor, frontier Dodge is hard at work helping Americans chart their moral landscape by existing as the archetypal bad civic example. Inserted into the national narrative, it prompts belief that things can never be as dreadful as they were in the Old West, thereby confirming in yet another idiom that we Americans have evolved into a civilized society.[3]

If the Dodge City of myth and make-believe reassures the American psyche, it also incites it to celebrate a frontier past believed to have been brimming with aggression and murderous self-defense. These lethal imaginings offer a spurious tradition for Americans' love of handguns and assault rifles. Writers intent on condemning violence have sometimes unwittingly supported such nonsense.[4]

A letter to the *Boston Globe* offered a caricature of the town that seemed agreeable to both sides in the ongoing gun-control debate. "In the Old West," claimed the writer,

Dodge City wasn't a safer place because everyone carried a firearm. Quite the contrary: It was a paradigm of the kind of dystopia that the English philosopher, Thomas Hobbes, warned us about, one in which there was a war of "everyman against everyman," and where the life of each was "poor, nasty, brutish and short."[5]

As if in direct reply, two National Rifle Association supporters writing that same year under the title "Goodbye Dodge City," exulted that recent criminological research "amounts to nothing short of the death-knell for the anti-gun lobby's fear-mongering 'Dodge City' prophecy."[6]

And so the metaphor lives. In 2012 and 2013 the NRA's uncompromising response to the massacre of children and teachers at Newtown, Connecticut prompted more citations. Its contention that "the best defense against deranged people armed with semiautomatic weapons is for everyone to be armed," wrote one criminologist, "is turning America into Dodge City." A journalist put it more concisely in an essay title: "Gun Control or Dodge City, America's Choice."[7]

The important subtext here is that frontier Dodge City is not contested terrain. The quoted writers all agreed: anarchic Dodge City was a historical reality. Since the metaphor evidently appeals to all political persuasions, it would seem we are gettin' outta Dodge whatever we put into it.

# APPENDIX:
# HOMICIDE VICTIMS, 1872-1886

1. August 1872 — Texas
2. September 5, 1872 — Jack Reynolds
3. November 14, 1872 — Unnamed Texan
4. November 14, 1872 — Unnamed Texan
5. November 22–23, 1872 — H. Essington
6. December 3, 1872 — Hennessy
7. December 3, 1872 — Charley Morehouse
8. December 28, 1872 — Matthew Sullivan
9. January 17–18, 1873 — Edward Hurley
10. January 30, 1873 — McDermott
11. February 9, 1873 — Ed Williams
12. February 9, 1873 — Charles Hill
13. March 11–12, 1873 — McGill
14. March 12–13, 1873 — Burns
15. June 3–4, 1873 — William Taylor
16. July 4–5, 1873 — Unnamed African American
17. July 20–21, 1873 — William Ellis
18. July 20–21, 1873 — David Burrell
19. January 14, 1876 — Unnamed German American
20. April 9, 1878 — Edward Masterson
21. April 9, 1878 — Jack Wagner
22. July 13, 1878 — Harry McCarty
23. July 26, 1878 — George Hoy
24. October 4, 1878 — Dora Hand
25. April 5, 1879 — Levi Richardson
26. September 8, 1879 — Barney Martin
27. November 16–17, 1880 — Henry Heck
28. July 22–23, 1881 — Joseph McDonald
29. July 9, 1883 — John Ballard
30. October 7, 1883 — William Smith

*(continued on next page)*

31. October 7, 1883      William Hilton
32. February 18, 1884      Keziah Morris
33. July 6, 1884      Kyle Choate
34. July 21, 1884      Thomas Nixon
35. May 10, 1885      David Barnes
36. April 15, 1886      Ed Julian

*Note:* If a source says a killing occurred in the "evening" of, say, May 1, then that is the date used. If it says "night" then May 1–2 is used.

# ACKNOWLEDGMENTS

A number of Kansans made important contributions to this project. Janice Scott, Dave Webb, and their colleagues at the Kansas Heritage Center in Dodge City offered absolutely first-rate assistance on more occasions than we care to count. Janice capably manages a research treasure, the encyclopedic notes from local news articles (1876–1929) compiled by Betty Bradford and later digitized by Jennie Burrichter. Dave curates a sizable collection of Dodge City photographs from which we have liberally borrowed; Nancy Sherbert and Lisa Keys of the Kansas State Historical Society in Topeka and Kathie Bell of the Boot Hill Museum in Dodge City also made relevant photos available. Jane Kelsey, Susan Forbes, and other librarians at the Kansas State Historical Society provided numerous documents. Joseph Snell of Topeka supplied personal photocopies of the Waldo Koop notes on cattle-town violence before donating them to the Kansas State Historical Society. Author Fredric Young of Dodge, an enthusiastic well-wisher of the project, graciously fielded multiple requests for information.

Other researchers and friends furnished essential information. Sara Berndt of Arlington, Virginia, hunted down materials at the US National Archives. Russell Wilhoit searched local records of interest in Greensburg, Indiana. Colleagues on the lookout for metaphorical references to Dodge City offered news clippings; thank you, Michael Bellesiles, Kenneth Moynihan, and Ivan Steen. And *molte grazie* to Marco Sioli of the University of Milan for supplying (in Italian) the epilogue title.

In Worcester, Massachusetts, we depended on the services of three outstanding institutions. The incomparable collections of the American Antiquarian Society yielded virtually every published book or historical journal we found a need to consult. Many thanks to its president, Ellen Dunlap, and its efficient and knowledgeable staff. Up the street we gratefully relied on the interlibrary loan services of Worcester Polytechnic Institute and the resourceful assistance of Betty Goodrich, Diana

Johnson, and Laura Robinson. The Worcester Public Library, besides maintaining a large collection of general-interest volumes, owns the best microfilm readers in town.

Other libraries and archives across the country made available various materials: Bancroft Library, University of California, Berkeley; Boston Public Library; Cincinnati History Library and Archives; Haley Memorial Library and History Center, Midland, Texas; Indiana Historical Society; University of Kansas Library; State Historical Society of Missouri; New York City Public Library; Northern Illinois University Library; San Francisco Public Library; Southwest Texas State University Library; and University of Texas Library, Austin.

This book profited enormously from the online offerings of Ancestry. com, notably the US newspaper collections and federal and state census records. These features multiplied many times over the ease of examining local historical materials from all over the nation.

Our appreciation goes to three publishers for granting permission to use previously printed (now substantially revised) material: New York University Press: "To Live and Die in Dodge City: Body Counts, Law and Order, and the Case of *Kansas v. Gill*," in *Lethal Imagination: Violence and Brutality in American History*, ed. Michael Bellesiles (New York, 1999), 210-226; Oxford University Press: "The Circle Dot Cowboys at Dodge City: History and Imagination in Andy Adams's *The Log of a Cowboy*," *Western Historical Quarterly* 33 (Spring 2002): 19–40; and the University of Utah Press: "Contesting Boot Hill: The Saga of Metaphorical Dodge City," in *Imagining the Big Open: Nature, Identity, and Play in the New West*, ed. Liza Nicholas, Elaine Bapis, and Thomas Harvey (Salt Lake City, 2003), 220–237.

# NOTES

## INTRODUCTION: GETTIN' OUTTA DODGE

1. *Hutchinson News,* September 5, 1872.

2. George W. Brown, "Life and Adventures of George W. Brown," ed. William E. Connelley, *Collections of the Kansas State Historical Society* 17 (1926–1928): 116. The *Topeka Commonwealth,* December 7, 1872, reports Morehouse's later death in Dodge City.

3. William Henry Powell, *Powell's Records of Living Officers of the United States Army* (Philadelphia: L. R. Hamersly, 1890), 602; Richard B. Fisher, *Joseph Lister, 1827–1912* (New York: Stein and Day, 1977), 121–197, 273. The first book published in the United States on the subject was Arpad G. Gerster, *The Rules of Aseptic and Antiseptic Surgery; a Practical Treatise for the Use of Students and the General Practitioner* (New York: Appleton, 1888). Almost a decade earlier Tremaine had described the Listerian surgical technique to members of the Kansas State Medical Association. *Atchison Champion* in *Ford County Globe* (Dodge City), May 20, 1879.

4. Joseph L. Byrne, "Medical History of Fort Dodge, Kansas, 1865–1972" (M.A. thesis, Fort Hays Kansas State College, 1972), 98.

5. David T. Courtwright, *Violent Land: Single Men and Social Disorder from the Frontier to the Inner City* (Cambridge, MA: Harvard University Press, 1996), 107. For apparently typical post-Vietnam military usages, see Charlie A. Beckwith and Donald Knox, *Delta Force: The Army's Elite Counterterrorist Unit* (New York: Avon Books, 2000), 153; Tom Clancy and John Gresham, *Special Forces: A Guided Tour of U.S. Army Special Forces* (New York: Berkley, 2001), 43.

6. Google Books Ngram Viewer, "Get Out of Dodge," https://books.google.com/ngrams/graph?content=get+out+of+Dodge&year_start=1975&year_end=2013&corpus=15&smoothing=3&share=&direct_url=t1%3B%2Cget%20out%20of%20Dodge%3B%2Cco; *Boston Globe* Archives, www.search.boston.com/local; Alan Feuer, "The Preppers Next Door," *New York Times,* January 27, 2013, p. MB1.

7. "Crime-Victim Travel Fund Sought," *Boston Globe,* May 8, 1981, no page; Jeffrey Goldberg, "Dodge City Agrees: D.C. Is No Dodge," *Washington Post,* February 16, 1989, p. A14; "3 Charged with Killing Boy in N.Y. Apartment," *Boston Globe,* August 1, 1990, National/Foreign sec., p. 69.

8. "We Must Get Tough—and Mean It," *Liverpool Post,* August 24, 2007, p. 14; Peter Mickelburough and others, "Binge City," *Melbourne Herald Sun,* June 9, 2007, p. 29; Jim Gordon, "Welcome to Scotland's Dodge City," *Glasgow Times,* October 13, 2007, p. 10; Dave Colbeck, "Not Dodge City," *London Telegraph,* April 21, 2006, Features sec., p. 25.

9. Eric Silver, "Law and Order under the Guns of 'the Boys,'" *London Guardian*, August 27, 1985, no page; Lawrence Weschler, "Letter from the Republika Srpska: High Noon at Twin Peaks," *New Yorker*, August 18, 1997, p. 29; "Dodge City on the Tigris," *London Economist*, US Edition, July 19, 2003, no page; Jan Stuart, "At Cannes, America Stars as the Wild West," *Boston Globe*, May 20, 2005, Arts sec., p. D9.

10. "The Mavens Word of the Day," January 4, 1999, http://www.randomhouse.com /wotd/index.pperl?date=19990104; B. Nooni, "Get the Hell Out of Dodge," December 13, 2005, http://www.urbandictionary.com/define.php?term=get+the+hell+out+of +dodge; "What Is the Origin of the Saying, 'Get Out of Dodge?'" August 17, 2006, http:// www.answerbag.com/q_view/70657; "Word for the Wise," July 27, 2006, broadcast, http://www.merriam-webster.com/cgi-bin/wftwarch.pl?072706; "Get out of Dodge," July 29–30, 2007, http://forum.wordreference.com/showthread.php?t=595322.

11. Robert M. Wright, *Dodge City: The Cowboy Capital and the Great Southwest* (Wichita: Wichita Eagle Press, 1913), rev. ed. with new pagination (Wichita, 1930). The earliest academics' books are Stanley Vestal, *Queen of Cowtowns: Dodge City, "The Wickedest Little City in America," 1872–1886* (New York: Harper and Row, 1952), republished as *Dodge City: Queen of Cowtowns* (Lincoln: University of Nebraska Press, 1972), and Odie B. Faulk, *Dodge City: The Most Western Town of All* (New York: Oxford University Press, 1977). The last work appropriates both its narrative and its source notes—without attribution—from the Dodge City sections of Robert R. Dykstra, *The Cattle Towns* (New York: Alfred A. Knopf, 1968); for details see *American Historical Review* 83 (June 1978): 824. The four books by C. Robert Haywood are *Trails South: The Wagon-Road Economy in the Dodge City–Panhandle Region* (Norman: University of Oklahoma Press, 1986); *Cowtown Lawyers: Dodge City and Its Attorneys, 1878–1888* (Norman: University of Oklahoma Press, 1988); *Victorian West: Class and Culture in Kansas Cattle Towns* (Lawrence: University Press of Kansas, 1991); *The Merchant Prince of Dodge City: The Life and Times of Robert M. Wright* (Norman: University of Oklahoma Press, 1998). Local historian Frederic R. Young has authored two indispensable works: *Dodge City: Up through a Century in Story and Pictures* (Dodge City, KS: Boot Hill Museum, 1972) and *The Delectable Burg: An Irreverent History of Dodge City—1872 to 1886* (Dodge City, KS: Boot Hill Museum, 2009). The most recent study, William B. Shillingberg, *Dodge City: The Early Years, 1872–1886* (Norman: Arthur H. Clark, 2009), is an overly detailed chronological narrative that sometimes lacks source citations, tends to ignore the secondary literature, and is not an easy read.

12. Mary Doria Russell, *Doc* (New York: Random House, 2011).

13. Dykstra, *Cattle Towns*, 293–354.


CHAPTER 1: PIONEERS

1. William G. Cutler, *History of the State of Kansas* (Chicago: A.T. Andreas, 1883), 1561; Lola A. Crum and others, eds., *Dodge City and Ford County, Kansas, 1870–1920: Pioneer Histories and Stories* (Dodge City: Ford County Historical Society, 1996),

305. Sitler was born in 1837, not, as stated in Cutler's biographical sketch, in 1827—obviously a misprint. More relaxed than Cutler's other word-portraits, it reads as though written by Sitler himself.

2. US Census, 1860: Pennsylvania, Crawford County, Summit Township, dwelling 2522; US Agricultural Census, 1860: Pennsylvania, Crawford County, Summit Township, 73–74; *Combined Atlas Map of Crawford County, Pennsylvania* (Philadelphia: Everts, Ensign and Everts, 1876), 95; *History of Crawford County, Pennsylvania* (Chicago: Warner, Beers, 1885), 466, 471, 1086; Samuel W. Tait, *The Wildcatters: An Informal History of Oil Hunting in America* (Princeton, NJ: Princeton University Press, 1946), 11–21; Lioy May, *Misplaced Glory: The Lost Soldiers of 1847–1865 in the Pennsylvania Oil Region* (Philadelphia, n.p., 1946), 50, 52. For Sitler's occupation in 1861 see Company Descriptive Book, Company I, 2d Pennsylvania Cavalry Regiment, Henry L. Sitler service records, Record Group 94, microfilm 554, roll 112, National Archives, Washington, DC.

3. Sitler enlisted on October 6, 1861, and was mustered in on November 25. A month later he was listed as a bugler, and in April 1862 was first described as a sergeant. Company Muster Roll, December 31, 1861, and Special Muster Roll, April 12, 1862, Company I, 2d Pennsylvania Cavalry Regiment, Sitler service records.

4. Samuel P. Bates, *History of Pennsylvania Volunteers, 1861–5*, 5 vols. (Harrisburg, PA: B. Singerly, State Printer, 1869–1871), 2: 325, 348; Miscellaneous correspondence, January–March 1865, Sitler service records; Eric J. Wittenberg, *Glory Enough for All: Sheridan's Second Raid and the Battle of Trevilian Station* (Washington, DC: Brassey's, 2001), 263–300; William Marvel, *Andersonville: The Last Depot* (Chapel Hill: University of North Carolina Press, 1994), 92.

5. For Sitler's recollection of his captivity see Cutler, *History*, 1561. For the official dates of that imprisonment (June 24 to November 26, 1864), see Miscellaneous correspondence, January–March 1865, Sitler service records. For Sitler's ailments, see Carded Medical Records, Volunteers, Pennsylvania: 2d Cavalry Regiment, H. L. Sitler, Record Group 94, entry 534, National Archives.

6. "A Few of the Old Timers in Dodge City," *Dodge City Globe*, July 23, 1914.

7. Pekka Hämäläinen, *The Comanche Empire* (New Haven, CT: Yale University Press, 2008, especially 20–37, 110–111, 161–165, offers the best survey of these complex developments. See also essays by James H. Gunnerson; Loretta Fowler; John H. Moore, Margot P. Liberty, and A. Terry Straus; Thomas W. Kavanagh; Jerrold E. Levy; Morris W. Foster and Martha McCollough; and Ives Goddard in *Handbook of North American Indians: Plains*, ed. Raymond J. DeMallie (Washington, DC: Smithsonian Institution, 2001).

8. David Kay Strate, *Sentinel to the Cimarron: The Frontier Experience of Fort Dodge, Kansas* (Dodge City, KS: Cultural Heritage and Arts Center, 1970), 17–21; Leo E. Oliva, *Fort Dodge: Sentry of the Western Plains* (Topeka: Kansas State Historical Society, 1998), 1–7; Thomas W. Kavanagh, *The Comanches: A History, 1706–1875* (Lincoln: University of Nebraska Press, 1996), 210–221, 348–351; Donald J. Berthrong, *The Southern Cheyennes* (Norman: University of Oklahoma Press, 1963), 23–24, 132–143. For a detailed

narrative of events near the later site of Fort Dodge, leading to the army's founding and subsequent abandonment of Forts Mann and Atkinson, see William B. Shillingberg, *Dodge City: The Early Years, 1872–1886* (Norman, OK: Arthur H. Clark, 2009), 14–27.

9. Berthrong, *Southern Cheyennes*, 301–310; Cutler, *History*, 1561; "Pioneer Citizen Died Last Night," *Dodge City Times*, October 31, 1917; *Junction City Union*, April 20, May 4, 11, 25, 1867; *Leavenworth Conservative*, July 10, 1867; "A Few of the Old Timers in Dodge City"; Leo E. Oliva, *Fort Hays: Frontier Army Post, 1865–1889* (Topeka: Kansas State Historical Society, 1980), 13–15, 54–60. Fort Harker was originally established as Fort Ellsworth in June 1864 and renamed in November 1866. Fort Hays was first established in October 1865.

10. Strate, *Sentinel*, 10–13, 22–28; Oliva, *Fort Dodge*, 7, 17–29; Richard Irving Dodge, *The Plains of the Great West and Their Inhabitants* (New York: G.P. Putnam's Sons, 1877), 22–23.

11. Berthrong, *Southern Cheyennes*, 339–344; Oliva, *Fort Dodge*, 69, 71; Cutler, *History*, 1561; Henry H. Raymond, "Notes on Diary of H. H. Raymond," typescript, Raymond Collection, Kansas State Historical Society (KSHS), Topeka; David K. Clapsaddle, "The Fort Hays–Fort Dodge Road," *Kansas History* 14 (Summer 1991): 100–112; "Pioneer Citizen Died Last Night"; "A Few of the Old Timers in Dodge City"; Samuel H. Williamson, "Seven Ways to Compute the Relative Value of a U.S. Dollar Amount, 1774 to present," MeasuringWorth, 2014, http://www.measuringworth.com /uscompare; Robert M. Wright, *Dodge City: The Cowboy Capital and the Great Southwest* (Wichita, KS: Wichita Eagle Press, 1913), 98.

12. Oliva, *Fort Dodge*, 31–32; Frederic R. Young, *Dodge City: Up through a Century in Story and Pictures* (Dodge City, KS: Boot Hill Museum, 1972), 15–16, 25. Since 1830, federal law had permitted a pioneer squatter to "preempt" a plot of land on the public domain in advance of a definitive government survey. Malcolm J. Rohrbough, *The Land Office Business: The Settlement and Administration of American Public Lands, 1789–1837* (New York: Oxford University Press, 1968), 205–219.

13. Cutler, *History*, 1561. For natural descriptions of southwest Kansas in pioneer days see Charles C. Lowther, *Dodge City, Kansas* (Philadelphia: Dorrance, 1940), 66; Samuel J. Crumbine, *Frontier Doctor* (Philadelphia: Dorrance, 1948), 43–44; Crum, *Dodge City and Ford County*, 76; Dodge, *Plains of the Great West*, 32–33, 38–40, 44.

14. David A. Dary, *The Buffalo Book: The Full Saga of the American Animal* (Chicago: Sage Books, 1974), 93–95; Charles M. Robinson III, *The Buffalo Hunters* (Austin, TX: Statehouse Press, 1995), 53–88; Andrew C. Isenberg, *The Destruction of the Bison: An Environmental History, 1750–1920* (New York: Cambridge University Press, 2000), 130–131; Young, *Dodge City*, 13–14; Dodge, *Plains of the Great West*, 116–117, 131–133, 140, 142. For the rapid constriction of the southwestern buffalo range between 1870 and 1875, compare maps in Ralph K. Andrist, *The Long Death: The Last Days of the Plains Indian* (New York: Macmillan, 1964), 173, with Dodge, *Plains of the Great West*, following xiv.

15. Glen Danford Bradley, *The Story of the Santa Fe* (Boston: Gorham Press, 1920), 85; James Marshall, *Santa Fe: The Railroad That Built an Empire* (New York: Random

House, 1945), 57–58, 396; Oliva, *Fort Dodge*, 31, 107; Young, *Dodge City*, 16–17, 25, 30; Dodge, *Plains of the Great West*, 140; *Leavenworth Times*, November 8, 1872.

16. Herman J. Fringer and Lyman B. Shaw affidavits, July 8, 1872, and Charter of the Dodge City Town Company of Ford County, August 15, 1872, Kansas Secretary of State Corporations Register, 4: 474–475, KSHS.

17. C. Robert Haywood, *The Merchant Prince of Dodge City: The Life and Times of Robert M. Wright* (Norman: University of Oklahoma Press, 1998), 25–27; Oliva, *Fort Dodge*, 89–93; Young, *Dodge City*, 12. Wright's name appears at the top of the 1872 list of company directors, and at the meeting of August 11, 1873, he is designated "President D.C. Town Company." Kansas Secretary of State Corporations Register, Amendments, A: 47, KSHS.

18. Universally referred to as Colonel Dodge because his wartime rank had been lieutenant colonel and, as was customary, he continued to hold it as a courtesy title. In official correspondence, however, Dodge identified himself by his permanent rank of major. Francis B. Heitman, *Historical Register and Dictionary of the United States Army*, 2 vols. (Washington, DC: Government Printing Office, 1903), 1: 377; Oliva, *Fort Dodge*, ii, 79. For the other original Fort Dodge officer/investors—Dr. William S. Tremaine and Captain Edward Moale—see Oliva, *Fort Dodge*, 101–102, 110. Three of the Fort Dodge civilian shareholders were connected with Robert Wright's post store: Andrew Anthony, his early business partner, and Herman Fringer and Alfred Peacock, store clerks. "Early History: Some Reminiscences of the Early Days of Dodge City," *Dodge City Democrat*, June 19, 1903. The fourth Fort Dodge civilian, Lyman Shaw, a quartermaster's clerk, died in Saint Louis in 1873. Saint Louis City Death Records, 1850–1902 (Saint Louis: Saint Louis Genealogical Society, 1999), 5: 287. The three off-site shareholders were Major David Taylor, Leavenworth paymaster; Samuel Weichselbaum, former Dodge and Larned clerk; and Alexander Johnson, the Santa Fe official tasked with handling the railroad's land sales. US Census, 1870: Kansas, Leavenworth County, Leavenworth City, Fourth Ward, dwelling 371; US Census, 1870: Kansas, Riley County, Ogden Township, dwelling 91; Young, *Dodge City*, 11, 20; Haywood, *Merchant Prince*, 39.

19. Congress had extended the preemption option to any bona fide group wishing to pool its resources and form a new community. For the pertinent federal and state laws on town site acquisition, see *Acts and Resolutions of the United States of America* (Washington, DC: Government Printing Office, 1867), 177–178; *The General Statutes of the State of Kansas* (Lawrence, KS: John Speer, 1868), 1073–1081. The July land description included a total of 314.47 acres. H. L. Sitler affidavit, July 13, 1872, and H. J. McGaffigan, Declaratory Statement, July 16, 1872, Ellis County Probate Court Record A, Ellis County Historical Society, Hays City, Kansas, 90.

20. David Taylor to A. Caldwell, February 20, 1873, Town Site Docket Case 87, Old Town Sites File, General Land Office, Record Group 49, National Archives, Washington, DC. For the 1868 survey map see Oliva, *Fort Dodge*, 31.

21. The August land description included 320 acres "more or less." Charter of the Dodge City Town Company of Ford County, August 15, 1872; Ford County Deed Record

A: 13–15, Office of the Register of Deeds, Dodge City. For the resurvey, see Ida Ellen Rath, *Early Ford County* (North Newton, KS: Mennonite Press, 1964), 32; *Leavenworth Times*, November 8, 1872. For a survey map of the established town, see "Plat of Dodge City, Ford Co. Kansas," *The Official State Atlas of Kansas: Compiled from Government Surveys, County Records and Personal Investigations* (Philadelphia: L. H. Everts, 1887), no page.

22. W. L. Jenkins to Willis Drummond, February 13, 1873 (enclosing depositions by Albert Emerson, W. S. Tremaine, and E. B. Kirk), Town Site Docket Case 87. Emerson was the company's Wichita attorney, and Major Ezra B. Kirk had purchased his shares a few months after the company's formation. R. M. Wright, "Personal Reminiscences of Frontier Life in Southwest Kansas," *Transactions of the Kansas State Historical Society* 7 (1901–1902), 75n.

23. A. Caldwell to Willis Drummond, March 15, 1873 (enclosing David Taylor to A. Caldwell, February 20, 1873), John Beatty to Willis Drummond, undated (received March 5, 1873), and W. L. Jenkins to Willis Drummond, May 13, 1873 (enclosing H. J. McGaffigan to W. L. Jenkins, May 9, 1873), Town Site Docket Case 87. For Taylor, see note 18. Tupper became a shareholder at the same time as Kirk. Wright, "Personal Reminiscences," 75n.

24. "To R[egister] & R[eceiver] May 24, [18]73, allowing change," endorsement on W. L. Jenkins to Willis Drummond, May 13, 1873, Town Site Docket Case 87; Kansas Land Tract Books, Wichita Land Office, Record Group 49, National Archives, Kansas City, 116: 72. The compilers of the later federal town site docket index mistakenly transcribed the docket number 87 for the final acreage received. Town Site Index [1], Old Town Sites File.

25. *Acts and Resolutions of the United States*, 177–178; *General Statutes of the State of Kansas*, 1073–1075; Ford County Deed Record A: 13–15, 62–63, 491–492, Office of the Register of Deeds, Dodge City; Kansas Secretary of State Corporations Register, Amendments, A: 47, KSHS. Unfortunately, only the July 8, 1872, list of town company shareholders is extant. Six of the nine shareholder/occupants (Wright, Peacock, Tremaine, Anthony, Fringer, and Sitler) purchased stock at the town company's formation and two (Kirk and Tupper) did so shortly thereafter. None of the remaining six original shareholders numbered among the nineteen occupants. Weichselbaum, Taylor, and Johnson had never been on site, Dodge and Moale transferred out of Fort Dodge in 1873, and Shaw had died. Oliva, *Fort Dodge*, 79, 110–111. Selling stock as late as December 1884, the company was dissolved in 1892. Rath, *Early Ford County*, 27, 30.

26. Cutler, *History*, 1561; Crum, *Dodge City and Ford County*, 305; US Census, 1880: Kansas, Chase County, Cottonwood Township, dwelling 164; *Ford County Globe* (Dodge City), March 7, June 13, 1882; *Dodge City Times*, January 22, 1885; *Kansas Cowboy* (Dodge City), May 2, 1885; Young, *Dodge City*, 15.

27. *Kinsley Valley Republican* in Craig Miner, *West of Wichita: Settling the High Plains of Kansas, 1865–1890* (Lawrence: University Press of Kansas, 1986), 96.

28. Ford County Deed Record, A: 13–15, 491–492, lists the town's official occupants and their spouses. George Hoover's lengthy interview in "Early History" con-

tains the arrival sequence of most of the pioneer businessmen. Young, *Dodge City*, 25, provides the initial locations of their businesses. For the spread of advanced literacy, see Thomas Augst, *The Clerk's Tale: Young Men and Moral Life in Nineteenth-Century America* (Chicago: University of Chicago Press, 2003).

29. Gerald Gribble, "George M. Hoover: Dodge City Pioneer" (M.A. thesis, Wichita State University, 1940), 1–2, 4; Howard J. Hoover, *Hoovers through the Ages* (Calgary, Alberta, Canada: Colin Bate Books, 1997), 150–151; US Census, 1870: Indiana, Warren County, Washington Township, dwelling 139 (Hoover's given name recorded as John); *Dodge City Times*, December 28, 1879; *Ford County Globe* , January 7, 1879; Kansas Census, 1875: Ford County, Dodge City, 13; Kansas Census, 1885: Ford County, Dodge City, dwelling 3; US Census, 1900: Kansas, Ford County, Dodge City, dwelling 65.

30. M. to *Topeka Commonwealth*, April 17, 1873; *Dodge City Globe*, June 18, 1914; *Dodge City Messenger*, February 26, 1874. Hoover's partner, John McDonald, became a heavy drinker and had to be let go some time before October 1876, eliminating him from consideration as a founding businessman. Margaret Carnahan, who in 1875 accompanied her parents to Dodge from Blanchester, Ohio, married Hoover in 1876. Gribble, "Hoover," 3–4.

31. Andrew Anthony and William Tremaine, the remaining original on-site shareholders, numbered among the nineteen official occupants, but Anthony laid out a cattle ranch west of Dodge and Tremaine continued to serve as post surgeon at Fort Dodge until transferred elsewhere in 1880. Cutler, *History*, 1560; Oliva, *Fort Dodge*, 102.

32. Haywood, *Merchant Prince*, 5–27, 41–42, 79–80; Young, *Dodge City*, 161. Wright's partner, Charles Rath, one of the nineteen legal occupants, dropped out of the business relationship in 1877, which is why he has not been included among the "first fellows." For Alice's parentage, see US Census, 1880: Kansas, Ford County, Dodge City, dwelling 235.

33. Cutler, *History*, 1561; US Census, 1850: Pennsylvania, Franklin County, Greene Township, dwelling 111; US Census, 1860: Ohio, Summit County, Green Township, dwelling 322; Company Muster-in and Descriptive Roll, May 2, 1864, Company C, 162d Regiment Ohio National Guard Infantry, Herman J. Fringer service records, Record Group 94, microfilm 554, roll 36, National Archives; Frederick H. Dyer, comp., *A Compendium of the War of the Rebellion* (Des Moines, IA: Dyer Publishing, 1908), 1552; US Census, 1880: Kansas, Ford County, Dodge City, dwelling 225.

34. The official records reveal that Alfred the Mormon teenager of 1856 and the later Alfred of Dodge City are one and the same—from their identical names (Alfred James Peacock) and dates of birth (around 1840) to Peacock's late-in-life sojourns in Salt Lake City. England Census, 1851: Hertfordshire County, Watford Parish, piece 1714, folio 216, p. 11; Passenger Lists of Vessels Arriving at New York, 1820–1957, microfilm 237, roll 163, line 1, list 490, p. 5, National Archives; David Roberts, *Devil's Gate: Brigham Young and the Great Mormon Handcart Tragedy* (New York: Simon and Schuster, 2008), 119–120, 185–193; James G. Willie Emigrating Company, Journal 1856, October 12, 1856, L.D.S. Church Archives, Salt Lake City, Utah; Quit Claim

Deeds, June 15, 1887, and November 15, 1888, and Warranty Deed, March 17, 1888 (all executed by Alfred and Emma Peacock at Salt Lake City), Abstract of Title for Lots 1 and 2 in Block 71, Ford County Register of Deeds, Kansas Heritage Center, Dodge City, Kansas.

35. US Census, 1870: Kansas, Ellis County, Hays City, dwelling 28; Kansas Census, 1875: Ford County, Dodge Township, 7; US Census, 1880: Kansas, Ford County, Dodge City, dwelling 51; US Census, 1870: Utah Territory, Cache County, Smithfield Township, dwelling 102.

36. "Early History"; Cutler, *History*, 1561; *Dodge City Messenger*, February 26, 1874; Young, *Dodge City*, 18, 25, 28, 42.

37. "The Old Scout Has Taken Last Trail," *Dodge City Kansas Journal*, September 13, 1912; F. A. Hobble, "Dodge City Pioneers and Buffalo Hunters," typescript copy of manuscript dated February 1922, 1–2, KSHS; D. Alexander Brown, *The Galvanized Yankees* (Urbana: University of Illinois Press, 1963). The sporting crowd nicknamed him "Dog" Kelley because of his devotion to a pack of hunting dogs. But contrary to modern accounts "this name," said one of Kelley's good friends, "was never applied to him by [the] Dodge City people." F. A. Hobble, "In Young Dodge," *Dodge City Globe*, February 26, 1941.

38. Kansas Census, 1875: Ford County, Dodge Township, 13; US Census, 1900: Kansas, Ford County, Dodge City, dwelling 363; *Leavenworth Times*, November 8, 1872; "Early History;" Report of Civilians Employed at Fort Hays, Returns from United States Military Posts, 1800–1916, Record Group 94, microfilm 617, roll 469, National Archives. Kelley's partner, Peter Beatty—not one of Dodge's official occupants—left the partnership in 1880. Ford County Deed Record, A: 5–6, Dodge City; *Dodge City Times*, March 29, May 24, 1879, December 11, 1880; *Ford County Globe*, April 6, 1880, January 4, 11, 1881; Young, *Dodge City*, 42–45, 64. Kelley and a woman named Nellie (birth surname unknown) married in the late 1880s. Kansas Census, 1895: Ford County, Dodge City, dwelling 228.

39. Crum, *Dodge City and Ford County*, 358–359; US Census, 1850 and 1860: New York, Genesee County, Pembroke Township, dwellings 905 and 202; Consent in Case of Minor, June 16, 1863, and Company Muster Role, November 1863–June 1864, 7th Michigan Cavalry Regiment, Alonzo B. Webster service records, Record Group 94, microfilm 545, roll 45, National Archives. Webster was hospitalized from November 1863 to May or June 1864 and from late July to December 1864. Carded Medical Records, Volunteers, Michigan: 7th Cavalry Regiment, Alonzo B. Webster, Record Group 94, entry 534, National Archives. For the remainder of his service see [Companies] M. and D. Roll of Men Transferred, November 17, 1865, and Company Muster-Out Roll, Company C, 1st Michigan Veteran Cavalry Regiment, Webster service records.

40. US Census, 1870: Kansas, Ellis County, Hays City, dwelling 11; Nyle H. Miller and Joseph W. Snell, *Why the West Was Wild* (Topeka: Kansas State Historical Society, 1963), 191, 197; R. W. Evans in *Ford County Republican* (Dodge City), April 20, 1887; Young, *Dodge City*, 161; Kansas Census, 1875: Ford County, Dodge Township, 13; US Census, 1880: Kansas, Ford County, Dodge Township (North of Arkansas River),

dwelling 1; *Dodge City Messenger*, February 26, 1874. For Amanda's birth surname and elopement, see *Kansas City Times,* May 10, 1883.

41. *The United States Biographical Dictionary: Kansas Volume* (Chicago: S. Lewis and Company, 1879), 411; Crum, *Dodge City and Ford County*, 146; Tim Wenzl, "Family Heritage Reaches from 'Gateway to the West' to Dodge," *Dodge City Globe*, June 4, 1979; "Dodge City Mayors," *Dodge City Journal*, August 25, 1938; US Census, 1860: Illinois, Jo Davies County, Woodbine Township, dwelling 4542; Dyer, *Compendium,* 1552; Mark K. Christ, *Civil War Arkansas, 1863: The Battle for a State* (Norman: University of Oklahoma Press, 2010); Company E, 2d Colorado Infantry Regiment, and Company C, 2d Colorado Calvary Regiment, Richard W. Evans service records, Record Group 94, microfilm 534, roll 1, National Archives. For Evans's multiple short-term hospitalizations, see his service record and Carded Medical Records, Volunteers, Colorado: 2d Cavalry Regiment, R. W. Evans, Record Group 94, entry 534, National Archives.

42. *The United States Biographical Dictionary: Kansas Volume*, 412; Crum, *Dodge City and Ford County*, 147; Young, *Dodge City,* 117, 161; Wenzl, "Family Heritage Reaches from 'Gateway to the West' to Dodge"; "Dodge City Mayors"; US Census, 1870: Illinois, Jo Davies County, Woodbine Township, dwelling 139 (Sarah's Illinois residence); US Census, 1870: Kansas, Ellis County, Hays City, dwelling 10; *Dodge City Messenger*, February 26, 1874; Kansas Census, 1875: Ford County, Dodge Township, 13.

43. Cutler, *History of Kansas*, 1562; *U.S. Biographical Dictionary*, 516–517; Crum, *Dodge City and Ford County*, 375–376; Young, *Dodge City*, 41–44, 54, 161, 148; *Dodge City Messenger*, February 26, 1874; Kansas Census, 1875: Ford County, Dodge Township, 7.

44. *Globe Live Stock Journal* (Dodge City), April 14, 1885; US Census, 1870: Colorado, Greenwood County, Kit Carson Township, dwellings 17 and 18; Young, *Dodge City*, 161. While living in Dodge, Jennie Collar said she was a member of the Episcopal Church. Yet when she died in 1899—a time when many American Jews were experiencing a renewed religiosity—Jennie was buried in the Jewish cemetery in Denver. Jonathan D. Sarna, *American Judaism: A History* (New Haven, CT: Yale University Press, 2004), 133–144; JewishGen, comp., *JewishGen Online Worldwide Burial Registry*, Provo, Utah: Ancestry.com Operations Inc., 2008; *Dodge City Democrat*, March 25, 1893; *Dodge City Globe Republican*, January 5, April 27, 1899.

45. Two documents confirm that by October 1872 the Collars had arrived in Dodge. Morris signed a memorial from Dodge to the Kansas governor on October 14, and Jacob was one of the first Dodge Citians to be enumerated in a special Ford County census begun on October 21, 1872. Ford County Commissioners Journal A: 1, KSHS; Ford County Census, 1873, Governors' Correspondence, T. A. Osborn, Correspondence Received (Counties), KSHS. See also Kansas Census, 1875: Ford County, Dodge Township, 7, 21; *Dodge City Messenger*, February 26, June 25, 1874; *Dodge City Times*, December 22, 1877; Young, *Dodge City*, 42–44.

46. US Census, 1860: Missouri, Saint Louis County, City of Saint Louis, Ward 8, dwelling 442; US Census, 1870: Missouri, Saint Louis County, City of Saint Louis, Ward 10, dwelling 223; Saint Louis Marriage Index, 1804–1876 (Saint Louis: Saint Louis Genealogical Society, 1999), 15: 574.

47. Cutler, *History*, 1350–1351, 1561. No George B. Cox anywhere near his age is listed in the approximately 80,000 records of Georgia's Confederate troops. For Cox's post–Civil War service, see "Register of Enlistments, United States Army [1867]," and "Alterations since Last Returns among the Enlisted Men," October 1867, and "Brief Record of Events during the Year [1867]," Company K, 3d United States Infantry Regiment, Record Group 94, microfilm 233, roll 33, and microfilm 665, roll 34, National Archives; US Census, 1870: Kansas, Pawnee County, Fort Larned, dwelling 1; US Census, 1860 and 1870: New Jersey, Mercer County, Lawrence Township, dwellings 147 and 162. In the postwar years Cox's parents lived in Lafayette, Alabama. *Ford County Globe*, September 21, 1880.

48. Cutler, *History*, 1561; Kansas Census, 1875: Ford County, Dodge Township, 21; *Newton Kansan*, November 28, 1872; Young, *Dodge City*, 43, 46, 58, 64.

49. C. Robert Haywood, *Victorian West: Class and Culture in Kansas Cattle Towns* (Lawrence: University Press of Kansas, 1991), 261, 268, and the entirety of chapter 13 for a discussion of Victorian women in the West.

50. Deane Monahan, *The Arkansas Valley and Its Great Railway* (Topeka: Kansas Magazine Publishing Company, 1873), engraving facing p. 18; Young, *Dodge City*, 25; "Plat of Dodge City, Ford Co. Kansas." For a block-by-block tour of downtown Dodge in the later 1870s see Fredric R. Young, *The Delectable Burg: An Irreverent History of Dodge City—1872–1886* (Dodge City: Boot Hill Museum, 2009), 48–61.

51. "Early History."


CHAPTER 2: YEAR OF LIVING DANGEROUSLY

1. Richard Irving Dodge, *The Plains of the Great West and Their Inhabitants* (New York; G. P. Putnam's Sons, 1877), 117; Richard Irving Dodge, *Our Wild Indians: Thirty-three Years' Personal Experience among the Red Men of the Great West* (Hartford: A. D. Worthington, 1882), 619, 623; Richard Dodge to Thomas Osborn, July 5, 1873, Governors' Correspondence, T. A. Osborn (Cities and Towns), Kansas State Historical Society (KSHS), Topeka.

2. "Early History: Some Reminiscences of the Early Days of Dodge City," *Dodge City Democrat*, June 19, 1903; Robert M. Wright, *Dodge City: The Cowboy Capital and the Great Southwest* (Wichita, KS: Wichita Eagle Press, 1913), 171.

3. We are indebted to Waldo Koop's compilation of Kansas newspaper reports of frontier violence (the Waldo Koop Collection) housed in the Kansas State Historical Society. Users should be aware, however, that it contains many transcription errors.

4. Wright, *Dodge City*, 169; "Early History." "Mr. Kelly" is founding businessman James Kelley.

5. *Hutchinson News*, September 5, 1872; George W. Brown, "Life and Adventures of George W. Brown," ed. William E. Connelley, *Collections of the Kansas State Historical Society* 17 (1926–1928): 116.

6. *Topeka Commonwealth*, September 8, 1872. Lewis Jansen's encounter with Reyn-

olds occurred some time before August 12, when the conductor suffered an on-the-job accident from which he died at Great Bend. Mentor to *Commonwealth*, August 17, 1872.

7. The original petition sent to Governor Harvey is no longer extant. Young's name and the dates on which he compiled the document appear on the special census. Ford County Census, 1873, Governors' Correspondence, T. A. Osborn (Counties), KSHS.

8. *Leavenworth Commercial*, November 21, 1872; *Wichita Beacon* in *Kansas City Times*, November 22, 1872. Kelley of Kelley & Hunt is the same James Kelley as in note 4 above.

9. Knarf in *Leavenworth Commercial*, November 21, 1872; *Kansas City Times*, November 17, 1872.

10. *Newton Kansan*, November 28, 1872; "Early History."

11. *Topeka Commonwealth*, December 7, 1872; Wright, *Dodge City*, 169. Wright confuses this Morehouse-Hennessy encounter with the earlier Morehouse-Langford brawl described in the Introduction. C. D. Morehouse to J. B. Edwards, December 9, 1872, Early Dodge City Letters, Kansas Heritage Center, Dodge City, Kansas.

12. *Oxford Press* in *Wichita Eagle*, January 2, 1873; Wright, *Dodge City*, 170.

13. Nyle H. Miller and Joseph W. Snell, *Why the West Was Wild* (Topeka: Kansas State Historical Society, 1963), 42–57, 118, 642–643, 645; Gary L. Roberts, "From Tin Star to Hanging Tree: The Short Career and Violent Times of Billy Brooks," *The Prairie Scout* (1975), 3: 23; Dodge City Census, 1873, entry 408. Bridges resided at Fort Dodge as late as June 1873, when he played a part in arresting the William Taylor murderers. *Kansas City Times*, July 15, 1873.

14. Federal Writers Project, *Kansas: A Guide to the Sunflower State* (New York: Viking Press, 1939), 180; William MacLeod Raine, "Dodge," *Liberty*, May 19, 1928, pp. 13–14.

15. Miller and Snell, *Why the West Was Wild*, 45. Roberts, "From Tin Star to Hanging Tree," 24–27, explores disagreement over the undocumented murders Brooks supposedly committed in Dodge City.

16. *Topeka Commonwealth*, December 31, 1872; B. Vesper, "The Pluck of a Poor German Boy," *The Trail Drivers of Texas*, ed. J. Marvin Hunter, rev. ed. (Nashville: Cokesbury Press, 1925), 893.

17. *Kansas City Times*, January 1, 7, 1873.

18. Dodge City Census, 1873, Herman J. Fringer, Notary Public, entries 9, 53, 260, 299, 477, 479, 577.

19. *Topeka Commonwealth*, August 17, 1872, January 23, 1873; Knarf to *Leavenworth Commercial*, February 26, 1873. The term "Woodhulleries" is a reference to feminist Victoria Woodhull, who in the 1870s gained widespread notoriety as a proponent of "free love."

20. *Newton Kansan*, January 23, 1873.

21. Johnson to *Topeka Commonwealth*, February 2, 1873; Harry (Sam) Young, *Hard Knocks: A Life Story of the Vanishing West* (Portland, OR: Wells and Company, 1915), 61–62.

22. Walker in *Topeka Commonwealth*, February 11, 1873.

23. *Kansas City Journal of Commerce*, February 15, 1873; *Kansas City Times*, February 15, 1873; C. W. M. in *Leavenworth Commercial*, February 16, 1873; *Denver Times*, February 17, 1873.

24. Dodge to Osborn, July 5, 1873, Governors' Correspondence. The technicalities of vigilance committee organization, as formalized in early San Francisco, are described in Hubert Howe Bancroft, *Popular Tribunals*, 2 vols. (San Francisco: History Company, 1887), 1: 211–212. For a recent reexamination of the San Francisco paradigm, see Kevin J. Mullen, *Dangerous Strangers: Minority Newcomers and Criminal Violence in the Urban West, 1850–2000* (New York: Palgrave Macmillan, 2005), 13–28. For a revisionist study of the equally famous vigilantism in Montana Territory, which more or less replicated the San Francisco model, see Frederick Allen, *A Decent, Orderly Lynching: The Montana Vigilantes* (Norman: University of Oklahoma Press, 2004).

25. Wright, *Dodge City*, 171.

26. Joseph W. Snell, "Diary of a Buffalo Hunter, 1872–1873," *Kansas Historical Quarterly* 31 (1965): 363; H. H. Raymond, "Notes on Diary of H. H. Raymond" (typescript), 7, KSHS.

27. *Atchison Patriot*, March 15, 1873.

28. "Peacock & Scott's billiard hall" is mentioned by Knarf in *Leavenworth Commercial*, February 26, 1873.

29. Wright, *Dodge City*, 171–172.

30. Snell, "Diary of a Buffalo Hunter," 364; Raymond, "Notes on Diary," 9–12.

31. Carl Ludvig Hendricks, "Recollections of a Swedish Buffalo Hunter, 1871–1873," *Swedish Pioneer Historical Quarterly* 32 (1981): 204; *Topeka Commonwealth*, March 21, 1873.

32. Ford County Commissioners' Journal A: 1, KSHS; Thomas A. Osborn to Herman J. Fringer, April 8, 1873, Governors' Letters, 2: 21, KSHS.

33. *State of Kansas, ex rel. Attorney General v. Board of Commissioners of Ford County, et al.* (1874), *Kansas Reports*, 12: 441–447.

34. Dodge to Osborn, July 5, 1873, Governors' Correspondence.

35. C. Robert Haywood, "'No Less a Man': Blacks in Cow Town Dodge City, 1876–1886, *Western Historical Quarterly* 19 (May 1988): 161–170; *Ford County Globe* (Dodge City), January 22, 1878, October 9, 1883; *Dodge City Times*, July 12, 1883; Kansas Census, 1870: Ford County, Fort Dodge, 10, dwelling 13; H. H. Raymond to J. Evetts Haley, December 6, 1934, Raymond Collection, KSHS; Wright, *Dodge City*, 172.

36. Scotty's Friend in *Topeka Commonwealth*, June 7, 1873. "B'hoy," New York music-hall slang, supposedly mimicked the Irish pronunciation of "boy." Luc Sante, *Low Life: Lures and Snares of Old New York* (New York: Farrar Straus Giroux, 1991), 77. A legacy of the bitter competition between the Irish immigrants and free blacks for the lowest of low-end employment on the East Coast, the Irish developed, as one labor historian put it, "an almost maniacal antagonism toward African-Americans." Bruce Nelson, *Divided We Stand: American Workers and the Struggle for Black Equality* (Princeton: Princeton University Press, 2001), xxxiv, xxxviii. See also Kerby A. Miller,

*Emigrants and Exiles: Ireland and the Irish Exodus to North America* (New York: Oxford University Press, 1985), 267, 318.

37. *Kansas City Times*, July 15, 1873.

38. Dodge to Osborn and Osborn to Dodge, June 4, 1873, Governors' Correspondence. For the telegraph line between the fort and the town see "Medical Histories of Posts," vol. 79 (Fort Dodge), Record Group 94, entry 547 (March 21, 1873), National Archives.

39. *Kansas City Times*, July 15, 1873; Dodge to Osborn, July 5, 1873, Governors' Correspondence; Special Order 79, June 5, 1873, Special Orders and Orders, 1866–1882, Fort Dodge, Kansas, Record Group 98, National Archives, KSHS; Snell, "Diary of a Buffalo Hunter," 375. Joseph Snell reads "Gilkerson" for what is most probably Gilson and "Mick's" for what is obviously the Hicks brothers. Taylor's well-attended funeral was held in his home town. *Leavenworth Commercial*, June 10, 1873.

40. *Newton Kansan*, June 12, 1873.

41. *Kansas City Times*, July 15, 1873; Glen Danford Bradley, *The Story of the Santa Fe* (Boston: Gorham Press, 1920), 95; "Proclamation of Reward for John Scott, July 21, 1873," Governors' Correspondence, T. A. Osborn (Crime and Criminals), KSHS.

42. Dodge to Osborn, July 5, 1873, Governors' Correspondence. For a brief survey of "socially constructive" vigilante committees taken over by criminal elements, see Richard Maxwell Brown, *Strain of Violence: Historical Studies of American Violence and Vigilantism* (New York: Oxford University Press, 1975), 121–123.

43. Criminal Docket A: 1, 8, 10, and Judge's Journal A: 7, 13, Ford County District Court Records, 1874–1910, KSHS; C. F. Dassler, *Compiled Laws of Kansas, 1879* (Saint Louis: W. J. Gilbert, 1879), 328–329; *Great Bend Register*, July 30, August 13, 1874; Kansas State Penitentiary Ledger A: 191–192, KSHS.

44. M. V. Cutler to Thomas Osborn, July 14, 1873, Governors' Correspondence, T. A. Osborn (Cities and Towns), KSHS. Cutler was the county attorney elected on June 5.

45. Dodge to Osborn, July 5, 1873, Governors' Correspondence; *Newton Kansan*, July 10, 1873.

46. Osborn to Cutler, July 9, 1873, Governors' Letters, 2: 131; *State of Kansas v. Ford County* (1874), *Kansas Reports*, 12: 441–447; *The Laws of the State of Kansas* (Lawrence, KS: George W. Martin, 1874), 8.

47. Coroner's jury verdict in *Topeka Commonwealth*, July 25, 1873; Roberts, "From Tin Star to Hanging Tree," 77–83. Bill Ellis's father commented on his son's descent into a "noisy brawler" in the *Leavenworth Commercial*, July 23, 1873.

48. J. B. D. in *Topeka Commonwealth*, July 25, 1873.

49. Clair V. McKanna Jr., *Homicide, Race, and Justice in the American West, 1880–1920* (Tucson: University of Arizona Press, 1997), 19–20.

50. Was Dodge City's *annus horribilis* a unique experience? The first year of life in another town on the Great Plains, North Platte, Nebraska, in 1866–1867, suggests that it was not. Mark R. Ellis, *Law and Order in Buffalo Bill's Country: Legal Culture and Com-*

*munity on the Great Plains, 1867–1910* (Lincoln: University of Nebraska Press, 2007), 20–21, 26–27.

51. This body count corrects the tabulated Dodge City entries for killings given in Robert R. Dykstra, *The Cattle Towns* (New York: Alfred A. Knopf, 1968), 144. The yearly data for Dodge City in the cowboy era should read:

| 1876 | 1877 | 1878 | 1879 | 1880 | 1881 | 1882 | 1883 | 1884 | 1885 | 1886 |
|------|------|------|------|------|------|------|------|------|------|------|
| 1 | 0 | 5 | 2 | 1 | 1 | 0 | 3 | 3 | 1 | 1 |

For scholars' contention over historical homicide rates, see Robert R. Dykstra, "Quantifying the Wild West: The Problematic Statistics of Frontier Violence," *Western Historical Quarterly* 40 (Autumn 2009): 334–335.

CHAPTER 3: DEADLY PROSE

1. Frederick Law Olmsted, *A Journey through Texas; or, a Saddle-Trip on the Southwestern Frontier* (New York: Dix, Edwards, 1857), 158–159; Albert D. Richardson, *From the Great River to the Great Ocean* (Hartford: American Publishing, 1867), 226; Horace Greeley, *An Overland Journey from New York to San Francisco in the Summer of 1859* (New York: C. M. Saxton, Barker and Company, 1860), 159.

2. *San Francisco California Chronicle*, December 30, 1854; Kevin J. Mullen to Robert Dykstra, March 18, 2008; Thomas J. Dimsdale, *The Vigilantes of Montana* (Virginia City: A. J. Noyes, 1866), 22; Frederick Allen, *A Decent Orderly Lynching: The Montana Vigilantes* (Norman: University of Oklahoma Press, 2004), 9, 117.

3. The dime novel (or "yellow-back" novel, since typically bound in a yellow or orange cover) was inaugurated in 1860 by the New York publishing firm of Beadle & Company. For the frontier as a common setting in these novels, see Russel Nye, *The Unembarrassed Muse: The Popular Arts in America* (New York: Dial Press, 1970), 200–207, 285–287; Daryl Jones, *The Dime Novel Western* (Bowling Green, OH: Popular Press, 1978), 6, 61–99; Bill Brown, "Reading the West: Cultural and Historical Background," *Reading the West: An Anthology of Dime Westerns*, ed. Brown (Boston: Bedford Books, 1997), 14–30, 34; Don Russell, *The Lives and Legends of Buffalo Bill* (Norman: University of Oklahoma Press, 1960), 192–208, 494.

4. Francis Bret Harte, *The Luck of Roaring Camp, and Other Sketches* (Boston: J. R. Osgood, 1870), 1; Mark Twain, *Roughing It* (Hartford: American Publishing, 1872), 339, 343–345; *The Compact Edition of the Oxford English Dictionary*, 3 vols. (New York: Oxford University Press, 1987), 3: 331; *Atlantic Monthly* 25 (May 1870): 633.

5. *Hutchinson News*, December 19, 1872; Geo. P. Rowell & Company, *American Newspaper Directory* (New York: Geo. P. Rowell, 1872), 61.

6. *Topeka Commonwealth*, September 8, December 7, 31, 1872, January 23, February 2, 11, June 7, 1873; *Newton Kansan*, June 12, 1873.

7. *Leavenworth Commercial*, July 23, 1873; *Wichita Eagle*, July 24, 1873.

8. *Newton Kansan*, December 12, 1872; *Wichita Eagle*, January 2, 1873; *Dickinson County Chronicle* (Abilene), February 20, 1873; *Lawrence Journal* in *Emporia News*, February 21, 1873; *Marion County Record* (Marion Center), March 29, 1873. The quotation is from the *Atchison Patriot*, March 15, 1873.

9. *Kansas City Times*, November 17, 22, 1872, January 1, 7, February 15, 1873; *Kansas City Journal of Commerce*, February 15, 1873.

10. *New York Times*, February 17, 1873; *New York Tribune*, June 16, 1873.

11. *Kansas City Times*, November 17, 1872, January 7, February 15, 1873; *Kansas City Journal of Commerce*, February 15, 1873; *Topeka Commonwealth*, January 14, March 18, 1873; *Atchison Patriot*, March 13, 1873; *Ellsworth Reporter*, March 27, 1873.

12. *Kansas City News* in *Topeka Commonwealth*, March 1, 1873; J. Freeland to *Topeka Commonwealth*, March 4, 1873; *Kansas City Journal*, March 14, 1873; C. in *Kansas City Journal of Commerce* in *Topeka Commonwealth*, March 14, 1873.

13. *New York Tribune*, June 16, 1873.

14. *Kansas City Times*, July 15, 1873; Judges Journal, A: 33–34, Ford County District Court Records; Ford County Commissioners Journal A: 1, 8, Kansas State Historical Society (KSHS), Topeka; Robert R. Dykstra, *The Cattle Towns* (New York: Alfred A. Knopf, 1968), 215–220, 266–284.

15. Judges Journal, A: 33–34, Ford County District Court Records; Ford County Commissioners Journal A: 1, 8; US Census, 1850: Massachusetts, Bristol County, New Bedford, dwelling 2179; *Kansas City Star*, January 7, 1896. For Bassett's military service, see Samuel P. Bates, *History of Pennsylvania Volunteers, 1861–5*, 5 vols. (Harrisburg: B. Singerly, 1869–71) 5: 436–437, 802, 815; Company Muster-in Roll, July 15, 1864, and Company Muster-out Roll, November 21, 1864, Company A, 196th Pennsylvania Infantry Regiment; Company Muster and Descriptive Roll, February 14, 1865, and Company Muster-out Roll, November 18, 1865, Company I, 213th Pennsylvania Infantry Regiment; Declaration of Recruit, December 13, 1865, 2d Regiment of US Cavalry, Charles E. Bassett service records, Record Group 94, microfilm 554, roll 6, National Archives, Washington DC; Nyle H. Miller and Joseph W. Snell, *Why the West Was Wild* (Topeka: Kansas State Historical Society, 1963), 31.

16. *Kansas City Star*, January 7, 1896; Ford County Census, 1873, Governors' Correspondence, T. A. Osborn, Correspondence Received (Counties), entry 306, KSHS.

17. Ford County Commissioners Journal A: 5, 22, 48; Miller and Snell, *Why the West Was Wild*, 217–221.

18. Voyageur in *Topeka Commonwealth*, October 22, 1873; *Dodge City Messenger*, February 26, 1874.

19. *Hutchinson News*, December 4, 1873; Jas. in *Topeka Commonwealth*, August 6, 1875; Criminal Docket A: 24, and Judges Journal A: 40, Ford County District Court Records, 1874–1910, KSHS; Ford County Commissioners Journal A: 90, 154, 156.

20. Donald J. Berthrong, *The Southern Cheyennes* (Norman: University of Oklahoma Press, 1963), 372–405; Thomas W. Kavanagh, *The Comanches: A History, 1706–1875* (Lincoln: University of Nebraska Press, 1996), 444–453; Dykstra, *Cattle Towns*, 16–62.

21. Judges Journal, A: 33–34, Ford County District Court Records; Kansas Census, 1875: Ford County, Dodge City; Carl F. Etrick, *Dodge City Semi-Centennial Souvenir* (Dodge City: Etrick Company, 1922), 6. For peace officers' positions and the names of men filling them, see Miller and Snell, *Why the West Was Wild*, 642–645. For the role of a police officer in Dodge and elsewhere, see Andrew C. Isenberg, *Wyatt Earp: A Vigilante Life* (New York: Hill and Wang, 2013), 92–93.

22. *Ford County Globe* (Dodge City), May 7, 1878; J. Marvin Hunter, ed., *The Trail Drivers of Texas*, rev. ed. (Nashville: Cokesbury Press, 1925), 453; *Topeka Commonwealth*, July 25, 1873; Harry E. Gryden, "Dodge City's Sensation," *National Police Gazette* (New York), July 21, 1883, p. 5.

23. The photo was taken between the day in late October 1878 that a Prickly Ash Bitters agent was posting up advertisements around town and the day in April 1879 that the town council ordered Front Street's disused wells filled in and their curbing dismantled. *Ford County Globe*, October 18, 1878; *Dodge City Times*, April 12, 1879; Frederic R. Young, *Dodge City: Up through a Century in Story and Pictures* (Dodge City, KS: Boot Hill Museum, 1972), 158–159. For the replacement notices, see *Dodge City Times*, June 7, 1879.

24. Ford County Commissioners Journal A: 25, 32; Dodge City Ordinance Book, 1: 4, KSHS; Wright, *Dodge City*, 174–175.

25. Stuart N. Lake, *Wyatt Earp: Frontier Marshal* (Boston: Houghton Mifflin, 1931), 143.

26. Pete Jinks in *Atchison Champion*, April 6, 1876; Roger Jay, "Close Shave for the Barber of Dodge City," *Wild West*, February 2008, pp. 50–53, 55; Criminal Docket, A: 29–30, 38, and Judges Journal, A: 72, Ford County District Court Records, 1874–1910, KSHS.

27. *Ford County Globe*, March 5, 1878; Miller and Snell, *Why the West Was Wild*, 291–292; Robert K. DeArment, *Bat Masterson: The Man and the Legend* (Norman: University of Oklahoma Press, 1979), 102.

28. Miller and Snell, *Why the West Was Wild*, 31–32, 295–297, 643. This particular Lone Star Dance Hall was in business from 1875 through 1878. Fredric R. Young, *The Delectable Burg: An Irreverent History of Dodge City—1872 to 1886* (Dodge City, KS: Boot Hill Museum, 2009), 57.

29. *Ford County Globe*, March 5, 1878.

30. DeArment, *Bat Masterson*, 103–108; Miller and Snell, *Why the West Was Wild*, 299–306; Bob Palmquist, "Who Killed Jack Wagner?" *True West* 40 (October 1993): 14–19.

31. *Dodge City Times*, April 20, May 11, May 18, 1878; *Ford County Globe*, May 14, 1878; Casey Tefertiller, *Wyatt Earp: The Life behind the Legend* (New York: J. Wiley, 1997), 22; *Kansas City Star*, January 7, 1896; *Dodge City Globe-Democrat*, January 9, 1896.

32. *Dodge City Times*, May 11, 18, August 10, 17, September 7, 1878; Many Citizens in *Dodge City Times*, August 3, 1878; Beppo in *Ford County Globe*, May 21, July 9 (city expenditures: $9,094), August 10, 1878; *Globe Live Stock Journal* (Dodge City), April 14, 1885.

33. Miller and Snell, *Why the West Was Wild*, 273–276.

34. On August 27, six days after Hoy's death, the *Ford County Globe* (Dodge City) mourned his passing. Tefertiller, *Wyatt Earp*, 23–25. Isenberg attributes Hoy's wounding to Earp and Bat Masterson, instead of his brother James. Isenberg, *Wyatt Earp*, 85.

35. Miller and Snell, *Why the West Was Wild*, 350–352.

36. *Dodge City Times*, October 14, 1876; *Ford County Globe*, January 29, 1878; Herbert to Dear Father in *Dodge City Times*, May 19, 1877; C. Emigrant to Dear Father in *Dodge City Times*, January 19, 1878; *Atchison Champion* in *Ford County Globe*, April 22, 1879.

37. *Ford County Globe*, January 29, 1878, March 18, 1879; *Topeka Commonwealth*, April 6, 1873; *Dodge City Times*, October 20, 1877; *Troy Budget* in *Dodge City Times*, April 13, 1878.

38. Pete Jinks in *Atchison Champion*, April 6, 1876; W.N.M. in *Hays City Sentinel*, March 23, 1877; F. in *Hays City Sentinel*, September 14, 1877; *Quincy Commercial Review* in *Dodge City Times*, April 27, 1878.

39. For a good discussion of the ever-fluctuating saloon and dance hall scene, see Young, *Delectable Burg*, chapter 3.

40. *Sterling Gazette* in *Dodge City Times*, June 22, 1878; Hamilton Bell in *Ford County Globe*, February 17, 1879; Eddie Foy and A. F. Harlow, *Clowning through Life* (New York: E. P. Dutton, 1928), 106; Kicking Bird in *Kansas City Times*, September 10, 1883; Samuel J. Crumbine, *Frontier Doctor* (Philadelphia: Dorrance, 1948), 26. For a contemporary photograph of the interior of one of these emporiums, see Dykstra, *Cattle Towns*, illustration 22.

41. Henri in *Kansas City Times* in *Dodge City Times*, June 9, 1877; *Sterling Gazette* in *Dodge City Times*, June 22, 1878. For an elaborate explanation of faro, see Isenberg, *Wyatt Earp*, 97–102.

42. *Kansas Cowboy* (Dodge City), September 26, 1885.

43. *Sterling Gazette* in *Dodge City Times*, June 22, 1878; unnamed New York City newspaper in *Dodge City Times*, November 16, 1878; L.S.A. in *Washington Star* in *Ford County Globe*, January 1, 1878; *New York Times*, June 17, 1878; *Kokomo Dispatch* in *Dodge City Times*, August 17, 1878.

44. *Dodge City Times*, December 29, 1877, March 16, 1878.

45. For a map of Dodge City in 1879–1882, and for the town's spatial configuration in August 1879 and in June 1882, see Young, *Dodge City*, 63 and front and back end papers.

46. *Ford County Globe*, April 22, May 6, August 12, November 11, 1879; *Dodge City Times*, September 27, 1879; Young, *Dodge City*, 160. For the name Gospel Ridge, see *Dodge City Times*, September 8, 1877. For illustrations of local civic, domestic, and religious architecture in the mid-1880s, see C. S. Burch, *Hand-Book of Ford County, Kansas* (Chicago: C. S. Burch Publishing, 1887), title page, 1–10, 15–20, 26. For the "respectable" community's middle-class mores, see C. Robert Haywood, *Victorian West: Class and Culture in Kansas Cattle Towns* (Lawrence: University Press of Kansas, 1991), 33–63, 90–111.

47. Young, *Dodge City*, 44, 54–58, 64; *Dodge City Times*, June 14, 1879; Compact Edition of the *Oxford English Dictionary* (New York: Oxford University Press, 1987), 1: 653.

48. Young, *Dodge City*, 59–60.

## CHAPTER 4: CASE HISTORIES

1. C. F. W. Dassler, *Compiled Laws of Kansas, 1879* (Saint Louis: W. J. Gilbert, 1879), 321–325, 733–773; *Ford County Globe* (Dodge City), January 24, 1880.

2. *Ford County Globe*, October 15, 1878, January 1, 1879. For a thumbnail sketch of the town's newspapers see Frederic R. Young, *Dodge City: Up through a Century in Story and Pictures* (Dodge City: Boot Hill Museum, 1972), 165. The Dodge City newspaper stories about the Hand killing and its aftermath are reprinted in Nyle H. Miller and Joseph W. Snell, *Why the West Was Wild* (Topeka: Kansas State Historical Society, 1963), 350–352, 361–365.

3. Miller and Snell, *Why the West Was Wild*, 350–351, 361; US Census, 1870: Missouri, Pettis County, Sedalia, dwelling 596; Theodore Hand–Dora Crews marriage, November 22, 1871, Saint Louis Marriage Index, 1804–1876 (Saint Louis: Genealogical Society, 1999), 15: 180; Theodore Hand service record in Iowa Adjutant General, *Roster and Record of Iowa Soldiers in the War of the Rebellion* (Des Moines: E. H. English, 1908), 5: 778; *Dora Hand v. Theodore Hand*, Records of the Ford County District Court, Civil Case Files, Kansas Heritage Center, Dodge City. Earle R. Forrest, "Dora Hand: The Dance Hall Singer of Old Dodge City," *Westerners Brand Book, Los Angeles Corral* 7 (1957): 47–58, claims to tell the "authentic story" of Dora Hand based on interviews in 1926 with Simpson and other old-timers. Virtually the entire Forrest article is romantic fiction.

4. Jane Clements Monday and Frances Brannen Vick, *Petra's Legacy: The South Texas Ranching Empire of Petra Vela and Mifflin Kenedy* (College Station: Texas A&M University Press, 2007), 168–169, 177, 182, 195, 292; Miller and Snell, *Why the West Was Wild*, 218; Robert K. DeArment, *Bat Masterson: The Man and the Legend* (Norman: University of Oklahoma Press, 1979), 116–118. Earp's latest biographer speculates that Kenedy was obsessed with Hand and intended to kill either Hand's supposed paramour, James Kelley, or Hand herself. Andrew C. Isenberg, *Wyatt Earp: A Vigilante Life* (New York: Hill and Wang, 2013), 95–96.

5. DeArment, *Bat Masterson*, 120–124; Miller and Snell, *Why the West Was Wild*, 352, 363–365; William G. Cutler, *History of the State of Kansas* (Chicago, 1883), 444.

6. Citing not a single source, Harry Sinclair Drago, in *The Legend Makers: Tales of the Old-Time Peace Officers and Desperadoes of the Frontier* (New York: Dodd, Mead, 1975), 76–81, tells the story of Mifflin Kenedy's October venture in Dodge and the supposed sellout of the town's lawmen.

7. DeArment, *Bat Masterson*, 124; Miller and Snell, *Why the West Was Wild*, 365; Monday and Vick, *Petra's Legacy*, 333–335.

8. DeArment, *Bat Masterson*, 124.

9. US Census, 1850 and 1860: Wisconsin, Green County, Sylvester Township, dwellings 24 and 2014; *Dodge City Times*, December 15, 1877; Stuart N. Lake, *Wyatt Earp: Frontier Marshal* (Boston: Houghton Mifflin, 1931), 223; Eugene Cunningham, *Triggernometry: A Gallery of Gunfighters* (Caldwell, ID: Caxton Printers, 1941), 417–418.

10. US Census, 1870: Missouri, Jackson County, Kansas City, Ward 3, dwelling 1; *Ford County Globe*, April 8, 1879.

11. War Department, *Daily Bulletin of Simultaneous Weather Reports . . . for the Month of April 1879* (Washington: Government Printing Company, 1879), 15–17; *Ford County Globe*, April 8, 1879. For a photograph of the Long Branch interior in the mid-1880s, see Miller and Snell, *Why the West Was Wild*, 117.

12. The *Ford County Globe*, April 8, 1879, featured a full account of the shootout, including the eyewitnesses' testimony. See also *Dodge City Times*, April 12, 1879; Lake, *Wyatt Earp*, 223–224; Stanley Vestal, *Queen of Cowtowns: Dodge City* (New York: Harper and Row, 1972), 194–195. According to DeArment, *Bat Masterson*, 125–126, Masterson also believed that Richardson had "fanned" during the gunfight.

13. *Ford County Globe*, April 8, 1879.

14. *Ford County Globe*, April 8, 1879; *Kansas City Times* in *Ford County Globe*, September 2, 1879.

15. War Department, *Daily Bulletin of Simultaneous Weather Reports . . . for the Month of September 1879*, 25; *Ford County Globe*, September 9, 1879; *Dodge City Times*, September 13, 1879.

16. *Ford County Globe*, September 9, 1879; *Dodge City Times*, September 13, 1879.

17. *Dodge City Times*, September 13, 1879; *Ford County Globe*, January 13, 1880; US Census, 1850 and 1860: Virginia, Prince George County, dwellings 405 and 424; Slave Inhabitants, 1850, no page; Slave Inhabitants, 1860, 32, 34. For Webb's vital statistics see entry 2103, Prison Ledger A, Kansas State Penitentiary, Kansas State Historical Society (KSHS), Topeka.

18. *Ford County Globe*, January 7, September 13, 1879. Arista is missing from his family's 1870 enumeration—US Census, 1870: Virginia, Nansemond County, Chuckatuck Township, dwelling 141. In 1860, when Arista was thirteen, his father's slaves included an unnamed ten-year-old female. Unfortunately, Arista and Christina Webb cannot be located in the 1870 census for either Iowa or Kansas. Robert R. Dykstra, *Bright Radical Star: Black Freedom and White Supremacy on the Hawkeye Frontier* (Cambridge, MA: Harvard University Press, 1993), 26, 177–178, 191–192; *The Statutes of the Territory of Kansas* (Topeka: Shawnee School, 1855), 488; Wyandotte Constitution, July 29, 1859, http://www.territorialkansasonline.org/~imlskto/cgi-bin/index.php?SCREEN=show_document&document_id=101119&FROM_PAGE=; *General Laws of the State of Kansas* (Topeka: J. H. Bennett, 1862), 332, 354, 469, 474, 488, 512, 691, 695–699.

19. *Ford County Globe*, October 1, 1878, September 2, 1879; Elise Virginia Lemire, *"Miscegenation": Making Race in America* (Philadelphia: University of Pennsylvania Press, 2002), 11, 57, 82–83, 110; Joshua D. Rothman, *Notorious in the Neighborhood: Sex and Families across the Color Line in Virginia, 1787–1861* (Chapel Hill: University of

North Carolina Press, 2003), 4–5, 50–52, 67–69; Annette Gordon-Reed, *The Hemingses of Monticello: An American Family* (New York: W. W. Norton, 2008), 366–371.

20. *Ford County Globe*, January 13, 1880; *Kansas City Journal* in *Ford County Globe*, September 16, 1879.

21. *Ford County Globe*, September 9, 1879, January 13, 1880; *Dodge City Times*, September 13, 1879; Dassler, *Compiled Laws*, 739.

22. *Ford County Globe*, January 13, 27, 1880; *Dodge City Times*, January 17, 24, 1880; Dassler, *Compiled Laws*, 329–330, 762; Ed D. Phillips in Application no. 83, Record of Pardons, State of Kansas, Book A, 1877–1885, KSHS; Criminal Case Record 64 and Judge's Journal A: 279–282, Ford County District Court Records, 1874–1910, KSHS.

23. US Census, 1880: Kansas, Leavenworth County, Lansing State Penitentiary; entry 2103, Prison Ledger A, Kansas State Penitentiary, KSHS; William B. Shillingberg, *Dodge City: The Early Years, 1872–1886* (Norman, OK: Arthur H. Clark, 2009), 252; Cutler, *History*, 431; US Census, 1880: Leavenworth County, City of Leavenworth, 3d Ward, dwellings 179 and 354. Arista and Christina Webb (whose name the 1880 census taker misspelled as "Christeina Web") most likely would have married in Iowa; the older child's birthplace is listed as Iowa, the younger's as Kansas.

24. Application no. 83; *Topeka Commonwealth*, May 23, 1885; *Dodge City Times*, May 28, 1885; *Dodge City Democrat*, May 30, 1885; Dassler, *Compiled Laws*, 762, 768; US Census, 1900: Virginia, Augusta County, Staunton, Ward 1, Western State Hospital for the Insane, patient 45.

25. Miller and Snell, *Why the West Was Wild*, 643–644; *Dodge City Times*, November 20, 1880; *Ford County Globe*, November 23, 1880.

26. US Census, 1880: Kansas, Ford County, Dodge Township South of the Arkansas River, 8, dwelling 1: *Dodge City Times*, May 6, 1877, July 27, August 3, 1878; *Ford County Globe*, April 30 (advertisement), June 11, 1878, November 23, 1880, January 25, 1881 (advertisement); H. B. Bell in *Leavenworth Press*, in *Ford County Globe*, February 17, 1879.

27. *Ford County Globe*, November 23, 1880; US Census, 1880: Kansas, Ford County, Dodge City, dwelling 94: entry 2395, Prison Ledgers A and B, Kansas State Penitentiary, KSHS.

28. *Ford County Globe*, October 8, 1878, November 23, 1880, January 25, 1881 (advertisement); *Dodge City Times*, November 20, 1880; C. Robert Haywood, *Trails South: The Wagon-Road Economy in the Dodge City–Panhandle Region* (Norman: University of Oklahoma Press, 1986), 80.

29. War Department, *Daily Bulletin of Simultaneous Weather Reports . . . for the Month of November 1880*, 48–50; *Dodge City Times*, November 20, 1880; *Ford County Globe*, November 23, 1880; Affidavit by Mrs. C. F. Lane, March 19, 1884, Pardon Papers 584 (John Gill), March 21, 1884, Kansas State Penitentiary Records, KSHS.

30. *Dodge City Times*, November 27, December 11, 1880; *Ford County Globe*, January 27, December 7, 1880; Dassler, *Compiled Laws*, 329.

31. *Ford County Globe*, January 27, December 21, 1880, January 25, 1881; *Dodge City*

*Times*, January 8, 1881; Criminal Docket A: 79, and Judge's Journal A: 329–330, Ford County District Court Records; Dassler, *Compiled Laws*, 328.

32. *Dodge City Times*, March 27, 1884; Pardon Papers 584.

33. Pardon Papers 584; US Census, 1880: Kansas, Ford County, Dodge City, dwelling 94; *Dodge City Times*, November 20, 1880; William A. Hammond, ed., *Military Medical and Surgical Essays Prepared for the United States Sanitary Commission* (Philadelphia: J. P. Lippincott, 1864), 177, 184, 196, 200–202; Robert Berkow, Mark H. Beers, and Andrew J. Fletcher, eds., *The Merck Manual of Medical Information: Home Edition* (Whitehouse Station, NJ: Merck Research Laboratories, 1997), 661, 938–942, 1289–1290.

34. Affidavits by Sallie Frazier and Mrs. C. F. Lane, March 19, 1884, Pardon Papers 584; C. Robert Haywood, *Cowtown Lawyers: Dodge City and Its Attorneys, 1876–1886* (Norman: University of Oklahoma Press, 1988), 207; C. Robert Haywood, "'No Less a Man': Blacks in Cow Town Dodge City, 1876–1886," *Western Historical Quarterly* 19 (May 1988): 167–168; Thomas S. Jones to George Glick, March 20, 1884, Pardon Papers 584.

35. James D. Young in *Dodge City Times*, April 3, 10, 1884; Pardon Papers 584; Request for Commutation, April 1890 (John Gill), Record of Pardons, State of Kansas, Book B, 1877–1885, KSHS; Dassler, *Compiled Laws*, 768.

36. *Dodge City Democrat*, February 23, 1884; *Ford County Globe*, April 8, 1879. The *Democrat* began publication on December 29, 1883.

CHAPTER 5: CIRCLE DOT COWBOYS

1. The earliest *OED* citation of this American slang expression is dated 1835. By 1844 it was described as "in very common use in Texas." *The Compact Edition of the Oxford English Dictionary*, 3 vols. (New York: Oxford University Press, 1987), 3: 232.

2. J. R. Humphries, "From the Nueces to the North Platte," *The Trail Drivers of Texas*, ed. J. Marvin Hunter, rev. ed. (Nashville: Cokesbury Press, 1925), 803.

3. Andy Adams, *The Log of a Cowboy: A Narrative of the Old Trail Days* (Boston: Houghton, Mifflin, 1903), 187–209. Subsequent quotations taken from chapter 13 will not be cited by page number.

4. For examples see Wilson M. Hudson, *Andy Adams: His Life and Writings* (Dallas: Southern Methodist University Press, 1964), 102, 104–107; Thomas W. Knowles and Joe R. Lansdale, eds. *Wild West Show!* (New York: Wings Books, 1994), 94; Casey Tefertiller, *Wyatt Earp: The Life behind the Legend* (New York: J. Wiley, 1997), 22–23.

5. The reader must look in two different places for the full identification of the narrator: Adams, *Log of a Cowboy*, 10 (given and middle names), 22 (last name).

6. For negative assessments see Barbara Quissell, "Andy Adams and the Real West," *Western American Literature* 7 (Fall 1972): 211–219; Don Graham, "Old and New Cowboy Classics," *Southwest Review* 65 (Summer 1980): 293–303. For the book's best literary

defense to date see Dayle H. Molen, "Andy Adams: Classic Novelist of the Trail," *Montana: The Magazine of Western History* 19 (Winter 1969): 28–30.

7. J. Frank Dobie, "Andy Adams, Cowboy Chronicler," *Southwest Review* 11 (January 1926): 93; Walter Prescott Webb, *The Great Plains* (Boston: Ginn, 1931), 462.

8. Joe B. Frantz and Julian Ernest Choate Jr., *The American Cowboy: The Myth and the Reality* (Norman: University of Oklahoma Press, 1955), 162; Graham, "Old and New Cowboy Classics," 294–295.

9. Mark Twain, *Roughing It* (Hartford: American Publishing, 1872), 339, 343–345. The latest study of Virginia City fails to clarify the precise extent to which Twain embellished gun violence. Ronald M. James, *The Roar and the Silence: A History of Virginia City and the Comstock Lode* (Reno: University of Nevada Press, 1998), 168.

10. Alfred Henry Lewis, *The Sunset Trail* (New York: A. S. Barnes, 1905).

11. Andy Adams to J. Evetts Haley, enclosing "Historical Memories of Andy Adams" (typescript), October 27, 1931, Haley Collection, J. Evetts Haley History Center, Nita Stewart Haley Memorial Library, Midland, Texas; J. Evetts Haley to Jean Shelley Henry, January 29, 1938, Haley Collection.

12. J. Frank Dobie, "Frank Dobie Recounts What He Knew of Andy Adams, Texas Cowboy Writer," *Austin American Statesman*, October 6, 1935; J. Frank Dobie, "Andy Adams: Man and Chronicler," *San Antonio Express*, October 13, 1935; May Frank, "Browsing Around," *Oklahoma City Oklahoman*, August 2, 1931.

13. US Census, 1880: Indiana, Thorn Creek Township, Whitley County, dwelling 110; Adams to Dobie, February 19, 1925 (typescript), Wilson Hudson Papers, Southwestern Writers Collection, Southwest Texas State University, San Marcos; Adams to Haley, "Historical Memories"; Hudson, *Andy Adams*, 22–25; Jean Shelley Jennings Henry, "Andy Adams" (M.A. thesis, Texas Christian University, 1938), 34–35, 38, 102; Harry C. Singer to J. Frank Dobie, June 25, 1932. Singer said that Frank Wishert, one of the cowboys riding with Adams, had told him the herd was driven to Dodge City. Singer's letter, cited by Dobie, is no longer extant.

14. "The Texas Drive," *Ford County Globe*, June 13, 1882. According to Hudson, Smith & Redmon was located at 301 South Flores Street. Although the 1882 San Antonio city directory is not extant, within two years the stockyard at that address was operated by William L. Smith, George Redmon, and W. M. Forrest. Hudson, *Andy Adams*, 22; *Texas State Gazetteer and Business Directory, 1884–85* (Chicago: R. L. Polk, n.d.), 622; George W. Saunders, "Reflections of the Trail," *Trail Drivers of Texas*, 449.

15. *Ford County Globe*, June 20, 1882; Dobie, "Frank Dobie Recounts." Chris Emmett's *Shanghai Pierce: A True Likeness* (Norman: University of Oklahoma Press, 1953), 126, is unforthcoming about the specifics of Pierce's visit to Dodge.

16. See A. H. Pierce Papers, Center for American History, University of Texas at Austin, which verify only that Pierce established his headquarters in Kansas City, Missouri, from late June through July of 1882, 1883, 1884, and 1885. The four Dodge City weeklies make no mention of other Pierce visits to Dodge.

17. Nyle H. Miller and Joseph W. Snell, *Why the West Was Wild* (Topeka: Kansas State Historical Society, 1963), 525; Robert R. Dykstra, *The Cattle Towns* (New York: Alfred

A. Knopf, 1968), 246–253; Fredric R. Young, *Dodge City: Up through a Century in Story and Pictures* (Dodge City: Boot Hill Museum, 1972), 160. For a discussion of the phenomenal increase in Kansas's evangelicals during the 1880s see Robert Smith Bader, *Prohibition in Kansas: A History* (Lawrence: University Press of Kansas, 1986), 109–111.

18. Bader, *Prohibition*, chapters 3–4; C. F. W. Dassler, *Compiled Laws of Kansas, 1885* (Topeka: G. W. Crane, 1885), 382–390; *Ford County Globe*, November 16, December 21, 1880, April 12, 1881.

19. *Ford County Globe*, February 15, April 5, April 12, 1881; *Dodge City Times*, March 3, April 7, April 14, 1881.

20. "The Mayor of Dodge in the Early Days," *Kansas Journal* (Dodge City), January 1, 1909. For the Battle of the Plaza see Robert K. DeArment, *Bat Masterson: The Man and the Legend* (Norman: University of Oklahoma Press, 1979), 204–210; Miller and Snell, *Why the West Was Wild*, 410–413.

21. *Dodge City Times*, April 21, 28, May 5, 1881; *Ford County Globe*, May 31, 1881; Frederic R. Young, *The Delectable Burg: An Irreverent History of Dodge City—1872 to 1886* (Dodge City: Boot Hill Museum, 2009), 50; Miller and Snell, *Why the West Was Wild*, 567–568.

22. *Ford County Globe*, December 13, 1881, April 4, June 6, 1882; *Dodge City Times*, December 15, 1881, March 30, 1882. On the IOGT, which lacks a full-length study, see Ernest Hurst Cherrington, Albert Porter, William Eugene Johnson, and Cora Frances Stoddard, eds., *Standard Encyclopedia of the Alcohol Problem*, 6 vols. (Westerville, OH: American Issue Publishing, 1926), 3: 1332–1341; Jack S. Blocker, *American Temperance Movements: Cycles of Reform* (Boston: Twayne Publishers, 1989), 50–51, 73, 78; Ann-Marie E. Szymanski, *Pathways to Prohibition: Radicals, Moderates, and Social Movement Outcomes* (Durham, NC: Duke University Press, 2003), 24, 29, 32–44, 156–157. On the Templars in Kansas see Bader, *Prohibition*, 27–29.

23. For membership numbers and male and female officers see *Ford County Globe*, June 6, August 15, 1882. For Rice see *Ford County Globe*, August 16, 1881. For Buzzell see *Ford County Globe*, January 30, 1883, and *Dodge City Globe*, December 8, 1925. For the Reynolds and Hard families see C. Robert Haywood, *Trails South: The Wagon-Road Economy in the Dodge City–Panhandle Region* (Norman: University of Oklahoma Press, 1986), 158–189; Becky Schulte to Robert R. Dykstra, February 4, 2013. The occupations of all others, as well as information on the entire sixteen, were found in the 1880, 1885, and 1900 US and Kansas manuscript censuses.

24. *Dodge City Times*, April 6, May 18, 1882; *Ford County Globe*, June 6, August 15, 1882. After serving two terms as governor, St. John ran for president of the United States as the National Prohibition Party candidate in 1884. William D. P. Bliss and Rudolph M. Binder, eds., *The New Encyclopedia of Social Reform* (New York: Funk and Wagnalls, 1908), 973.

25. William G. Cutler, *History of the State of Kansas* (Chicago: A. T. Andreas, 1883), 1560–1561; *Ford County Globe*, February 1, November 8, 1881, June 6, June 13, September 12, 1882.

26. *Dodge City Times*, February 9, June 15, 1882; *Ford County Globe*, June 13, 1882.

Harland's lack of law-enforcement experience is indicated by his absence from the lists of Dodge City and Ford County officers in Miller and Snell, *Why the West Was Wild*, 642–645.

27. *Ford County Globe*, June 13, 1882; "Police Regulations," *Dodge City Times*, June 22, 1882.

28. *Dodge City Times*, June 15, 22, 1882. For a discussion of these assessments, expressly forbidden by the 1871 Kansas law establishing prerequisites for third-class cities, see Dykstra, *Cattle Towns*, 125–128.

29. *Ford County Globe*, June 27, September 12, 1882; *Dodge City Times*, June 29, 1882, November 8, 1883.

30. *Ford County Globe*, June 20, 1882; *Dodge City Times*, June 22, July 13, 1882.

31. Charles A. Siringo, *A Lone Star Cowboy* (Santa Fe: Charles A. Siringo, 1919), 101–102. In 1925 Adams wrote that he remembered the Turkey Track Ranch having been located in northwest Texas, but that he had forgotten the owner's name. Hudson, *Andy Adams*, 241.

32. *Dodge City Times*, July 27, August 24, 1878, July 12, 1883; *Ford County Globe*, July 30, August 27, 1878, May 2, 1882, July 10, 1883. For two uses of the "parting salute" trope see *Ford County Globe*, August 17, 1880, September 27, 1881.

33. Remington depicts four mounted cowboys firing their six-shooters into the air. One art historian describes the four as *entering* a town rather than leaving it, which would have proved foolishly hazardous. Why the artist titled the piece as he did remains an open question. Rupert Matthews, *Frederic Remington* (London: Grange Books, 1997), 74; Peggy Samuels and Harold Samuels, *Frederic Remington: A Biography* (Garden City, NY: Doubleday, 1982), 327–328.

34. Hudson, *Andy Adams*, 78–79. The earliest example of popular nonfiction that focuses on Dodge is most probably E. C. Little, "The Round Table of Dodge City," *Everybody's Magazine* 7 (November 1902): 432–439.

35. *Ford County Globe*, February 17, 1880; Robert M. Wright, *Dodge City: The Cowboy Capital and the Great Southwest* (Wichita: Eagle Press, 1913), 211–212; DeArment, *Bat Masterson*, 144–146.

36. *Dodge City Times*, June 22, 1882; C. Robert Haywood, *The Merchant Prince of Dodge City: The Life and Times of Robert M. Wright* (Norman: University of Oklahoma Press, 1998), 108.

37. *Dodge City Times*, June 15, 1882.

38. *Dodge City Times*, January 1, 1881, July 20, 1882; US Census, 1880, Kansas: Ford County, Dodge City, dwelling 27; Floyd B. Streeter, *Ben Thompson: Man with a Gun* (New York: F. Fell, 1957), 183–185.

39. Young, *Delectable Burg*, 36–81. Information on local prices is hard to come by. For beer—two glasses for twenty-five cents in 1884—see Dykstra, *Cattle Towns*, 278. For dancing—seventy-five cents per set in 1878—see *Dodge City Times*, June 22, 1878.

40. *Dodge City Times*, June 8, 1882.

41. Even Adams's biographer so misinterprets the text: "Quince confronts the bouncer and they fire without wasting words; the bouncer goes down." And: "Quince

Forrest gets into a shooting scrape in Dodge City. . . . He shoots the bouncer in a dance hall." Hudson, *Andy Adams,* 94; Wilson M. Hudson, *Andy Adams: Storyteller and Novelist of the Great Plains* (Austin, TX: Steck-Vaughn, 1967), 23.

42. As explained in chapter 3 above, the deaths of both Ed Masterson and Harry McCarty occurred in 1878. Six years later, in 1884, came the fatal shooting of another Dodge City officer, Assistant Marshal Thomas Nixon.

43. The killing occurred on June 22, 1882, as first reported by the Caldwell press on June 29, providing the source for Klaine's commentary. Miller and Snell, *Why the West Was Wild,* 58–66.

44. *Dodge City Times,* June 29, 1882.

45. Ibid.

46. Miller and Snell, *Why the West Was Wild,* 42–47.

47. *Dodge City Times,* July 12, 1883; *Ford County Globe,* July 17, 1883; Wright, *Dodge City,* 173–174.

48. Dykstra, *Cattle Towns,* 121–122.

### CHAPTER 6: DODGE CITY'S SENSATIONS

1. *National Police Gazette* (New York), August 10, 1878, p. 2.

2. Frank Luther Mott, *A History of American Magazines, 1865–1885* (Cambridge, MA: Harvard University Press, 1938), 7, 198, 209, 218; Dan Schiller, *Objectivity and the News: The Public and the Rise of Commercial Journalism* (Philadelphia: University of Pennsylvania Press, 1981), 98–99; Edward Van Every, *Sins of New York as "Exposed" by the Police Gazette* (New York: Frederick A. Stokes, 1930); Edward Van Every, *Sins of America as "Exposed" by the Police Gazette* (New York: Frederick A. Stokes, 1931).

3. *National Police Gazette,* April 27, 1878, p. 2.

4. *National Police Gazette,* August 10, 1878, p. 13.

5. *Dodge City Times,* July 27, 1878.

6. *National Police Gazette,* July 21, 1883, p. 5.

7. *Globe Live Stock Journal* (Dodge City), September 2, 1884.

8. "Harry Eric Gryden," *The United States Biographical Dictionary: Kansas Volume* (Chicago: S. Lewis, 1879), 846–847; Erick M. Gryden, Index to Declarations of Intent for Citizenship, Book 1 (1851–1879), Ripley County Courthouse, Versailles, Indiana; *Ripley County History, 1818–1988* (Osgood, IN: Ripley County Historical Book Committee, 1988), 90; US Census, 1860: Ohio, Hamilton County, Cincinnati, Ward 16, dwelling 628.

9. Henry E. Gryden service records, Record Group 94, microfilm 1290, roll 3, National Archives, Washington, D.C. For the activities in December 1864 of Captain Jesse Merrill's detachment, of which Gryden was a member, see J. Willard Brown, *The Signal Corps, U.S.A. in the War of the Rebellion* (Boston: US Veteran Signal Corps Association, 1896), 282–285, 558–563. According to Ray Anthony, "H. E. Gryden," *Dodge City Globe,* December 2, 1914, Harry also signaled the famous message telling the be-

sieged Union garrison at Allatoona, Georgia, to "hold the fort, for we are coming," which, reworked as a Christian hymn, became a camp-meeting staple in the Gilded Age. But Gryden was never stationed in northern Georgia.

10. "Harry Eric Gryden," 846–847; US Census, 1870: Indiana, Ripley County, Jackson Township, family 28; Deed Books 40:470 and 45:70, Ripley County Courthouse; *Ford County Globe* (Dodge City), May 20, 1879; *Dodge City Times*, September 4, 1884; US Census, 1880: Kansas, Ford County, Dodge City, dwelling 26; Judge's Journal A: 50, Ford County District Court Records, 1874–1910, Kansas State Historical Society (KSHS), Topeka.

11. C. Robert Haywood, *Cowtown Lawyers: Dodge City and Its Attorneys, 1876–1886* (Norman: University of Oklahoma Press, 1988), 74, 79–84; *Ford County Globe*, January 1, 1878; *Dodge City Times*, August 10, 1878.

12. *Dodge City Times*, October 14, 1876, July 14, 1877, April 20, August 31, 1878, August 7, 1880; *Ford County Globe*, April 2, 1878, March 2, April 13, June 8, 1880, April 5, 1881, June 13, 1882, January 30, 1883, April 15, 1884; *Dodge City Democrat*, April 12, August 30, 1884; *Kansas Cowboy* (Dodge City), September 6, 1884.

13. *Dodge City Times*, August 28, 1884; Haywood, *Cowtown Lawyers*, 83–84; *Dodge City Democrat*, August 30, 1884; Samuel Galland in *Yates Center News*, September 9, 1880; *Ford County Globe*, September 14, 1880, April 15, September 2, 1884. Gryden mentioned these specific friends in H. E. Gryden to Bat Masterson, *Dodge City Times*, June 9, 1881.

14. *Dodge City Times*, October 5, 1878; *National Police Gazette*, October 19, 1878, pp. 5, 10. For Gryden as Hand's divorce attorney see *Ford County Globe*, October 1, 1878.

15. *National Police Gazette*, April 19, 1879, p. 10.

16. Nyle H. Miller and Joseph W. Snell, *Why the West Was Wild* (Topeka: Kansas State Historical Society, 1963), 35–36, 643; Anthony, "H. E. Gryden."

17. *Kansas City Times*, May 29, 1880; *Ford County Globe*, June 1, 15, 1880.

18. Haywood, *Cowtown Lawyers*, 85–86.

19. *Ford County Globe*, May 24, 1881; *Fort Wayne Gazette*, July 24, 1881; Miller and Snell, *Why the West Was Wild*, 567–568.

20. Miller and Snell, *Why the West Was Wild*, 415–420; *Dodge City Times*, November 17, 1881. The *Sun* article, reprinted in the *Ford County Globe*, November 22, 1881, also appeared elsewhere, for example in the *Chicago Tribune*, November 11, 1881, and the *Butte Miner*, November 30, 1881.

21. *Dodge City Times*, December 15, 1881, March 16, April 6, 20, 1882; *Ford County Globe*, March 21, April 11, June 13, December 5, 1882.

22. *National Police Gazette*, July 21, 1883, p. 5; *Kansas City Star*, May 9, 1883; *Chicago Times*, May 10, 1883; *New York Times*, June 8, 1883.

23. *Ford County Globe*, February 6, April 3, May 8, 1883; *Dodge City Times*, August 10, 1878, October 13, 21, 27, 1881; *Kansas City Times*, May 10, 1883; Miller and Snell, *Why the West Was Wild*, 519–524; Robert R. Dykstra, *The Cattle Towns* (New York: Alfred A. Knopf, 1968), 271–273.

24. *Kansas City Star*, May 9, 1883; *Kansas City Times*, May 10, 1883; *Chicago Times*,

May 10, 11, 12, 16, 1883; *Helena Independent*, May 10, 1883; *Butte Miner*, May 10, 1883; *New York Tribune*, May 11, 1883; *New York Times*, May 11, 1883.

25. Miller and Snell, *Why the West Was Wild*, 530–534, 537; *Chicago Times*, May 14, 16, 17, 18, 1883; *Chicago Tribune*, May 17, 18, 1883; *Topeka Capital*, May 18, 1883; *Topeka Journal*, May 23, 1883; *New York Tribune*, May 19, 1883; Citizens of Dodge City to Governor George W. Glick, May 15, 1883, http://www.kansasmemory.org/item/208008.

26. *Chicago Times*, May 16, 18, 1883; *New York Tribune*, May 19, 1883; *Kansas City Journal*, May 15, 1883; *Topeka Capital*, May 16, 1883; Miller and Snell, *Why the West Was Wild*, 533, 549. On May 23, the day Short rejected the ten-day offer in the *Topeka Journal*, the *New York Times* reported it as a refusal of "the compromise." For Beeson see Frederick R. Young, *Dodge City: Up through a Century in Story and Pictures* (Dodge City: Boot Hill Museum, 1972), 67.

27. *Chicago Times*, May 22, 1883; *Chicago Tribune*, June 3, 1883; Horace E. Mather, *Lineage of Rev. Richard Mather* (Hartford, CT: Lockwood and Brainard, 1890), 391; Miller and Snell, *Why the West Was Wild*, 449–472, 644; Jack DeMattos, *Mysterious Gunfighter: The Story of Dave Mather* (College Station, TX: Creative Publishing, 1992).

28. *Topeka Journal*, May 23, 1883; "Wyatt Earp's Tribute to Bat Masterson," *San Francisco Examiner*, August 16, 1896; *Chicago Tribune*, June 3, 4, 1883; *Topeka Commonwealth*, June 5, 1883; Miller and Snell, *Why the West Was Wild*, 555, 557.

29. "Luke L. Short Dictation, Fort Worth, Texas, 1886," MS, Bancroft Library, University of California, Berkeley; *Chicago Times*, June 5, 1883; *Chicago Tribune*, June 3, 4, 5, 6, 1883; *New York Times*, June 5, 1883; "Wyatt Earp's Tribute"; W. B. (Bat) Masterson, *Famous Gunfighters of the Western Frontier* (Mineola, NY: Dover Publications, 2009), 17–19.

30. Miller and Snell, *Why the West Was Wild*, 558; *Chicago Times*, June 5, 1883; *Chicago Tribune*, June 5, 6, 1883.

31. *New York Times*, June 8, 9, 1883; *New York Tribune*, June 9, 1883.

32. *Dodge City Times*, June 7, 1883; Miller and Snell, *Why the West Was Wild*, 556–557; *Ford County Globe*, June 12, 1883; *Topeka Commonwealth*, June 9, 1883.

33. *National Police Gazette*, July 21, 1883, p. 5; Miller and Snell, *Why the West Was Wild*, 355.

34. *Chicago Tribune*, July 10, 1883; *Ford County Globe*, July 10, 1883; *Dodge City Times*, July 12, 1883; C. F. W. Dassler, *Compiled Laws of Kansas, 1879* (Saint Louis: W. J. Gilbert, 1879), 328–329; Robert M. Wright, *Dodge City: The Cowboy Capital and the Great Southwest* (Wichita: Eagle Press, 1913), 173–174.

35. *New York Commercial* in *Dodge City Globe*, July 24, 1883; *Chicago Press* in *Dodge City Times*, September 20, 1883; unnamed British newspaper in *Dodge City Times*, November 29, 1883.

36. The story ran in the *Colorado Springs Gazette*, July 8, 1884; the *Perry Pilot* (Iowa), July 16, 1884; and no doubt other papers. The *Atchison Globe*, July 8, 1884, printed a slightly longer piece.

37. J. Marvin Hunter, ed., *The Trail Drivers of Texas*, rev. ed. (Nashville: Cokesbury Press, 1925), 737–738; *Dodge City Democrat*, July 5, 12, 1884; *Ford County Globe*, July 8,

1884; *Dodge City Times*, July 10, 1884; *Kansas Cowboy*, July 12, 1884; *Globe Live Stock Journal*, July 15, 1884. In printing the witness accounts, the newspapers, of course, substituted combinations of letters and two-em dashes for "son-of-a-bitch" and "damned ass."

38. *Fort Wayne Gazette*, July 24, 1884; *Galveston News*, July 23, 1884; *Colorado Springs Gazette*, July 23, 1884; *Freeborn County Standard* (Albert Lea, MN), July 30, 1884; *New York Sun*, July 23, 1884; *Dunkirk Observer*, July 23, 1884; *Globe Live Stock Journal*, July 22, 1884. For the practice of "pony report" abstracts see S. N. D. North, *History and Present Condition of the Newspaper and Periodical Press of the United States, with a Catalogue of the Publications of the Census Year* (Washington, DC: Government Printing Office, 1884), 108.

39. *Dodge City Democrat*, April 12, May 24, 1884; *Ford County Globe*, May 27, 1884; *Larned Optic* in *Dodge City Times*, June 12, 1884; *Kansas Cowboy*, July 26, 1884.

40. *Dodge City Democrat*, July 19, 26, August 2, 23, December 20, 1884, January 3, 1885; *Globe Live Stock Journal*, July 22, 29, August 5, October 28, 1884; *Dodge City Times*, July 24, 31, August 7, 21, 1884; *Kansas Cowboy*, July 26, August 2, 9, 23, 1884, January 3, 1885; *Kinsley Mercury* in *Globe Live Stock Journal*, January 6, 1885, and in *Dodge City Times*, January 8, 1885.

41. Haywood, *Cowtown Lawyers*, 79–80; *Ford County Globe*, October 9, 1883; *Dodge City Times*, July 12, October 11, 1883.

42. *Ford County Globe*, February 19, 1884; *Dodge City Times*, February 21, 1884; *Dodge City Democrat*, February 23, 1884; Criminal Docket A: 150, Ford County District Court Records, KHS; Prison Ledgers A and F, entry 3287, Kansas State Penitentiary, KHS. None of the local papers covered Chambers's trial.

43. Gryden died on August 29, 1884. *Globe Live Stock Journal*, August 26, September 2, 1884; *Dodge City Democrat*, August 30, 1884; *Dodge City Times*, September 4, 1884; *Kansas Cowboy*, September 6, 1884.

CHAPTER 7: END GAMES

1. *New York Herald* and *Saint Louis Globe Democrat* in *Kansas Cowboy* (Dodge City), July 12, 1884; Kirke Mechem, "The Bull Fight at Dodge," *Kansas Historical Quarterly* 2 (August 1933): 294, 300.

2. Whitney R. Cross, *The Burned-Over District: The Social and Intellectual History of Enthusiastic Religion in Western New York, 1800–1850* (Ithaca, NY: Cornell University Press, 1950); Webster funeral oration in *Dodge City Times*, April 21, 1887.

3. *Dodge City Times*, October 21, 27, November 3, 1881, April 12, 1883; *Ford County Globe* (Dodge City), November 1, 8, 1881.

4. L. E. Deger to Citizens of Dodge City, *Dodge City Times*, March 29, 1883.

5. For the Santa Fe Railroad's threats to locate elsewhere see *Dodge City Times*, August 23, 30, 1883; *Ford County Globe*, August 28, 1883. For the number of Front Street

saloons in 1884 see fire map in William B. Shillingberg, *Dodge City: The Early Years, 1872–1886* (Norman, OK: Arthur H. Clark, 2009), end papers.

6. *Dodge City Times*, December 20, 1883, March 6, February 14, April 10, 1884; A. B. Webster in *Dodge City Democrat*, March 8 1884; *Dodge City Democrat*, January 19, April 12, May 24, 1884, October 20, 1888; *Ford County Globe*, March 11, March 18, April 8, 15, 1884. For the founding officers of the Dodge City Democrat Publishing Co. see *Ford County Globe*, December 25, 1883.

7. *Dodge City Times*, May 8, June 12, 19, 26, 1884; *Ford County Globe*, June 17, 1884; *Dodge City Democrat*, June 21, 28, 1884; *Globe Live Stock Journal* (Dodge City), October 28, 1884; Criminal Docket A: 163–175, Ford County District Court Records, 1874–1910, Kansas State Historical Society (KSHS), Topeka, Kansas; J. C. Strang to John A. Martin, July 5, 1885, Governors' Correspondence, John A. Martin (General Correspondence), KSHS; *State of Kansas v. Gleason* (1884), *Kansas Reports*, 32: 245–248.

8. Mechem, "Bull Fight at Dodge," 294–297; *Ford County Globe*, May 13, 1884; *Dodge City Democrat*, June 21, 1884; *Dodge City Times*, June 26, 1884.

9. Mechem, "Bull Fight at Dodge," 299–301; *Dodge City Times*, May 29, 1884; *New York Herald*, July 4, 1884; *Cincinnati Enquirer* in Mechem, "Bull Fight at Dodge," 296–297; *Topeka Commonwealth* in *Dodge City Times*, May 29, 1884; *Wichita Eagle* in *Ford County Globe*, June 3, 1884; *New York Times*, July 10, 1884.

10. Mechem, "Bull Fight at Dodge," 300–308; Frederic R. Young, *Dodge City: Up through a Century in Story and Pictures* (Dodge City: Boot Hill Museum, 1972), 83–86; *Dodge City Democrat*, July 5, 1884; *Ford County Globe*, July 8, 1884; *Larned Chronoscope* in *Dodge City Times*, July 17, 1884.

11. Robert K. DeArment, *Bat Masterson: The Man and the Legend* (Norman: University of Oklahoma Press, 1979), 270–271; *New York Herald*, July 4, 1884; *Fort Wayne Gazette*, July 20, 1884; *Reno Gazette*, July 31, 1884; *Cincinnati Enquirer* in *Dodge City Democrat*, July 17, 1884.

12. Clifford P. Westermeier, "The Dodge City Cowboy Band," *Kansas Historical Quarterly* 19 (1951): 1–7; Young, *Dodge City*, 150–152; *Great Bend Register* in *Ford County Globe*, June 24, 1884; *St. Paul & Minneapolis Pioneer Press*, November 28, 1884; *Chicago Inter Ocean* in *Kansas Cowboy*, November 29, 1884; *Harper's Weekly*, December 6, 1884, pp. 198, 805; *Frank Leslie's Illustrated Newspaper*, December 6, 1884, pp. 241, 253. The group's banner conspicuously hyphenated the word "cowboy."

13. *Minneapolis Journal*, November 26, 1884; *Minneapolis Tribune*, November 27, 1884; *St. Paul & Minneapolis Pioneer Press*, November 27, 28, 1884; *Kansas Cowboy*, December 6, 1884, January 3, 1885; *Lawrence Herald Tribune* in *Dodge City Times*, January 15, 1885.

14. *Kansas Cowboy*, December 27, 1884.

15. *Globe Live Stock Journal*, November 25, 1884; *Topeka Commonwealth* in *Dodge City Times*, April 30, 1885; *Dodge City Times*, May 21, 1885; Nyle H. Miller and Joseph W. Snell, *Why the West Was Wild* (Topeka: Kansas State Historical Society, 1963), 468–472.

16. *Dodge City Democrat*, May 10, 1884; T. in *Lyons Prohibitionist* in *Dodge City Times*, March 19, 1885; *Globe Live Stock Journal*, April 7, June 23, 1885; *Kansas Cowboy*, May 30, 1885.

17. *Dodge City Times*, April 10, 1884; James C. Malin, "Was Governor John A. Martin a Prohibitionist?" *Kansas Historical Quarterly* 1 (November 1931): 63–73.

18. S. Galland in *Dodge City Times*, January 22, 1885. For the names of temperance activists as of 1884 see *Dodge City Times*, February 28 (contributors to the KSTU), May 15 (committee on arrangements for the A. B. Campbell reception), August 21 (bondsmen for Dave Mather), 1884; *Ford County Globe* March 18 ("Holy Water" ticket), 1884. The reason reformers supported Mather is that he eliminated Nixon, a leading antiprohibition figure. Robert R. Dykstra, *The Cattle Towns* (Alfred A. Knopf, 1968), 278.

19. S. Galland in *Dodge City Democrat*, February 23, March 1, 1884; S. Galland in *Dodge City Times*, January 8, 15, 22, 1885; *Kansas Cowboy*, June 27, 1885; Malin, "Was Governor John A. Martin a Prohibitionist?" 65; *Dodge City Democrat*, January 10, 1885; Chat in *Dodge City Times*, February 19, 1885. For the KSTU through the 1880s see Robert Smith Bader, *Prohibition in Kansas: A History* (Lawrence: University Press of Kansas, 1986), 36, 46, 75–77.

20. C. F. W. Dassler, *Compiled Laws of Kansas, 1885* (Topeka: G. W. Crane, 1885), 386; *Dodge City Democrat*, February 21, 1885; *Globe Live Stock Journal*, March 3, 10, 1885; *Dodge City Times*, February 26, March 5, April 16, 1885.

21. *Kansas Cowboy*, June 27, 1885; *Dodge City Democrat*, June 27, 1885; Miller and Snell, *Why the West Was Wild*, 432–434; *Topeka Capital*, July 2, 1885; *St. Louis Globe Democrat* in *Manhattan Nationalist*, July 10, 1885.

22. *Manhattan Nationalist*, July 10, 1885; *Globe Live Stock Journal*, March 17, 1885, April 14, 1885; G. M. Hoover, "Saloon Account Book, Dodge City (1883–1885)," KSHS; Samuel H. Williamson, November 10, 2016, "Seven Ways to Compute the Relative Value of a U.S. Dollar Amount, 1774 to Present," MeasuringWorth, 2016, www.measuringworth.com/uscompare/; Dassler, *Compiled Laws, 1885*, 386; *Dodge City Democrat*, May 2, 1885.

23. *Globe Live Stock Journal*, March 17, April 14, 21, 1885; *Dodge City Times*, March 19, April 9, 23, 1885; *Dodge City Democrat*, March 21, May 2, 9, 1885; *Kansas Cowboy*, April 11, 1885; Dassler, *Compiled Laws, 1885*, 382–383.

24. *Dodge City Democrat*, July 11, 1885; *Topeka Capital*, July 11, 1885; Dassler, *Compiled Laws, 1885*, 386; *Dodge City Times*, December 10, 1885; Bader, *Prohibition in Kansas*, 48–51, 59, 79–81, 92–100; Ann-Marie E. Szymanski, *Pathways to Prohibition: Radicals, Moderates, and Social Movement Outcomes* (Durham, NC: Duke University Press, 2003), 42–43.

25. John A. Martin to R. M. Wright, October 29, 1885, Governors' Letters, 62: 127–137, KSHS; *Dodge City Democrat*, May 23, 1885. Calculating the number of saloons from the data in the *Globe Live Stock Journal*, November 17, 1885, is a matter of dividing the amount of money the town collected for "soda water licenses" by the $20 monthly payment by each saloon.

26. John A. Martin to P. F. Sughrue and Martin to B. F. Milton (county attorney,

Ford County), October 29, 1885, Governors' Letters, 62: 123–126, 138–140; B. F. Milton to John A. Martin, October 30, 1885, and P. F. Sughrue to Martin, October 31, 1885, and R. M. Wright to Martin, October 31, 1885, and W. M. Sutton to Martin, November 1, 1885, Governors' Correspondence.

27. R. M. Wright to John A. Martin, November 5, 1885, Governors' Correspondence; *Dodge City Times*, March 5, 1885.

28. *Dodge City Times*, September 17, October 8, November 5, 12, December 3, 17, 1885; *Dodge City Democrat*, October 10, November 7, 1885; *Kansas Cowboy*, October 10, 17, November 7, 1885; *Globe Live Stock Journal*, December 1, 8, 1885; Dykstra, *Cattle Towns*, 283.

29. John A. Martin to R. M. Wright, November 7, 1885, Governors' Letters, 62: 272–280; *Globe Live Stock Journal*, November 10, December 29, 1885; *Kansas Cowboy*, November 11, 21, 1885; *Dodge City Democrat*, November 14, 28, 1885; *Dodge City Times*, November 26, December 3, 1885; Bader, *Prohibition*, 77, 80.

30. *Dodge City Democrat*, December, 5, 12, 19, 1885; *Dodge City Times*, December 3, 10, 1885; *Topeka Capital*, November 28, 1885.

31. *Dodge City Times*, December 3, 1885; *Dodge City Democrat*, November 28, 1885; *Globe Live Stock Journal*, December 1, 15, 1885; *Kansas Cowboy*, December 1, 1885.

32. John A. Martin to J. C. Strang, December 9, 1885, Governors' Letters, 63: 267–276; *Kansas City Journal*, December 10, 1885; *Medicine Lodge Cresset*, December 31, 1885.

33. J. C. Strang to John A. Martin, December 15, 24, 1885; M. W. Sutton to John A. Martin, December 10, 17, 22, 1885, Governors' Correspondence; M. W. Sutton to Simon B. Bradford, March 10, 1886, Attorney Generals' Correspondence, KSHS; *Globe Live Stock Journal*, December 15, 1885; *Dodge City Times*, December 17, 31, 1885, January 7, 1886.

34. *Dodge City Democrat*, November 28, 1885; *Globe Live Stock Journal*, December 1, 15, 1885; *Kansas Cowboy*, December 1, 1885; *Dodge City Times*, December 3, 1885; Robert M. Wright, *Dodge City: The Cowboy Capital and the Great Southwest* (Wichita: Eagle Press, 1915), 319–320.

35. *Dodge City Democrat*, December 12, 1885; *Globe Live Stock Journal*, December 15, 1885; Malin, "Was Governor John A. Martin a Prohibitionist?" 69–70; Dykstra, *Cattle Towns*, 287–290.

36. *Abilene Chronicle*, December 29, 1898; *Abilene Reflector*, December 27, 1898; Bader, *Prohibition*, 158; William D. P. Bliss and Rudolph M. Binder, *The New Encyclopedia of Social Reform* (New York: Funk and Wagnalls, 1908), 720. For a balanced assessment of Carrie Nation's activism see Bader, *Prohibition*, 150–155.

37. *Dodge City Democrat*, February 6, 20, 1886; *Globe* Live Stock *Journal*, March 9, April 6, 13, 1886; *Dodge City Times*, March 11, 1886.

38. *Globe Live Stock Journal*, March 9, 16, 23, 30, 1886; *Dodge City Democrat*, March 13, April 3, April 10, 1886; R. M. Wright to John A. Martin, November 5, 1885, Governors' Correspondence; Criminal Docket A: 231–240, Ford County District Court Records; M. W. Sutton to Simon B. Bradford, March 10, 1886, Attorney Generals' Correspondence.

39. *Globe Live Stock Journal*, March 23, 30, 1886; *Dodge City Times*, April 1, 1886; *Dodge City Democrat*, April 17, 24, October 23, 1886; A. J. Abbott to Simon B. Bradford, March 30, 1886, Attorney Generals' Correspondence. Bradford had appointed Abbott, of Garden City, to assist the Ford County attorney in prosecuting the liquor cases.

40. *Dodge City Democrat*, April 10, 17, November 20, 1886; *Globe Live Stock Journal*, April 20, 1886; *State of Kansas v. Ben Daniels*, Criminal Docket A: 254, 272–276, 279–281, Ford County District Court Records.

41. *Globe Live Stock Journal*, March 23, 30, 1886; *Dodge City Democrat*, April 17, 1886.


CHAPTER 8: CONTESTING BOOT HILL

1. *New York Times*, October 27, 1889.

2. Kenneth S. Davis, *Kansas: A Bicentennial History* (New York: Norton, 1976), 122–127; Robert M. Wright, *Dodge City: The Cowboy Capital and the Great Southwest* (Wichita: Eagle Press, 1913), 328. For the Texas cattle trade's last years at Dodge see Robert R. Dykstra, *The Cattle Towns* (New York: Alfred A. Knopf, 1968), 334–342.

3. For Fringer: *Globe Livestock Journal* (Dodge City), February 10, 24, 1885; *Kansas Cowboy* (Dodge City), February 14, 1885. For Webster: *Dodge City Times*, April 14, 21, 1887; *Ford County Republican* (Dodge City), April 20, 1887. For Zimmerman: *Ford County Republican*, January 25, 1888. For Peacock: *Dodge City Globe Republican*, February 18, 1891; Utah Death Registers, 1847–1966, 1890 volume, p. 76, entry 2418, Provo, Utah: Ancestry.com Operations, 2010. For Jacob Collar: *Dodge City Democrat*, March 25, 1893; *Dodge City Globe Republican*, January 5, April 27, 1899; JewishGen, comp., *JewishGen Online Worldwide Burial Registry*, Provo, Utah: Ancestry.com Operations, 2008. For Morris Collar: Chris Pearsall to Betty Bradford, November 2, 1993, Kansas Heritage Center, Dodge City, Kansas. For Kelley: *Topeka Journal*, January 13, 1911; *First Biennial Report of the Kansas State Soldiers' Home, Dodge City, 1889–90* (Topeka: Clifford C. Baker, 1890), 5; *Kansas Journal* (Dodge City), September 13, 1912. For Cox: *Dodge City Globe Republican*, September 2, 10, 1891; *Dodge City Journal*, March 26, 1918.

4. C. Robert Haywood, *The Merchant Prince of Dodge City: The Life and Times of Robert M. Wright* (Norman: University of Oklahoma Press, 1998), 162–179.

5. For Hoover: Gerald Gribble, "George M. Hoover, Dodge City Pioneer" (M.A. thesis, University of Wichita, 1940), 22–29, 30–35, 83–84. For Evans: Lola A. Crum et al., eds., *Dodge City and Ford County, Kansas, 1870–1920: Pioneer Histories and Stories* (Dodge City: Ford County Historical Society, 1996), 147; *Dodge City Globe*, May 27, 1912. For Sitler: *Dodge City Times*, October 31, 1917.

6. A. K. Sims, *The Dandy of Dodge; or, Rustling for Millions*, Beadle's Half-Dime Library No. 568 (June 12, 1888); Albert Johannsen, *The House of Beadle and Adams and Its Dime and Nickel Novels: The Story of a Vanished Literature*, 3 vols. (Norman: University of Oklahoma Press, 1950), 2: 299–300; Will Wright, *Sixguns and Society: A Structural Study of the Western* (Berkeley: University of California Press, 1975), 32.

7. *Dodge City Globe Republican*, November 30, 1899; Fredric R. Young to Robert R. Dykstra, April 19, 2013; Fredric R. Young, *The Delectable Burg: An Irreverent History of Dodge City—1872 to 1886* (Dodge City: Boot Hill Museum, 2009), 159.

8. Fredric R. Young, *Dodge City: Up through a Century in Story and Pictures* (Dodge City: Boot Hill Museum, 1972), 146–147; *Topeka Capital*, August 6, 1910; *Kansas City Star*, April 2, 1916; Joseph S. Vernon, *Dodge City and Ford County, Kansas: A History of the Old and a Story of the New* (Larned, KS: Tucker Vernon, 1911), 17.

9. Owen Wister, *The Virginian: A Horseman of the Plains* (New York: Macmillan, 1902), chapter 35; William K. Everson, *The Hollywood Western* (Secaucus, NJ: Carol Publishing Group, 1992), 26–27.

10. E. C. Little, "The Round Table of Dodge City: Border Men Knights-Errant Who Surpassed the Achievements of Heroes of Romance," *Everybody's Magazine* 7 (November 1902): 432–439.

11. Little, "Round Table of Dodge City," 436; Horace C. Mather, *Lineage of Rev. Richard Mather* (Hartford, CT: Case, Lockwood and Brainard, 1890), 391. For a contemporary account of the Las Vegas shooting see Nyle H. Miller and Joseph W. Snell, *Why the West Was Wild* (Topeka: Kansas State Historical Society, 1963), 451.

12. Andy Adams, *The Log of a Cowboy: A Narrative of the Old Trail Days* (Boston: Houghton, Mifflin, 1903), 177–209.

13. Alfred Henry Lewis, "The Deep Strategy of Mr. Masterson: The Story of a Stampeded Election," *Saturday Evening Post*, December 17, 1904, pp. 8–9, 23–24; compare with the actual election documented in Miller and Snell, *Why the West Was Wild*, 327–328. The other stories were "Diplomacy in Dodge," *Metropolitan Magazine* 20 (April 1904): 90–102; "An Invasion of Dodge: The Story of a Craven Desperado," *Collier's Weekly*, April 16, 1904, pp. 19–20; and "The Fatal Gratitude of Mr. Kelly," *Collier's Weekly*, September 17, 1904, pp. 16–17. For Lewis's friendship with Masterson see Robert K. DeArment, *Bat Masterson: The Man and the Legend* (Norman: University of Oklahoma Press, 1979), 371–372, 380, 389.

14. Casey Tefertiller, *Wyatt Earp: The Life behind the Legend* (New York: J. Wiley, 1997), 299; Alfred Henry Lewis, *The Sunset Trail* (New York: A. S. Barnes, 1905).

15. W. B. Masterson, "Famous Gunfighters of the Western Frontier," *Human Life* 4 (January 1907): 4–5, 8–9, 12–13; (February): 9–10, 22; (April): 9–10, 20; (May): 5–6; (July): 11–12. Lewis's chapter was "The King of the Gun-Players: William Barclay Masterson," *Human Life* 4 (November 1907): 7–9. These articles were reprinted as a small book, most recently republished as W. B. (Bat) Masterson, *Famous Gunfighters of the Western Frontier* (Mineola, NY: Dover Publications, 2009).

16. Arthur Chapman, "The Men Who Tamed the Cow-Towns," *Outing* 45 (November 1904): 138; "The Seven Able Gun Fighters from Kansas City," *Kansas City Star*, January 13, 1918; "The Man Who Put Goodness into the 'Wickedest Town,'" *Literary Digest*, August 22, 1925, p. 46; William MacLeod Raine, "Dodge," *Liberty*, May 19, 1928, p. 12.

17. DeArment, *Bat Masterson*, 35; *Topeka Capital*, August 6, 1910; Charles A. Siringo, *Riata and Spurs: The Story of a Lifetime Spent in the Saddle as Cowboy and Detective* (Boston: Houghton Mifflin, 1927), 37.

18. *Ford County Globe* (Dodge City), February 10, 1880; photo titled "Prairie Grove Cemetery: A B Webster's Funeral," Kansas State Historical Society (KSHS), Topeka; Young, *Dodge City*, 47; Young, *Delectable Burg*, 159; *Dodge City Globe*, December 16, 1926.

19. US Census, 1870 and 1880: Kansas, Atchison County, Shannon Township, dwellings 97 and 25; Kansas Census, 1875 and 1885: Atchison County, Shannon Township, dwellings 110 and 1, both on p. 26; *St. Joseph, Missouri Directories, 1887–90*, Provo, Utah: Ancestry.com The Generations Network, 2000; US Census, 1900: Oklahoma Territory, Oklahoma City, dwelling 146; US Census, 1930: Missouri, Jackson County, Kansas City, dwelling 236.

20. Jan Cohn, *Creating America: George Horace Lorimer and the Saturday Evening Post* (Pittsburgh: University of Pittsburgh Press, 1989), 165–166; Fred E. Sutton and A. B. Macdonald, "Fill Your Hand," *Saturday Evening Post*, April 10, 1926, pp. 14–15, 168, 173–174, 177; "Hands Up!" *Saturday Evening Post*, April 24, 1926, pp. 32–33, 70, 72, 74, 76, 78, 80, 82; Fred E. Sutton and A. B. Macdonald, *Hands Up! Stories of the Six-Gun Fighters of the Old Wild West* (Indianapolis: Bobbs-Merrill, 1927). The quotation is from the forward to *Hands Up!*, 7.

21. Sutton and Macdonald, "Fill Your Hand," 15, 168; Sutton and Macdonald, *Hands Up!* 20, 104.

22. Sutton and Macdonald, "Fill Your Hand," 15; Miller and Snell, *Why the West Was Wild*, 198–199. Sutton later provided a fictitious wrap-up on himself and Wild Bill. Fred E. Sutton, "My Personal Contact with James Butler Hickok," *Pony Express Courier* 4 (June 1937): 11.

23. Sutton and Macdonald, *Hands Up!* 109, 116–117, 225; Sutton and Macdonald, "Fill Your Hand," 15, 173; DeArment, *Bat Masterson*, 81, 87, 182, 217.

24. *Topeka Capital*, October 13, 1922.

25. *Dodge City Journal*, July 16, 1925; *Dodge City Globe*, August 13, 14, 18, 1925.

26. *Dodge City Globe*, July 16, August 21, 1925, February 4, 1927, June 13, August 1, 1929; *Dodge City Journal*, August 27, 1925; William B. Shillingberg, *Dodge City: The Early Years, 1872–1886* (Norman, OK: Arthur H. Clark, 2009), 394; Kevin Britz, "'Boot Hill Burlesque': The Frontier Cemetery as a Tourist Attraction in Tombstone, Arizona, and Dodge City, Kansas," *Journal of Arizona History* 44 (Autumn 2003): 215–218.

27. *New York Times*, August 18, 1929, sec. 3, p. E6.

28. Stuart N. Lake, "Straight-Shooting Dodge," *Saturday Evening Post*, March 8, 1930, p. 25.

29. *New York Times*, August 18, 1929; Lake, "Straight-Shooting Dodge," 148; "Boot Hill," *Time*, November 11, 1929, p. 66; *Kansas City Star*, November 4, 17, 1929; Young, *Dodge City*, 189. In the days following the celebration Billy Sunday continued to preach from Boot Hill, turning his appearance into a traditional "protracted revival."

30. *Kansas City Star*, November 4, 1929.

31. . Lake, "Straight-Shooting Dodge," 24. For Lake's background see Tefertiller, *Wyatt Earp*, 325–326; Allen Barra, *Inventing Wyatt Earp: His Life and Many Legends* (New York: Carroll and Graf Publishers, 1998), 380; Andrew C. Isenberg, *Wyatt Earp: A Vigilante Life* (New York: Hill and Wang, 2013), 213–214.

32. Stuart N. Lake, "The Frontier Marshal," *Saturday Evening Post*, November 15, 1930, p. 104.

33. Stuart N. Lake, *Wyatt Earp: Frontier Marshal* (Boston: Houghton Mifflin, 1931); Tefertiller, *Wyatt Earp*, 342; Barra, *Inventing Wyatt Earp*, 10; Isenberg, *Wyatt Earp*, 48.

34. In his flyleaf inscription in a second edition at the American Antiquarian Society, Worcester, Massachusetts, book collector George T. Watkins wrote: "I was told in Dodge City the second edition was printed simply to supply the 'home folks' in and around the old 'cowboy capital.'"

35. Young, *Dodge City*, 189; *Kansas City Star*, November 4, 1929; *Kansas City Times*, November 4, 1929; *Topeka Journal*, August 18, 1937; *Dodge City Globe*, February 27, 1947; *Wichita Eagle*, October 23, 1949; Britz, "'Boot Hill Burlesque,'" 218–224.

36. Everson, *Hollywood Western*, 54. For the 1936 remake see *IMDB*, "Dodge City Trail," http://www.imdb.com/title/tt0003854/?ref_=fn_al_tt_1. For the storyline, cast, and details of other movies mentioned here consult http://www.imdb.com/ and provide titles.

37. Barra, *Inventing Wyatt Earp*, 344–345; *Topeka Capital*, April 2, 1939; *Topeka Journal*, April 3, 1939; *Dodge City Globe*, February 24, 1947; Rudy Behlmer, ed., *Inside Warner Bros. (1939–1951)* (New York: Viking, 1985), 80–81.

38. George N. Fenin and William K. Everson, *The Western: From Silents to the Seventies*, rev. ed. (New York: Penguin Books, 1973), 243. For a discussion of Earp films see Barra, *Inventing Wyatt Earp*, 342–347; Isenberg, *Wyatt Earp*, 217–218.

39. David D. Courtwright, *Violent Land: Single Men and Social Disorder from the Frontier to the Inner City* (Cambridge, MA: Harvard University Press, 1996), 104–105. A remarkably informative essay on *Gunsmoke* and the radio version that preceded it can be found at *Wikipedia*, "Gunsmoke," http://en.wikipedia.org/wiki/Gunsmoke.

40. Britz, "'Boot Hill Burlesque,'" 224–225; *Dodge City Globe*, February 24, 1947, June 7, 1950, February 13, 1956; *Wichita Eagle*, October 23, 1949; *Topeka Capital*, June 1, 1958.

41. *Topeka Capital*, June 1, 1958; *Kansas City Star*, July 30, 1958; *Wichita Eagle*, September 25, 1958; Shirley Christian, "Where Wyatt Earp Stood Tall," *New York Times*, January 17, 1999, sec. 5, pp. 18, 28.

EPILOGUE: HOMICIDE, MORAL DISCOURSE,
CULTURAL IDENTITY

1. US Census Bureau, Urban and Rural Definitions, http://www.census.gov/population/censusdata/urdef.txt; *American Fact Finder*, Dodge City, Kansas, http://factfinder.census.gov/faces/tableservices/jsf/pages/productview.xhtml?src=bkmk; Dodge City Ford County Development Corporation, *Doing Business*, "Existing Industry," http://www.dodgedev.org/doing-business/existing-industry.

2. Janice Scott, Kansas Heritage Center, Dodge City, to Robert Dykstra, October 7, 2010, April 4, 2011; *Dodge City Globe*, May 5, 1942, August 9, 1944; Peter Biskind, *Easy*

*Riders, Raging Bulls: How the Sex-Drugs-and-Rock-'n'-Roll Generation Saved Hollywood* (New York: Simon and Schuster, 1998), 43, 73–75. Hopper died in California in 2010.

3. Theorists of nationalism such as Benedict Anderson and E. J. Hobsbawm have long emphasized the cultural authority of its media and literature in defining a nation's values. See Anderson, *Imagined Communities: Reflections on the Origin and Spread of Nationalism* (London: Verso, 1983), 61–79; Hobsbawm, *Nations and Nationalism since 1780: Programme, Myth, Reality* (New York: Cambridge University Press, 1990), 90, 94.

4. Stewart L. Udall, concluding remarks, in "How the West Got Wild: American Media and Frontier Violence—A Roundtable," *Western Historical Quarterly* 31 (Autumn 2000): 295. A former US secretary of the interior, Udall criticized historians who, in his opinion, passively accepted the story of unlimited interpersonal gun violence in the Old West.

5. Paul Nevins, "Guns Are Everywhere, but I Don't Feel Safer," *Boston Globe*, June 22, 1998, p. A18.

6. Paul Gallant and Joanne Eisen, "Goodbye Dodge City: How the Antis Torpedoed Their Own Movement," *Guns & Ammo* 42 (December 1998): 12–16.

7. David H. Bayley, "NRA Defies Common Sense," *Albany Times Union*, January 4, 2013, p. A8; John Ruane, *Chicago Now*, "Gun Control or Dodge City, America's Choice," December 18, 2012, http://www.chicagonow.com/newsboy/2012/12/gun-control-or-dodge-city-americas-choice/.

# INDEX

Adams, Andy
  as cowboy, 86–87, 102
  *The Log of a Cowboy*, 84–85, 86, 87–88,
    93–100, 102, 167
African Americans
  cowboys, 36, 125
  dance halls, 36, 125
  Dodge City residents, 36, 74
  entrepreneurs, 36–40, 55
  Gryden and, 125
  gunfights, 125
  interracial marriage, 73–74, 75
  murder committed, 55–56
  murder victims, 23
  prejudice against, 56
  residential area, 36
  vigilante attacks on, 36–40, 41
  women, 73–74, 75, 76–77, 82
alcohol. *See* prohibition; saloons
Allison, Clay, 94
Anthony, Andrew, 191n18, 193n31
Arkansas River
  bridge, 137 (photo), 179
  flooding, 9
  Fort Dodge site, 9, 10
  Native American settlements, 7–8
arson, suspected, 158, 159
Associated Press (AP), 111, 113–114, 123
Atchison, Topeka & Santa Fe Railroad,
    10–11, 35, 53, 65, 144, 155
*Atchison Patriot*, 33, 48
*Atlantic Monthly*, 46

Ballard, John, 102, 122
Barnes, David, 150–151

Barra, Allen, 175
Bassett, Charley
  as city marshal, 56, 58, 68, 71, 74
  Dodge City War and, 119, 120
  life of, 51–52
  as sheriff, 51, 52, 53, 54
  studio portrait, 139 (photo)
  train robbery investigation, 109
*Bat Masterson* (television series), 3, 177
Battle of the Plaza, 89–90, 109, 148
Beamer, Peter, 91–92, 93, 98–99, 101,
    102–103
Beatty, John, 13
Beeson, Chalkley, 116, 148, 178
Bell, Hamilton, 61, 78, 79, 80, 82, 172–173,
    176. *See also* Elephant Livery Stable
*Big Hand for the Little Lady, A*, 177
bison. *See* buffalo
blacks. *See* African Americans
Bloom, Jacob, 164
Blunt, James, 18
Boot Hill, 127 (photo)
  burials, 23, 34–35, 168–169, 170, 174
  city hall and jail built on, 172–173
  excavations, 165, 169
  "Last Round-Up" (1929), 173–174
  proposed city purchase, 171–172
  relocated graves, 168
  school, 64, 165, 168, 169, 172
  symbolism, 173–174
  as tourist attraction, 60, 172, 175, 178,
    180
  view from, 128 (figure)
Boot Hill Museum, 178, 180
*Boston Globe*, 3

Bowen, P. T., 41
boxing matches, 150
Bradford, Simon, 154, 156, 157
Bridges, Jack
    as city marshal, 101–102, 113, 117, 122
    at Fort Dodge, 197n13
    as US marshal, 27–28, 38, 39
Brooks, Billy "Bully," 25, 27, 28–29, 31, 42
Brown, George W., 1–2
Brown, Neil, 78, 80
Brown (yard master), 27
buffalo
    commercial hunting, 10, 11, 52
    hides, 5, 128 (photo)
Bullard, S. A., 152
bullfight, 143, 145, 146–147, 164
Burns (victim), 34, 35
Burrell, Dave, 41, 43, 47–48, 54
businesses
    banks, 14, 163–164
    billiard hall, 16, 33, 129 (photo)
    bird's-eye view, 137 (figure)
    downtown, 21, 64–65, 128 (figure)
    drug stores, 142 (photo), 154, 156–157, 160
    dry goods store, 18
    early buildings, 13, 128 (photo), 129 (photo)
    general stores, 15, 19–20, 21
    gun and hardware store, 19, 72–73, 113, 129 (photo), 131 (photo), 157
    hotels, 20, 26, 42–43, 65, 96–97, 152, 153, 163
    See also dance halls; Front Street; saloons
business owners
    African American, 36–40, 55
    concerns about gun violence, 24, 28, 30–31, 64
    elected officials as, 50–51
    opposition to prohibition, 151
    pioneers, 11, 12, 14–20, 29, 163–164

Tyler's bondsmen, 55–56
vigilance committee, 30, 31–33
Buzzell, Anson and Florence, 91
Byler, Frank, 86

Caldwell, Alexander, 13
Caldwell (Kansas), 5, 100, 151, 159
Cameron, William, 77
cattle dealers, 87–88
cattle drives, 87, 150, 161. See also cowboys
cattle towns, 5, 53, 156, 159, 161
cemeteries. See Boot Hill; Prairie Grove Cemetery
Chambers, Henry, 125
Cheyenne Autumn, 177
Chicago, Dodge City visitors, 149
Chicago Press, 122
Chicago Times, 113–114, 115, 116, 117, 118, 119
Chicago Tribune, 113, 117, 118, 119, 122
Chipman, Clark, 92, 93, 98–99, 116
Chisholm Trail, 53
Choate, Julian Ernest, Jr., 85
Choate, Kyle "Bing," 123, 147
churches. See evangelicals; Gospel Ridge
Cincinnati Enquirer, 146
Circle Dot cowboys. See Log of a Cowboy, The
Civil War
    Andersonville, 7
    Galvanized Yankees, 17
    veterans, 6–7, 9, 14, 16, 17–18, 20, 51–52, 92, 106, 189n3
    western battles, 18
Clark, T. E., 27
Cody, "Buffalo Bill," 46
Collar, Jacob, 130 (photo)
    background, 19–20
    country estate, 64
    death, 163
    Dodge City War and, 115
    elected office, 51

opposition to prohibition, 151
Tyler case and, 55
Collar, Jennie, 19, 195n44
Collar, Morris
background, 19–20
country estate, 64
death, 163
elected offices, 51
opposition to prohibition, 151
petition for Gill's pardon, 82
store, 129 (photo)
Conrad, George, 91
Cook, Rufus, 68, 69, 72
coroner's juries
Ballard case, 122
Choate case, 123
Ellis case, 41, 42–43, 54
Hand case, 68
Heck case, 80
Martin case, 74–75
procedures, 66
Richardson case, 71–72, 83
cowboys
African American, 36, 125
cattle drives, 87, 150, 161
deaths, 59
in Dodge City, 53, 56, 84, 86–88,
94–100, 102
fictional, 84–86, 93–94
gunfights, 57–58, 105
guns checked by, 55, 94
meals, 138 (photo)
parting salutes, 94–95, 100, 105, 122
saloon fights, 25
victims of random gunshots, 122
See also Dodge City Cow-Boy Band
Cox, Amy Bennett, 20, 138 (photo)
Cox, George, 138 (photo)
background, 20
death, 163
Dodge City War and, 115
elected offices, 51, 145
hotel, 20, 26, 42–43, 163

later life, 163
opposition to prohibition, 151
petition for Gill's pardon, 82
Tyler case and, 55
Cullen, Barney, 30, 47
cultural myths. See mythology of Dodge
City
Custer, George, 17

Dade, Wallace, 41
Dade County Crime Watch, 3
dance halls
closed by city, 156
in fiction, 98–100
gunfights, 30, 105, 125
musicians, 148
number of, 61
outlawed, 124
prices, 98
racial segregation, 36, 125
on south side, 79, 128 (photo), 156
women, 61, 65, 113
Woodhulleries (term), 197n19
Dandy of Dodge, The (Sims), 164
Daniels, Ben, 160–161
Deadwood (South Dakota), 5, 104
Deger, Lawrence, 112–113, 114, 115, 116,
119, 121, 144
Democratic Party, 152. See also Glick,
George; Gryden, Harry
Denver (gambler), 23
Denver Times, 32
depression (1890s), 162, 163
dime novels, 45–46, 60, 85, 200n3. See
also Western novels
Dobie, J. Frank, 85, 86
Dodge, Richard
background, 11
on buffalo hunting, 10
film portrayals, 176
Ford County organization and, 35
on racial violence, 41
rank, 191n18

Dodge, Richard, *continued*
  Taylor murder reports, 38, 39–40
  on troublemakers, 22
  on vigilance committee, 32
Dodge City
  bird's-eye view, 136–137 (figures)
  as cattle town, 5, 53, 156, 161
  courthouse, 54, 64
  cultural metaphor, 2–5
  entertainment district, 12, 21, 65, 84,
    88, 128 (figure)
  founding, 11–13
  histories, 4
  middle class, 64, 88
  nighttime entertainment, 44, 61–64,
    65, 98, 156
  population, 53, 64, 88, 121, 179
  post–frontier era, 162–165, 166
  public school, 64
  reformers, 112–113, 114, 143–144
  semicentennial, 170–171
  site, 11, 12–13
  today, 179–181
  tourism, 60, 150, 172, 175, 178, 180–181
  *See also* Fort Dodge; mythology of
    Dodge City; pioneers
*Dodge City* (movie), 176
Dodge City Cow-Boy Band, 140 (figure),
  148–150, 164, 181
*Dodge City Democrat*, 83, 144–145, 157
Dodge City government
  as city of second class, 160
  as city of third class, 53, 54
  mayors, 51, 56, 112–113
  taxes, 58, 107
  *See also* elections
*Dodge City Journal*, 171
*Dodge City Messenger*, 52
*Dodge City: The Cowboy Capital* (Wright), 4,
  163, 175
*Dodge City Times*
  Deger's announcement, 144
  editorials, 59, 82, 90, 91, 100–101

on gunfights, 105, 124
murder coverage, 56, 66, 67, 68, 78,
  108
Dodge City Town Company, 11–13, 191n18,
  192n25
*Dodge City Trail, The* (movie), 176
Dodge City War (1883), 111–115, 116–121,
  144
Dodge House, 20, 26, 42–43, 163
downtown businesses. *See* businesses;
  Front Street
Drake, H. P., 145
drug stores, 142 (photo), 154, 156–157,
  160
Duffey, William, 68, 71, 74, 78
*Dunkirk Observer*, 111

Earp, Wyatt, 131 (photo)
  as assistant city marshal, 58, 59, 68,
    69, 105
  biographies, 55, 70, 174–175
  Dodge City War and, 116, 117–118, 119,
    121–122
  fame, 121–122, 165–166, 167, 175
  fictionalized stories, 170
  in films and television, 3, 176, 177, 178
  gunfights, 59, 105, 203n34
  later life, 167
  on Richardson, 71
  statue, 180
  studio portrait, 121, 139 (photo)
elections
  Ford County, 50–51, 156
  fraud, 156, 160
  municipal, 51, 107, 112–113, 114, 124,
    144–145, 151, 160
elephant, seeing, 84
Elephant Livery Stable, 65, 79, 137 (photo)
Ellis, Bill, 41, 42–43, 47–48, 54
Ellis County, 12, 24
Ellsworth (Kansas), 5, 8, 17, 52, 67
entrepreneurs. *See* business owners
Essington House, 20, 25, 26

evangelicals
  criticism of bullfight, 146
  revivals, 173
  support of prohibition, 88, 90, 91,
    152–153
  Webster and, 143–145, 160
  *See also* Independent Order of Good
    Templars (IOGT); Sunday, Billy;
    temperance activists
Evans, Richard, 16, 18–19, 64, 115, 151, 164
*Everybody's Magazine*, 166

Flynn, Errol, 176
Ford, John, 177
Ford County
  census, 24, 28, 29, 35
  courthouse, 54, 64
  district attorney, 56
  district court, 66, 75–76, 81, 107, 145,
    160
  elections, 36, 50–51, 107, 156
  gun control, 54
  officials, 40–41, 50–51, 52, 54
  organization, 24, 35–36, 41
  schools, 107
  *See also* sheriffs
*Ford County Globe*
  cattle drive lists, 87
  editorials, 56, 59–60, 72, 92
  files, 165, 174
  on lax gun control, 57
  on Loving, 70
  murder coverage, 66, 69, 78–80, 83
  train robbery story, 109
Fort Dodge, 127 (photo)
  civilian employees, 9, 11, 15, 16, 191n18
  establishment, 17
  hospital, 2, 69
  military reservation, 9–10, 11, 12
  railroad, 11
  site, 9
  soldiers from, 26–27
  Soldiers' Home, 163

supply trains, 8–9
  tourism, 181
Fort Harker (Ellsworth, KS), 8, 17, 190n9
Fort Hays, 8, 17, 18
Fox, Richard Kyle, 104
*Frank Leslie's Illustrated*, 149
Frantz, Joe B., 85
Frazier, Sally, 82
Fringer, Herman
  background, 15–16
  as county clerk, 35
  death, 163
  elected offices, 51
  Ford County census and, 29
  at Fort Dodge, 15, 16, 191n18
  opposition to prohibition, 151
  property, 64
  Taylor murder and, 37–38, 40
Front Street
  businesses, 15, 16, 65, 128 (figure), 129
    (photo)
  fire (1885), 157, 158–159, 179
  gun control sign, 55, 132 (photo)
  hotels, 20
  night life, 62
  rebuilding, 160
  replica as tourist attraction, 178, 180
  saloons, 14–15, 72, 88, 144, 156, 157
  site, 12
Frost, Daniel, 109, 115, 147, 156, 160, 161
Fryer, Blencowe, 69

Galland, Samuel, 91, 152, 153
Gallup Saddlery Company, 135 (photo)
gamblers
  cheating, 25, 123
  fines and taxes, 58, 90, 93, 107
  gunfights, 1, 23, 25, 123, 150–151
  private security, 28
  professional, 70, 79, 80, 97
  regulating, 93, 113
  troublemakers, 22, 70
  *See also* Dodge City War

gambling
    in saloons, 62, 97, 150–151, 156
    tolerance of, 64
Garrettson, Fannie, 67
"get out of Dodge" metaphor, 2–3, 4, 180
Gill, John "Concho," 79, 80–83, 109
Gilson, Christopher, 31, 33, 38, 48
Glick, George
    bullfight and, 146, 147
    defeat in 1884 election, 152
    Dodge City War and, 114–115, 116, 119
    Gryden and, 107
    petition for Gill's pardon, 81, 83
    Webb case, 77
Gospel Ridge, 64, 136 (figure), 146, 152,
        160, 181
Graham, Don, 85
Great Western Hotel, 65, 152, 153
Greeley, Horace, 45
Griffin, Albert, 153, 167
Gryden, Harry, 141 (photo)
    background, 105–106, 107
    as city attorney, 107–108, 109, 123, 124
    death, 125
    debts, 109
    friends, 107
    law practice, 75, 76, 77, 106–107, 108,
        109, 114
    as militia officer, 119
    at mock wedding, 74
    newspaper stories by, 104–105, 108–
        111, 113–114, 115, 116, 117, 118–119,
        120, 121–122, 123–126
    petition for Gill's pardon, 82
    political activities, 107
gun control
    current debates, 181–182
    Dodge City ordinance, 54–55, 61, 94,
        102
    enforcement, 54, 55, 56, 57, 72, 94
    signs, 55, 132 (photo)
    supporters, 41–42, 54
Gunsmoke, 3, 177–178

gun violence
    Battle of the Plaza, 89–90, 109, 148
    in cattle trading period, 44, 55, 94–95
    concerns of business owners, 24, 28,
        30–31, 64
    at dance halls, 105, 125
    decline, 44, 52–53, 54, 56, 162
    fictional accounts, 84–85, 99–100, 166
    first recorded gunfight, 1–2, 23
    newspaper accounts, 23–27, 28, 29–30,
        31–32, 33, 35, 36–38, 46–50, 56,
        108–112, 122–126
    residents' accounts, 22–23, 27, 32–35
    Wild West mythology, 45–46, 166
    See also law enforcement; mythology of
        Dodge City; troublemakers
gun violence casualties
    in 1872–1873, 22–30, 34–35, 41–44, 42
        (table), 46–49
    in 1873–1875, 44, 52–53
    in 1876–1886, 44, 55–56, 57–59,
        94–95, 102, 109–110, 122, 123, 147,
        150–151, 160–161, 200n51
    lawmen, 57–59, 100, 123–124, 211n42
    See also Boot Hill; homicides

Hackett, Jerome, 52
Hand, Dora, 59, 66–69, 79, 108, 134
        (photo), 167
Hand, Theodore, 67
Hanrahan, James, 33
Hard, Olin and Inez, 91
Harland, Lee, 92, 98–99
Harper's Weekly, 140 (figure), 149
Harris, William, 112–113, 115, 118
Harrison, Benjamin, 164
Harte, Bret, 46, 167
Harvey, James, 24
Hays City (Kansas), 8, 9, 16, 17, 18, 27,
        60–61, 89, 170, 174
Haywood, C. Robert, 20–21, 36, 125
Haywood, Nate, 56, 57, 58
Heck, Henry, 78–81, 82, 109

Heinz, Charles, 98
Hennessey (soldier), 26–27, 47
Hickok, J. B. "Wild Bill," 46, 50, 170
Hicks, Bill, 37, 38, 39, 40
Hill, Charles, 31, 47
Hilton, Bill, 125
Hinkle, George, 78, 81, 114, 116, 119
Hogue, Edward, 52
Holliday, John "Doc," 116, 167, 177
homicides
    in 1878–1880 period, 66–83, 108–109
    death sentences, 76
    Dodge City's reputation, 153
    of Hand, 66–69, 108, 167
    indictments, 36, 53
    insanity defense, 75–76, 77
    justifiable, 123, 161
    legal proceedings, 66, 83, 124
    trials, 40, 56, 59, 75–76, 107, 161
    by vigilantes, 30, 31–33, 36–40, 44, 48
    See also coroner's juries; gun violence
        casualties
Hoover, George
    background, 14–15
    on church element, 88
    coroner's jury, 72
    death, 164
    Dodge City War and, 115, 116
    on early businesses, 21
    elected offices, 51
    gun control support, 41
    on gun violence in early days, 22, 23, 44
    later life, 163–164
    liquor wholesale business, 153–154
    marriage, 193n30
    as mayor, 51, 124, 145
    opposition to prohibition, 151
    saloons, 11, 14–15, 57–58, 129 (photo),
        145
    Tyler case and, 55
    at Webb trial, 76
Hopper, Dennis, 180
Hoy, George, 59, 105, 203n34

Hudson, Nate, 107
Hungerford, Charley, 42, 74
Hurley, Edward, 29–30, 47
Hustis, Ida, 91
Hutchinson (Kansas), railroad, 11
Hutchinson News, 1, 23

Illustrated Police News, 109
Independent Order of Good Templars
    (IOGT), 91, 151, 154
Indian wars, 8–9, 17, 18, 53. See also Native
    Americans
interracial marriage, 73–74, 75
IOGT. See Independent Order of Good
    Templars
Iowa Constitution, 73
Isenberg, Andrew C., 175

James, Jesse, 46
Jansen, Lewis, 24, 196–197n6
Jews, 19. See also Collar, Jacob; Collar,
    Morris
Johnson, Alexander, 191n18
Jones, Thomas, 82, 168
journalism. See newspapers
Julian, Ed, 160–161
Junction Saloon, 150–151, 157, 159

Kansas
    attorneys general, 35, 40–41, 150, 154,
        156
    constitution, 73, 88, 152
    prohibition, 88–89, 90, 151–152, 156
    state legislature, 51, 152
    state militia, 119
    See also Kansas governors
Kansas Cattle Growers' Association, 148
Kansas City Journal, 109, 116, 158
Kansas City Journal of Commerce, 31, 49–50
Kansas City News, 50, 161
Kansas City Star, 111, 113, 168, 173
Kansas City Times, 26, 29, 31, 32, 37, 38–39,
        48, 49–50, 109, 113, 114

*Kansas Cowboy*, 77, 150
Kansas governors
    Ford County organization, 24, 29, 35, 41
    law enforcement, 38, 39
    prohibition enforcement, 90, 91, 151–152
    *See also* Glick, George; Martin, John; Osborn, Thomas
Kansas Heritage Center, 181
Kansas State Temperance Union (KSTU), 152–153
Kansas Supreme Court, 35–36, 41, 145, 156
Keenan, Fannie. *See* Hand, Dora
Kelley, James, 130 (photo)
    background, 16–17
    Dodge City War and, 115
    elected offices, 51, 145
    fictional accounts, 86
    friends, 107
    later life, 163
    marriage, 194n38
    as mayor, 51, 58, 68
    murder attempt on, 59, 67, 68, 69
    nickname, 194n37
    saloon, 17, 23, 25
    Taylor murder and, 40
    on vigilance committee, 33
Kenedy, James, 67–70
Kenedy, Mifflin, 67, 69, 204n4
*Kinsley Mercury*, 124
Klaine, Nicholas
    book, 163
    on bullfight, 146
    Gryden and, 108, 109, 125
    personality, 66
    petition for Gill's pardon, 82
    on prohibition, 90, 91, 152, 156
    reports on police force, 92, 93, 101
    on saloon fires, 157, 158
    See also *Dodge City Times*
KSTU. *See* Kansas State Temperance Union

Lady Gay Dance Hall, 57, 59, 89, 98, 105
Lake, Stuart N., 174–175
Langford, John, 1–2, 23
Lansing State Penitentiary, 76–77, 81, 83
Larned (Kansas), 20, 56
law enforcement
    funding, 58
    priorities, 50–51, 89, 101
    unofficial, 28
    *See also* gun control; gun violence; vigilantes
lawmen
    Battle of the Plaza, 89–90, 109, 148
    city marshals, 53–54, 56–58, 91–93, 98–99, 101–103
    in Ford County, 53–54
    killed, 57–59, 100, 123–124, 211n42
    legendary, 95, 147–148, 165–167, 169–170, 174–175
    police, 53–54, 58, 90, 91–92
    posses, 68–69
    tolerance of illegal entertainment, 64
    unofficial, 28
    US marshals, 27–28, 38, 39, 58–59
    *See also* Earp, Wyatt; gun control; Masterson, Bat; sheriffs
*Leavenworth Commercial*, 24–25, 31, 32, 47–48
legends. *See* lawmen; mythology of Dodge City
Lewis, Alfred Henry, 167
liquor. *See* prohibition; saloons
liquor wholesalers, 153–154, 156–157, 160
Lister, Joseph, 2
Little, E. C., 166
*Log of a Cowboy, The* (Adams), 84–85, 86, 87–88, 93–100, 102, 167
Lone Star Dance Hall, 56, 202n28
Lone Star Saloon & Restaurant, 98
Long Branch Saloon, 132 (photo)
    coroner's jury, 74
    fights, 59, 70–71, 108–109
    fire, 157

gambling, 97
owners, 112–113
singers, 113
*See also* Dodge City War
Lovett, Harry, 52
Loving, Frank "Cockeyed Frank," 70–72,
    83, 108–109

Macdonald, A. B., 173–174
Martin, Barney, 72–73, 74–76, 107, 109
Martin, John, 77–78, 145, 150, 151–152,
    155–156, 157–158, 159, 160
Masterson, Bat, 131 (photo)
    articles by, 167
    Battle of the Plaza, 89–90, 109, 148
    departure (1886), 160
    Dodge City War and, 116, 118, 119, 120,
      121
    enforcement of prohibition, 160
    exile from Dodge City, 90, 114, 118
    fame, 109, 147, 165–166, 168
    fictionalized stories, 167, 169–170
    in films and television, 3, 176, 177
    friends, 107
    gunfights, 57, 58, 109, 147–148, 168,
      203n34
    later life, 167, 168, 170
    memoir, 119
    practical joke and, 96
    return to Dodge City, 119, 120, 147, 153,
      155
    as sheriff, 56–57, 68–69, 74, 170
    studio portrait, 121, 139 (photo)
    Webster and, 143–144
Masterson, Edward
    as city marshal, 56–57, 95
    death, 57–58, 95, 102, 107, 167, 168,
      211n42
    fictional accounts, 170
Masterson, George, 62
Masterson, James
    as city marshal, 78, 81
    feud with Peacock, 89

Hand murder investigation, 68
    Hoy shooting, 59, 105, 203n34
Mather, Cotton, 166
Mather, David "Mysterious Dave," 140
    (photo)
    as assistant city marshal, 117
    Barnes killing, 150–151
    fictional accounts, 170
    gunfights, 166
    Nixon killing, 123–124
    petition for Gill's pardon, 82
    Remington illustration, 166
    reputation, 117
Mather, Josiah, 150–151
McAdams, Louisa, 91
McCarty, Harry, 58–59, 211n42
McCarty, Thomas, 37–38, 40
McDermott (murder victim), 30, 47
McDonald, John, 193n30
McDonald, Joseph, 90, 109
McGaffigan, H. J., 12, 13
McGill (buffalo hunter), 32–33, 34
McNulty, Richard, 94
Milde, Charley, 80–81
Minnesota, Dodge City visitors, 149–150
Moonlight, Thomas, 116, 118, 121
Moore, Caroline, 79–80, 81, 82
Morehouse, Charles, 1–2, 23, 26–27, 47
Mormons, 16, 163
Morris, Keziah, 125
Morrow, "Prairie Dog Dave," 107, 117
movies, Western, 166, 176–177
murders. *See* homicides
musicians. *See* Dodge City Cow-Boy Band
mythology of Dodge City
    bullfight and, 146–147
    as cattle town, 5
    Cow-Boy Band and, 148–150
    cultural production, 181–182
    differences from reality, 56, 161, 162,
      165
    in films and television, 3, 176–178
    historic preservation and, 171–172, 180

mythology of Dodge City, *continued*
    influence of early years, 44, 46–50
    legendary lawmen, 95, 147–148, 165–
        167, 169–170, 174–175
    media attention, 5, 46–50, 147–148
    newspaper sensationalism, 111–112,
        116, 122
    in novels, 4–5, 60, 84–86, 164
    pride in, 145–146
    symbolic of Wild West, 6, 104, 181–182
    tourism based on, 60, 172, 175, 178,
        180–181
    in twentieth century, 165–166, 168–
        171, 172–178
    *See also* Boot Hill; gun violence;
        reputation of Dodge City

Nation, Carrie, 159
*National Police Gazette*, 104–105, 108–109,
    110, 121–122
National Rifle Association, 182
National Stockmen's Convention, 148–
    149
Native Americans, 7–8, 10, 15. *See also*
    Indian wars
newspapers
    roles in creating Dodge City mythology,
        5, 46–50
    sensationalism, 111–112, 116, 122
    tabloid journalism, 104–105, 108
    on vigilante actions, 48–49, 111–112
    *See also* Associated Press; Gryden,
        Harry; *individual newspapers*
*Newton Kansan*, 26, 30, 38, 41, 48
*New York Commercial*, 122
*New York Herald*, 146, 147
*New York Sun*, 109, 111
*New York Times*, 49, 63, 111, 113, 114, 118–
    121, 146, 162, 172, 173, 178
*New York Tribune*, 49, 50, 111, 113, 114, 116,
    119, 120
Nixon, Thomas, 123–124, 211n42
novels. *See* Western novels

O'Brian, Hugh, 178
Old House Saloon, 72, 109
Olive, Isom "Print," 67–68
Olmsted, Frederick Law, 45
opera house (public auditorium), 65, 152
Opera House Saloon, 124, 157
Osborn, Thomas, 29, 35, 38, 41
*Oxford Press*, 27, 48

*Pawnee County Herald*, 56
Peacock, Alfred
    background, 16
    billiard hall, 16, 33, 129 (photo)
    death, 163
    elected office, 51
    feud with Masterson, 88, 109, 148
    fictional accounts, 86
    at Fort Dodge, 15, 191n18
    at Gill trial, 81
    gun control support, 41
    saloon, 30, 33
    Taylor murder and, 39, 40
Peters, Samuel, 75–76, 81
Petillon, W. F., 139 (photo), 145
Pierce, A. H. "Shanghai," 87–88, 93–94,
    97–98, 102, 208n16
pioneers
    businessmen, 11, 12, 14–20, 29, 163–
        164
    in census, 29
    deaths, 163, 164
    "Last Round-Up" (1929), 172–174
    memoirs, 4, 96, 163, 175
    Sitler's land claim, 9–10
    women, 20–21
police, 53–54, 58, 90, 91–92. *See also*
    lawmen
Prairie Grove Cemetery, 168–169, 174
prohibition
    bootleggers, 159
    as election issue, 144–145
    enforcement, 88, 145, 153–155, 156–
        157, 160

ignored in Dodge City, 88–89, 90, 91, 97, 144, 151, 164
in Kansas, 88–89, 90, 151–152, 156
private enforcement, 152, 153, 159, 161
saloons converted to drug stores, 142 (photo), 154, 156–157
supporters, 90–93, 112, 144–145, 151–153, 157–158
*See also* temperance activists
prostitutes, 133 (photo)
at dance halls, 61, 113
fines and taxes, 58, 90, 107, 113
sporting houses destroyed by fire, 159
tolerance of, 64, 65
Prouty, Samuel, 150, 153

racial segregation, 36, 125. *See also* African Americans
racial violence, 36–40, 41
Ramsey, Charles, 91
Rath, Charles, 40, 193n32
Ratzell, Sarah "Sadie," 133 (photo)
Raymond, Henry, 32–33, 34, 38
Remington, Frederic
*Coming Through the Rye*, 95, 210n33
magazine illustration, 166
Republican Party, 151–152
reputation of Dodge City
for lawlessness, 44, 46–50, 162
for rowdy nightlife, 61–64, 65, 154–155, 156
for violence, 3–4, 59–61, 111–112, 153, 165, 181–182
*See also* mythology of Dodge City
Reynolds, Jack, 23–24, 47
Reynolds, Philander and Lemira, 91
Rhodes, William "Dad," 178
Rice, Robert and Susan, 91
Richardson, Albert D., 45
Richardson, Levi, 70–72, 83, 108–109
Robbins, R. A., 91
Roosevelt, Theodore, 166, 168
Russell, Mary Doria (author of *Doc*), 4–5

Saint James Saloon, 133 (photo)
saloons
attacked by temperance activists, 159
city fees, 154
closed by city, 156
Dodge City's reputation, 61–64, 154–155, 156
feuds between owners, 112–113
fights, 25–27, 28–29, 44, 63, 72
fires, 157, 158–159
on Front Street, 88, 144, 156, 157
gambling, 62, 97, 150–151, 156
gunfights, 70–72, 123, 147, 150–151
of Hoover, 11, 14–15, 57–58, 129 (photo), 145
in Kansas, 159
of Kelley, 17, 23, 25
late-night entertainment, 61–64, 65, 156
liquor licenses, 88, 90
local acceptance, 64, 88, 151
makeshift, 11
number of, 61
under prohibition, 88–89, 142 (photo), 151, 153–155, 160
sizes, 61–62
on south side, 65, 144
Sunday closings, 160
of Webster, 112–113, 144, 145, 154, 160
Santa Fe Railroad, 10–11, 35, 53, 65, 144, 155
Santa Fe Trail, 8, 9, 15, 17, 180–181
*Saturday Evening Post*, 169, 174
Scott, John "Scotty," 33, 37, 38–39, 40
Shaw, Lyman, 191n18
Sheridan, Philip, 9
sheriffs
Bassett as, 51, 52, 53, 54
deputies, 53–54
Ford County, 53
Masterson as, 56–57, 68–69, 74, 170
Webster as, 88–89, 95
*See also* lawmen

Sherman, Tom, 31, 34, 38, 40, 41–42, 53
Shinn, Lloyd, 66, 75, 78–80, 81, 87, 92, 93, 94–95. See also *Ford County Globe*
Short, Luke
  articles on, 167
  Dodge City War and, 113–114, 115, 116, 117, 118, 119
  saloon, 112, 113
  studio portrait, 121, 139 (photo)
Simpson, O. H., 67, 173, 175
Singer, Frederick, 78, 81, 109
Siringo, Charlie, 168
Sitler, Emma Harper, 9, 152
Sitler, Henry
  businesses, 8–9, 13–14
  in Civil War, 6–7, 189n3
  death, 164
  land claim, 9–10, 11, 12
  life of, 6–7, 8–9
  sod house, 10, 127 (photo), 128 (figure)
  Tyler case and, 55
Smith, William L., 87, 125
Smith & Redmon, 87, 208n14
Society for the Prevention of Cruelty to Animals (SPCA), 146
Spencer, Pony, 32
St. Claire, Dave, 123, 147
Stevens, Henry "Uncle Henry," 94, 97, 102
St. John, John, 90, 91, 209n24
Stock Exchange Saloon, 112–113, 117, 123, 144, 157
Strang, Jeremiah, 145, 158
Straughn, John, 71, 74, 80
Sturm, Henry, 154, 160
Sughrue, Patrick, 80, 82, 91–92, 145, 154, 161, 166
Sullivan, James, 91
Sullivan, John L., 150
Sullivan, Matt, 25, 28–29, 44, 47, 48
Sunday, Billy, 173, 220n29
*Sunset Trail, The,* 85–86
Sutton, Fred E., 169–170, 173

Sutton, Michael, 82, 141 (photo), 152, 155, 156, 157–158, 168
Sweeney, William, 53

Taylor, David, 13, 47, 191n18, 199n39
Taylor, William, 36–40
Tefertiller, Casey, 175
television series, Western, 3, 177–178
temperance activists
  as city marshals, 91–93
  in Dodge City, 151–153, 158, 159
  organizations, 90–91
  suspected in fires, 157, 159
  violence, 159
  Webster and, 143–145
  women, 21, 154, 159
  *See also* prohibition
Templars. *See* Independent Order of Good Templars
Tex (murder victim), 23
Texas
  gun violence, 45
  Live Oak County, 87
  ranches, 53, 67, 94
  *See also* cowboys
Thompson, Ben, 97, 102, 167, 170
Tilghman, William, 68, 167, 169–170
Tombstone (Arizona), 5, 121, 176, 180
*Topeka Capital,* 115, 116, 153
*Topeka Commonwealth,* 23–24, 26, 28, 31, 35, 36–37, 42–43, 46–47, 52–53, 146
*Topeka Journal,* 115, 116
tourism, 60, 150, 172, 175, 178, 180–181
Tremaine, William, 2, 193n31
troublemakers
  buffalo hunters, 22, 52
  in early days, 22
  gamblers, 22, 70
  killed by vigilance committee, 31–33
  rowdy nightlife, 62–63
  vigilantes, 39, 41
Tupper, Tullius, 13

Tuttle, A. J., 80, 81
Twain, Mark, 46, 85, 153
Tyler, John, 55–56

Varieties Theatre and Dance Hall, 79
Vietnam War, 3
vigilantes
   committee of businessmen, 30, 31–33
   defense of, 114
   murders, 30, 31–33, 36–40, 44, 48
   newspaper accounts, 48–49, 111–112
   opposition to, 83
   racial violence, 41
   warnings, 113
violence. *See* gun violence; homicides
*Virginian, The* (Wister), 166

Wagner, Jack, 57, 58, 168
Walker, Alfred, 57, 58
*Washington Evening Critic*, 111–112
*Washington Post*, 111
WCTU. *See* Women's Christian Temperance
   Union
Webb, Arista, 72–78, 83, 107, 109
Webb, Christina, 73–74, 75, 76–77
Webb, Walter Prescott, 85
Webster, Alonzo, 129 (photo)
   background, 16, 17–18, 143
   bullfight and, 143, 145, 146–147
   coroner's jury, 80
   country estate, 64
   death, 163, 168
   Deger and, 144
   elected offices, 51
   evangelicals and, 143–145, 160
   feud with Harris, 112, 114, 115, 117, 119
   fictional accounts, 86
   as mayor, 51, 89–90, 91–93, 101–103,
      143–144, 160
   reputation, 89
   saloon, 112–113, 144, 145, 154, 160
   as sheriff, 88–89, 95
Weichselbaum, Samuel, 191n18

West. *See* Wild West
Western movies, 166, 176–177
Western novels
   classical plot, 164
   dime novels, 45–46, 60, 85, 200n3
   factual basis, 85–86, 95–96, 97, 102
   gunfight scenes, 166
   set in Dodge City, 4–5, 84–86, 164
   *The Log of a Cowboy* (Adams), 84–85,
      86, 87–88, 93–100, 102, 167
Western television series, 3, 177–178
Whitman, Walt, 17
*Wichita Beacon*, 25
*Wichita Eagle*, 47–48, 146
Wild West
   Dodge City's symbolism, 6, 104, 181–
      182
   gun violence mythology, 45–46, 166
   movies, 166, 176–177
   mythology, 169–170, 181–182
Wild West shows, 46
Williams, Ed, 31, 47
Wister, Owen, (author of *The Virginian*),
   166
women
   African American, 73–74, 75, 76–77,
      82
   middle-class, 65
   pioneers, 20–21
   temperance activists, 21, 154, 159
   *See also* prostitutes
Women's Christian Temperance Union
   (WCTU), 154
Woodbine (Kansas), 159
Wright, Robert
   attack on Sutton house, 157–158
   background, 15
   businesses, 21, 55, 57, 93, 96–97, 157
   coroner's jury, 122
   on depression, 162
   Dodge City War and, 115, 116, 118, 119
   on gun violence in early days, 22, 27,
      44

Wright, Robert, *continued*
    later life, 163
    as mayor, 51, 151, 155–156, 157, 160
    memoir, 4, 96, 163, 175
    opposition to prohibition, 151
    petition for Gill's pardon, 82
    as post trader, 11, 191n18
    on saloon fires, 158–159
    in state legislature, 51
    on vigilance committee, 32, 33
Wright, Will, 164
Wright & Beamer, 93
Wright House, 96–97

Young, Isaac, 24, 28, 29, 35
Young, James, 81, 82–83

Zimmerman, Frederick
    background, 19
    coroner's jury, 122
    country estate, 64
    death, 163
    elected offices, 51
    gun and hardware store, 19, 72–73, 113,
        129 (photo), 131 (photo), 157
    opposition to prohibition, 151
    school committee, 64